Social Work in a Multi-Racial Society

Peter Ely
and
David Denney

Gower

Published by
Gower Publishing Company Limited,
Gower House, Croft Road,
Aldershot, Hants GU11 3HR,
England.

Gower Publishing Company,
Old Post Road, Brookfield,
Vermont 05036, USA.

Reprinted 1989

British Library Cataloguing in Publication Data

Ely, Peter
    Social work in a multi-racial society.—
    1. Social group work — Great Britain
    2. Social work with minorities — Great
    Britain.
    I. Title   II. Denney, David   III. Series
    362.8'4'00941   HV245

Library of Congress Cataloging-in-Publication Data

Ely, Peter
    Social work in a multi-racial society.
    Bibliography: p.
    Includes index.
    1. Social work with minorities — Great Britain.
    2. Race awareness — Great Britain. I. Denney, David.
    II. Title.   III. Series.   III. Series.
    HV245.D36   1986   362.8'4   86—14908

ISBN 0 566 00939 0
       0 566 05814 6 (Pbk)

Printed and bound in Great Britain at
The Camelot Press plc, Southampton

Contents

Figures

Table

1 Introduction

Biological 'race'

In Britain, when black players get possession of the ball at association football matches, the crowd responds with noises intended to imitate the language of apes. This exuberant celebration of white ethnicity conveys that 'man is descended from the apes', and that the white man, by descending furthest of all, is now at a more advanced stage of biological evolution than the other races.

Even in more polite circles, such mistaken beliefs about human biology may well prevent or cloud with embarrassment any discussion of the physical aspects of race. Man did not 'descend from the apes', though both apes and man probably developed from similar earlier forms of life.

Nor can one race be said to be unequivocally 'closer' to the modern apes than another. As regards skeletal features, whites when compared with negroes or mongoloids are 'farthest' in respect of jaw protrusion, but 'closer' to apes in respect of their pronounced brow ridges. The pronounced concavity of the spine in the negroes' lower back region makes them the least ape-like of human groups in body form. In non-skeletal features, the thin lips and greater hairiness of the whites place them 'closer' to the apes than are negroes. It is clear that different human biological 'races' cannot be ranked as consistently closer to or further from the apes on these criteria.

The biological differences between human races are relatively minor, and all races are far more similar to each other than to any modern ape. No two human beings living today are likely to be further apart than fiftieth cousins.

When white people associate negroes with apes they utilise their habitual form of selective perception, attributing overwhelming importance to skin colour. Skin colour is inherited polygenically, and involves the interaction of from three to six pairs of genes. Every human has the same distribution of cells (melanocytes) producing the brown pigment melanin. How fair or dark a person is is determined by the level of activity of the melanocytes and resulting concentration of melanin granules in the skin. This is primarily controlled by inheritance, secondarily by environmental factors such as exposure to sunlight (Harrison and Owen 1964). Variations in skin colour hardly signal profound biological differences nor is racial mixing disadvantageous genetically (Stern 1973).

The biological variation among human populations has its origins in the tendency for the 'gene pools' of geographically separated breeding populations to come to differ from each other, because they are constantly evolving through the inter-action of mutation, variation and natural selection. This results in aggregate differences in genetically inherited characteristics. Although, apart from identical twins, each individual is genetically unique, differences between populations emerge with regard to the frequency with which certain inherited characteristics occur. These gene frequencies change through time, so that populations are subject to 'genetic drift'. All modern populations have also been subject to 'inter-breeding' to the extent that it would now be difficult to find a 'racial frontier' on land anywhere. Instead, in long-settled human populations, genes for specific inheritable characteristics exhibit 'clines', gradual changes in frequency across geographical regions.

For example, in West Africa we find high frequencies of dark skin, wiry hair, broad nose and everted (outward turned) lips. These associated characteristics occur in several of the world's regions of equatorial heat. If we map the 'clines' in an eastward direction, by the time we reach East Africa we find a similar frequency of wiry hair, associated with a lower frequency of very dark skin and everted lips, and a higher frequency of high nasal profile.

Equivalent problems emerge with attempts at classifications based on non-visible characteristics, such as blood types:

> In many respects, peoples of widely different physical appearance have many less visible traits in common . . . while peoples who have been grouped together into one race on grounds of physical appearance turn out to be quite distinct in other genetic dimensions (Banton and Harwood 1975, p. 53).

All this makes classification on the basis of distinct racial 'types' impracticable. No classificatory scheme yet devised has been able to group human populations into discrete categories without ignoring much inconvenient information.

However, attempts to dismiss biological 'race' as a figment of the imagination, founder on the common-sense ability to distinguish a Chinese person from an African. Conventional groupings such as Europeans (or 'Caucasians'), Asians or Africans do have marked group differences in their overall pattern of gene frequencies, but they are in no sense genetically discrete groupings, for very few of these differences are of the all-or-none kind. As there are no clear-cut biological indications of which differences are the most important, there are no biological grounds for deciding which individuals and which populations should go into the same category.

The positive contribution of physical anthropology is therefore to reveal common misconceptions about human physical differences. Banton and Harwood (1975) provide a learned review of the scientific evidence, or lack of it, for the ideas that 'racial genes' control cultural level, brain size, IQ test scores, religious beliefs, moral standards, or 'innate' feelings of racial antagonism. It seems that less repressive race relations policies are not under threat from anything so far 'discovered' in this field, and much to gain from studies that challenge the evidence supporting supposedly 'scientific' speculation related to the dominant political ideologies of the time. It is important for the scientific status of racial beliefs to be tested. Biological differences are bound to be used politically, but ignorance about them can only foster the suspicion that there is a 'scientific' biological rationale for racist policies and practices.

Banton (1977) traces the history of 'race' in Europe as an idea, and Poliakov (1974) takes the story back to the time before Africans or apes were widely known of in Europe, showing how the Lapps were then unfavourably compared to dogs. Banton (1977) concludes that:

> It looks as though there were many influences which contributed to the growth of prejudice. Its story is the story of Western Europe itself and it is impossible to separate the various items into a unique sequence of events.

Feelings about racial differences have a very long history indeed.

The significance of biological 'race' for social work is not generally obvious to social workers at this time, because the recognition and acknowledgment in oneself of feelings that are provoked by biological racial differences is too rare an event in Britain outside of overtly racist circles. The very idea tends to be met with a numb neutrality. It is tempting to avoid facing one's own *racial* feelings, in favour of learning about differences in cultural backgrounds or economic status, which are far easier to cope with on an intellectual level. However, unless subconscious ideas of racial hierarchy are first acknowledged, a racialist perspective will infuse any understanding of structural issues or cultural relativity with the automatic assumption that difference equals inferiority. If social workers do not incorporate awareness of their own racial feelings into their professional relationships on a conscious, but not necessarily explicit level, then the more assertive black clients will often do it for them: 'Ah don't tek no coffee from no white boy . . . .'

Social race in social work
There is no reason to suppose that race relations are different in kind from the relations between other unequal categories or groups or persons:

> human societies utilise natural differences and natural relations as ways of organising social relations. There is a sexual difference between a man and a woman, and there are biological relations between parents and children. Human societies develop gender roles which go beyond the biological imperatives of sexuality. They create kinship roles which go beyond principles of genetics and the relationships necessary to child-rearing. In the same way humans utilise the physical differences that are thought of as racial to help create and identify social roles. They utilise the facts of common language, culture and shared experience to develop notions of nationality. Some might say that they elaborate on the division of labour to formulate ideologies of class relations, and though this suggests a somewhat different kind of relationship, there is sufficient similarity for it to be worth remarking (Banton and Harwood 1975, pp. 150–1).

The development of racial ideology does not reflect the state of knowledge about racial differences, but is an aspect of social conflict. To be aware of how 'race' functions in practice, we need to focus on the social use made of biological differences. The functions of racial ideology in Britain today parallel those categorised twenty years ago by Nash (1962) for the United States. Racial beliefs: provide a moral rationale for systematic disprivilege; allow the members of the dominant group to reconcile their values with their activities; aim to discourage the subordinate group from making claims on the society; rally their adherents to political action in a 'just' cause; and defend the existing division of labour as eternal.

Traditional and popularised explanations of prejudice linked it to rigid personality structures or neurotic disturbance in individuals (Adorno *et al.* 1950) or to man's animal background in terms of instinct or territorial aggression (Lorenz 1966). Extreme racist beliefs are sometimes associated with personality disturbance but Davey (1983) researching racial awareness in schoolchildren, concludes that it was quite unnecessary to account for the development of prejudice by using concepts implying pathology or irrationality. In line with Paiget's framework for intellectual development, Davey finds that prejudice develops in children as 'part of the essentially rational process of trying to make sense of the world'. The segmentation of the environment into groups of items, which are treated as if they were equivalent for some purpose, lies at the root of our intellectual development. By constructing categories to fit our environment and simplifying the environment to fit our categories, we provide ourselves with 'the means for rapid identification and a guide to action'. Thus:

> we allocate people to categories on a fraction of their attributes such as: their sex, their wealth, their language or their pigmentation, and treat each complex individual as if he or she was a perfect example of the group as a whole (Davey and Norburn, 1980).

Inevitably this has the effect of emphasising the similarities of people within a group, and exaggerating the differences between groups.

Children will perceive differences in skin colour, hair form, dress, speech and so on, and these can become the basis for a classification process. An awareness of racial and ethnic differences emerges between the ages of four and five. It is society that determines how much attention should be paid to these differences, and that teaches how they should be evaluated. The categories that children choose for 'chunking up' their world are those available to them through their own culture and will therefore reflect the preferences and biases of their society. The learning and utilisation of his society's scheme of categories and the evaluation system related to it are the principal means by which a child is 'socialised'.

Davey points out that the motivation for the child to adopt the values and attitudes of those around him is his fundamental need to establish his own identity. He must be able to perceive the differences between the major groups in his community and identify the one to which he belongs: he must learn the signs by which people are classified as members or non-members of a group: and he must learn the appropriate behavioural and attitudinal response towards people classified in a particular way. Self-identification can only be acquired within the context of the system of preferences and biases which exist in a society.

Racial categorisation is thus part learning process, part cultural transmission and part of the development of self-identity. In contemporary Britain it tends to result in a society where 'people of all classes believe that people's physical appearance is indicative of their intellectual and cultural abilities and standards' (Miles 1982).

Physical and cultural differences are utilised to create groups and categories by the process of inclusion and exclusion. In so far as the process is used by the dominant white group to exclude those who are different from certain sectors of the economy, it functions to validate in reality the apparent correlation between physical and cultural variation, occupational status, wealth and education, which tends to confirm the prejudice of the dominant group:

> Moreover, such is the acculturation process that later in life, the individual will not be able to recognise the part played by the socio-economic structures of society in creating his out-group images. He will, in fact, claim them as the reality which confirms his independent evaluations and judgements (Davey 1975, p. 33).

Thus Davey identifies the link between psychological processes and economic (material) relations. The established pattern of economic relations between black and white groups in Britain is as much a cause of inter-group hostility as stereotyped attitudes containing a large proportion of error and projection. Both economic relations and attitudes are linked to global economic arrangements in which the military defeat of black peoples, colonialism and imperialism have now developed into trading arrangements that impoverish the Third World to the material advantage of white countries (Segal 1976).

To those who regard economic determinants as primary, white British racialist beliefs can be regarded as merely adjuncts to economic arrangements that work to the advantage of the white majority. In a world of scarcity, racialist attitudes can be interpreted as part of an essentially rational defence of privilege, in the sense in which 'rational choice' is used in economics to signify behaviour that maximises gains and minimises losses (Banton 1977). Racism helps preserve the near-monopoly of prestigious occupational roles and desirable residential locations enjoyed by middle class whites: for poorer whites, it is available to articulate competition with blacks for scarce resources such as jobs and housing.

Ballard (1983) points out that, in 1870, Marx considered that the competition for employment from cheaper Irish labour accounted for the political weakness of the English working class, despite their organisation. This competition fuelled a lively hostility on both sides. Later Marxist commentators have tended to claim that today's racism originates from a purposive strategy of the bourgeoisie to divide the working class and thus handicap its struggle against capital. Marxist economic reductionism relegates 'race' to an aspect of 'class' and ethnic minority communities to the status of a 'class fraction', though Ballard (1983) alleges that it is unclear whether this latter concept 'will withstand closer examination any better than do typologies of biological races'.

The social class dimensions of the racial issue are indeed of salient importance, and, together with the role of capital in structuring the problem, have merited the attention that Marxists have paid to them. However, unfortunately Marxist analyses can generally find little room for the distinctive cultural and historical experiences of ethnic groups. For instance, to Sivanandan (1981) ethnicity is 'some kind of bootstrap' by which you are supposed to pull yourself up. Ethnic conflicts, like religion itself, may be regarded as aspects of 'false consciousness' generated by the ideology of the dominant class, 'culture' a mystification of more important structural factors such as racism. These explanations seem inadequate:

> Contrary to conventional understanding, deep-rooted non-class conflicts have long been, and remain, a *normal* feature of urban industrial societies. Alongside the successive tensions surrounding the Irish, Jewish and now Black presence in Britain one can place those surrounding Turks in Germany, Algerians in France, Italians in Switzerland, Hispanics in California, 'Southerners' in Bombay, Chinese in Hanoi, Ghanaians in Nigeria, Bengalis in Assam... the list is endless. What is conventionally described as 'race' relations in Britain emerges, in this context, as the manifestation of a much wider structural phenomenon (Ballard 1983).

Though there are features specific to the British situation, to reduce ethnic group identification to social class is to ignore many inconvenient aspects of reality.

Both Phillips (1982), from the West Indian community, and Mukherji (1982), in relation to the Sikhs, express resentment that the interests of their communities are invariably assumed to be identical to those of the white working class. They also point out that the centrality of religious beliefs to the lives of many ethnic minority members should not be seen as a relic of colonialism, an escape, a retreat or a symptom of a peculiar black susceptibility to superstition, but as an invaluable resource and a basis for community organisation in which leadership is not inevitably correlated with occupational position.

In the preceding two sections we have attempted to show that it is unnecessary to explain the distribution of political and economic rewards in terms of the biological superiority or inferiority of races: and that prejudiced beliefs and behaviour, acquired in childhood as part of the normal developmental process, function to sustain existing relations of inequality. By inviting the majority group individual to step outside of his usual frame of reference about these two aspects of 'race', we have not intended to ignore the differences between groups. Before exploring this further, we need to point out that racialist attitudes do not have a monopoly of 'rationality'. As professional social workers, it is in our own self-interest to widen political support for services by involving as many individuals and communities as possible, and providing service delivery that appears effective, appropriate and equitable. It is unnecessary to combat racism by relying solely on the argument that racism represents a moral failure.

'Race' and ethnicity

Tajfel (1978) identifies the small number of psychological strategies available to minority groups and individuals faced with a majority group that maintains barriers to participation in society. The first possibility is to accept the negative view of one's identity held by the majority group, and internalise an unfavourable self-image. Projective tests done on minority children in several countries before the 1960s confirmed that this was then the common solution. The second possibility is to insulate and isolate one's community so that one rarely comes into contact with the majority or its opinions in any significant way. This solution is an unstable one, because it is usually impracticable to sustain separation in the economic sphere, and because succeeding generations are likely to be increasingly influenced by majority group influences.

The third option is assimilation with the majority, in which case the group may well cease to exist as a distinguishable entity. Assimilation is seldom available in a complete form save to a few exceptional individuals. These may be left with a continuing negative self-image of their residual differences from the majority, or may over-compensate by behaviour or attitudes that take their new group identification to extreme lengths.

The fourth option is the one that has generated the worldwide upsurge of ethnic and national affiliations since the 1960s. This is to develop an emotional investment in one's membership of a minority, and to put forward new claims for equality based on this group's right to be different as defined in their own terms, not in terms of the majority's negative evaluation. The minority revalues its difference from the majority in a positive way, so that what was previously a reason for humiliation is celebrated as a source of pride.

Ethnic groups are those to which people subjectively and consciously belong, and feel are distinctive, because they share some historical experience or national origin, or perceive features common to their present position, or to their possible collective futures. They are usually based around some biological or cultural difference, which has shaped their experience in society. Moreover they are also interest groups, and there is a social class dimension to ethnicity. If minority group members occupy a lower position in the system of social stratification than their self-respect will tolerate, they collaborate to improve their status. Religious belief has often played a crucial part in the process of commitment to cultural distinctiveness and the rejection of the low status conferred by the majority. While some of the cultural objectives may diverge from those of the majority, the economic objectives do not, for by organising as an ethnic minority the members obtain material advantages for themselves:

> ethnicity as a stratification phenomenon is based on the idea that ethnic groups are interest groups, committed to increasing their share of the scarce resources valued by society such as income, good jobs, good housing, good schooling, prestige and political power. Therefore the mobilisation of ethnic groups and the pursuit of ethnic interests are a strategy for the achievement of goals or cultural values desired by everybody (Lal 1983, p. 156).

Numerous writers have pointed out that the 'pluralist' society towards which the celebration of ethnic identity seems to point is an alternative mechanism of social control, both conceptual and institutional; particularly when it is recognised in government policies. However since power is an element in all relationships between individuals and between groups, and social control is inherent in social life, the issue is the purpose to which the power and control is put. If pluralism were to create social arrangements reminiscent of 'indirect rule' by 'traditional' leaders, or result in Bantustan-type developments in some policy areas, then it would not reduce inequality nor be intended to do so. If, however, it results in more positive arrangements for sharing power, it will be more equitable. Social workers will need to accommodate ethnic minority interests in their distribution of resources and in their law enforcement roles.

It is necessary to emphasise that the 'whites' are as 'ethnic' as any other group, and that ethnic organisation is the product of interactions between two (or more) ethnicities, one of which is the majority white group. It is reinforced by hostility. The most relevant aspects of white English ethnicity are those by which the inclusive and exclusive boundary of their group is maintained. The white interpretation of biological race draws a very 'hard', definite boundary which few individuals will be able to cross. It assumes that any detectable trace of non-European ancestry disqualifies from full membership of the group. This makes 'race' into a matter of 'white' or 'black'. Khan (1982) suggests that it would be just as logical to assume that a person with any detectable trace of European blood qualified for inclusion, but this would then provide a 'soft' boundary.

As it happens, both West Indian and Asian societies of origin have 'soft' but still contested associations of colour with status. On the Indian subcontinent, lighter skin colour is associated with the political and economic dominance of North India over the more heavily pigmented peoples of the South. It is also associated with higher status in the caste system, which was imposed by lighter-skinned Sanscrit-speaking invaders during the second millennium BC. Caste endogamy (marriage within the caste) has preserved a higher frequency of lighter skin colour among the upper castes, whereas the lower castes show more evidence of intermarriage with aboriginal peoples, previous invaders, and Mongoloid groups in eastern areas. The importance of caste is contested by the Muslim and Sikh ideals of equality before God, and by the Ghandian and secular philosophies of the Indian State, where the lowest castes are helped by legal and political safeguards.

As regards the West Indies, in the days of slavery the Africans who were 'house slaves' suffered more sexual exploitation by white male plantation staff than the 'field slaves' and were sometimes allowed more family continuity. Their descendants were in a better position to acquire artisan posts and the like, and later to rise above the post-Emancipation peasantry and form the 'middle classes'. Thus higher social class came to be associated with lighter skin. Since the emigration to Britain, political developments in the West Indies have somewhat ameliorated the position of darker-skinned people there, while West Indians in Britain have become more aware of the disadvantages of being black (Foner 1979).

An important difference between these attitudes to colour and the white English one is that the boundaries are not 'hard' and not primarily biological, but are aspects of caste and of class respectively. Returning to the salient features of white ethnicity, we may note that English racism is closely associated with nationalism, a point capitalised on by Enoch Powell and by the National Front. A belief in common descent is part of the stress on the continuity of English history and contemporary school children are encouraged to identify with previous inhabitants of these islands. The English language is another unifying force for whites and its imagery in which blackness is persistently associated with wickedness, evil, hostility, death, despair, depression and failure (as in black-hearted, black day, black look, black outlook, black magic, blackmail, blackguard, etc) may well have predisposed the English to abhor dark skins even before they encountered any, and must have parallel effects today.

The 'culture' of a society or of an ethnic grouping involves both personal meanings and systems of ideas rooted in its economic base. Khan (1982) uses the concept to refer to 'the system of shared meanings developed in a social and economic context which has a particular historical and political background'. Culture is thus not a fossilised relic but is constantly evolving to provide concepts for understanding the current situation. If we relate this to white ethnicity, we can understand why minority cultural factors such as kinship patterns, dress, religion and diet have come to be regarded as somewhat 'safe' topics, compared to the feelings aroused by physical differences. If white social workers have not first become aware of their feelings about biological race, then understandings of minority 'cultural differences' are bound to reflect negative valuations (Ahmed 1983).

Khan (1982) suggests that whites tend to believe that human development proceeds along a single path, on which they have advanced the furthest. The concepts of valid divergent developments, or parallel developments, do not readily occur to them. The upshot is that whites tend to think that 'culture' is something that blacks have, whereas whites have civilisation. It follows that minority culture is an interesting exotica or 'esoteric misguided system of beliefs and/or quaint behaviour held by others'. Thus 'if they become Westernised/English-assimilated they will become civilised/rational beings'. To regard culture as a backward artefact belonging only to minorities is to comprehend minority cultures in terms of what they are not (that is, they are not white English), their deficit, rather than understanding them as alternative social systems, a means to self-preservation, material gain and identity. Minority cultures are regarded as dispensable. The English may tend not to take minority cultures very seriously because relatively few English people are aware of their own racial feelings or that discrimination exists save on an individual level, so that the political meanings of the maintenance of ethnic identity (the assertion of difference, of dignity, of resistance) are not appreciated.

Nor does the English conception of minority cultures relate these to the economic base of ethnic communities. Most of the original 'immigrants' arrived here through the process of 'chain' migration whereby they took up employment and housing opportunities found for them by relatives already here. It was natural and beneficial for them to locate themselves in the midst of members of their own group, where a shared language, shared memories and cultural heritage provided a bridge between their past and present worlds. The ethnic press is often a most important source of information about the new country, and travel agencies, estate agents, banks, grocers, places of worship can all be established on an ethnic community basis. Since the dress, language and other differences that were signs of self-respect in the old country are now regarded by the majority with contempt and made an occasion for humiliation, participation in ethnic community life and institutions provides self-esteem and the means to procure a satisfying social identity through participation in a recognised social group. Finally, the institutions of the ethnic community provide a substitute for the traditional mechanisms of social control in the communities of the homeland (Lal 1983, pp. 159—65). This is reinforced in some communities by continuing integration with the economic base of their country of origin (Anwar 1979, Philpott 1977).

Ethnic minority institutions are adaptations of the original cultures. Social workers need to know of local ethnic organisations and services. They also need to be familiar with minority systems of cultural preferences. Whites trying to learn about other cultures often seek to reduce them to a set of prescriptive (often religious) rules, by which the behaviour of individuals is determined and explicable. This leaves no room at all for choice between alternative courses of action, and whites would not dream of explaining their own behaviour in terms of such 'rules'. The process may be a stage in 'translating' from our system or may reflect our view of minority cultures as rigid and unserviceable, incapable of development. 'Rules' are more properly regarded as emphases, cultural preferences, or as an idiom or ideology with which people discuss relationships. They may well reflect the cultural ideal rather than actual behaviour, and to confuse one of these with the other is a very frequent mistake. The 'rule', for instance, that Muslim women do not go out to work seems to be as 'real' a determinant of behaviour as the 'rule' that white British marriage is a lifetime monogamous union (Allen 1980). There seems to be no alternative to learning systems of cultural preferences, but what these are said to be will vary from one client/informant to another — inevitably so, since a culture is larger than any one person's interpretation of it, and because the explanation will vary with the context, and also the purpose for which it is being asked.

A further consideration is the extraordinarily diverse backgrounds of ethnic minorities in Britain. 'West Indians' are neither a homogenous nor a national group, and cultural preferences vary widely between those of mainly African descent in different social classes and on different islands, and between other ethnic groups within the islands (Chinese, Moslem and Hindu Indians, Syrians, etc). Asians coming to Britain from India are divided into ethnic minorities such as Sikhs and Gujeratis, those from Pakistan into Mirpuris, Chhachhis, Campbellpuris, other Punjabis, and Pathans. Asians from East Africa include Sikhs and Gujeratis but also Christian Goans, and Muslim sectarian minorities (Khojas) such as the Ismailis (Morris 1968). Ethnic affiliation in Britain may be enhanced by concentrated homogeneous settlement, as of Mirpuris in Bradford. In areas of more dispersed heterogeneous settlement such as South London, there is more interaction across 'fundamental linguistic, religious and cultural boundaries' within the Asian community, and more identification of themselves as 'Asians'. (Khan 1982).

The cultural characteristics of every group change through

time. Particular emphases may be heightened by distant world events in Amritsar, in Delhi, in Iran, in Grenada or in the Falklands. New generations have new ideas and support different strategies towards other groups. Significant differences emerge between the first generation and their descendants. The former tend to retain as a point of reference an idealised picture of the cultural preferences of their homeland at the time of their departure. The culture of the homeland, however, continues to develop after they leave, so that returning for a visit can be a salutary 'culture shock'. They may realise that they no longer fit in there and they may re-evaluate their position in Britain (Dahya 1973, Foner 1977). Their descendants will not carry with them the same 'time capsule' of cultural preferences as their parents, and, being exposed to different social and educational experiences and more oriented to the economy of the new country, they are bound to reinterpret their parent's 'conservative' beliefs. Surveys reveal that the extent to which this is done is sometimes surprising (CRC 1976a).

Any ethnic minority community, however distinctive it appears to an outsider, is likely to be divided internally between sections advocating different strategies in relation to other groups. This is not merely because individuals and sections may have divergent interests in the short term. It also reflects disagreement about ultimate objectives, because, although ethnic minority leaders may be in the business of heightening awareness of differences now, in the long term enhancing the influence of the minority with the majority is likely to make it easier for members to participate in the majority society. In so far as this may render them more likely to be influenced by this society and feel less ethnic solidarity, it can arouse anxiety. This seems to be one factor making for difficulties in departmental consultations with ethnic communities.

Social workers are also likely to encounter persons with no very strong links to their ethnic community of origin. The latter may not be well represented in this country, or the individuals' ascribed status in it may be very low, or their relationship may have been severed in some way, perhaps by choice. This result may be part of a situation of social isolation, or alternatively of a lifestyle that reflects the fact that ethnic group membership is only one source of identity among many other affiliations.

Many individuals may be identified, or may identify themselves, as 'black', solely on the basis of racial difference and the resulting social experience of discrimination; there may be no cultural dimension to their difference from the white majority. They may be the descendants of black people settled here for generations, or accidents of their life history may have separated them from the socialising effects of their community, or they or their parents may have tried the path of assimilation. Persons of ethnically mixed parentage may be 'fluent' in both cultures. The ability to move in more than one cultural milieu is valued by many black people born here.

In social work the leading exponents of the black perspective have used the white racial boundary as the inclusive boundary of their own community: since all individuals with dark skins will suffer discrimination from whites, their place is with other black people, who alone can show them how to cope with prejudice. Ethnic groups require leadership to encourage at least a substantial section of the leading elements of each community to turn away from the ideal of assimilation, and use racial or cultural identification to promote ethnic consciousness, and teach the black person to prefer to be black.

More definitions

As whites we are writing for white social workers with black clients, though it shall occasionally be relevant for the reverse situation, so we have followed the white practice of referring to all 'non-whites' as 'black'. We have limited ourselves to making our points with reference to the relations between whites and the ethnic communities of West Indian origin (the literature tends to take those of Jamaican descent as its point of reference) and of 'Asian' origin. We use 'Asian' to describe those who were originally from what are now India, Pakistan, Sri Lanka and Bangla Desh.

There is material published on the background and social needs of most other communities. For the literature on West African residents in Britain see Ellis (1978) and for those of Chinese origin see Lau (1984) Watson (1975 and 1977) and the Second Report of the Home Affairs Committee (HCP 102—I 1985). For those from Vietnam, who are mostly ethnic Chinese, see Jones (1982) and the Joint Committee

(1982). Dench (1975) has written on the Maltese in London, and Constantinides (1977) and Ladbury (1977) on the Greek and Turkish Cypriot communities. Benson (1981) looks in depth at a number of families with both black and white members.

Apart from the meanings of 'race' already described, the term has been applied in a more mystical way to language groups (for example, Aryans), to national or cultural groupings (British, Nordic), to religious groups (Jewish) and to all living mankind (the 'human race'). These meanings all imply that the line of descent is a salient factor in the current situation of these groups.

Cashmore and Troyna (1983) provide a great deal of information relevant to the position of black people in Britain and we have generally adopted the following current definitions of key terms which they offer:

Prejudice 'An inflexible mental attitude towards specific groups of others based on unreliable, possibly distorted, stereotyped images of them' (Cashmore and Troyna 1983, p. 36).

Ethnocentric 'A view of the world in which oneself or one's group is at the centre of things: a failure to take into account the perspectives of others' (*ibid*, p. 154).

Racism The doctrine that the world's population is divisible into discrete categories based on genetically transmitted physical differences. Invariably, this leads to a conception that the categories can be ordered hierarchically so that some elements of the world's population are superior to others' (*ibid*, p. 35). Often used interchangeably with:

Racialism 'The action of discriminating against particular others by using the belief that they are racially different, and usually inferior. It is the practical element of the race concept' (*ibid*, p. 33).

Institutional racism 'The policies of institutions that work to perpetuate racial ideology without acknowledging that fact. Glasgow (1980) refers to this as camouflaged racism, meaning that it is not open and visible but is concealed in the routine practices and procedures of organisations such as industries, political parties and schools' (*ibid*, p. 60).

When existing practices are challenged, they are

usually defended not by reference to racist beliefs, but by appeal to a value that society holds superior to sectional interests. In social work the white ethnic boundary against changes in personnel or policy has been defended by the appeal to 'equality' — 'we treat everyone equally'. This 'colour blind' policy has the outcome that the services provided are designed to be appropriate for the white majority, and there is thus less access for black people, and no room to develop services that are particularly appropriate to black people.

Positive discrimination (known as 'affirmative action' in the USA) fully analysed by Edwards (1986). In employment 'A policy usually directed by central government in an attempt to reverse the historical trend that has consigned many minority groups to positions of occupational disadvantage. It involves actually encouraging employers, administrators, and so on to grant access to or promote members of disprivileged groups — even though, at times, white candidates may have commensurable qualifications.' (*ibid*, p. 93).

In social work, positive discrimination may be used by whites to describe *any* provision for black people, such as the appointment of any black social worker, or providing a service to black people where previously the service was only to whites (for example, providing Asian meals-on-wheels). Similarly, even limited organisational arrangements distinguishing the provision of a service appropriate for black people can be labelled 'separatism', with its connotations of forming a separate autonomous state.

'Racialist' is commonly used to describe any practice or policy likely to disadvantage a black person or group. Sometimes its effect in this respect will be beyond dispute. Sometimes it will not, and then racialism takes on the same pervasive qualities as the concept of original sin. Writers against racialism are in danger of facing the same dilemma as the North London councillor who recently punched an opponent for calling him a fascist. Readers will doubtless find evidence of our own racist and racialist assumptions in this book. Social work across racial or ethnic boundaries requires a healthy lack of confidence in one's own motives as well as a degree of trust in the black community.

We would not wish to over-emphasise the extent to which racial attitudes have hardened, nor to suggest that racial feeling is necessarily significant in every interaction. We would not attempt to over-simplify what is a very complex phenomenon. Using projective tests on school children, Davey (1983) finds that when they were choosing collaborators in co-operative activities (such as playing football), race was a less important guide to preference than competence. He concludes that in problem-solving situations, mutual dependence is more important than ethnicity. Perhaps this is the key to the 'feel' of many constructive social work interactions on both a personal and a policy level.

2 Getting to where we are now: policy development 1945-1986

From economics to politics 1945—1961
Black people have now been living in Britain for more than four centuries. During almost the whole of that period elements of the white population have voiced fears about their numbers, fears about black men having relations with white women, fears that cheap black labour would undermine wage rates, and fears that black people are or will become a burden on the public purse. Blacks have experienced discrimination, threats and acts of explusion, violent assaults and occasional race riots. They have also experienced acts of kindness and found allies among the whites who would help them personally and politically. Black people have formed organisations for their own advancement, the black presence has persisted, and there is a record of black achievement (Shyllon 1977, Fryer 1984). The 'problem' of today which seems so 'new', shows continuities with a situation existing since blacks were first brought here. It also shows parallels with the Irish and Jewish immigration of the nineteenth and twentieth centuries.

Many more black people live here now than did four decades ago. Before the Second World War, black people were concentrated in a few large ports, and were mainly following occupations connected with shipping. During the 1940s this picture began to alter as the post-war demand for labour for reconstruction and the expansion of the British economy led to upward mobility among the white workforce, and an acute shortage of labour in less attractive occupations. This need was met partly by the immigration of displaced nationals from Eastern Europe, and partly by immigration from the Caribbean, and later the Indian subcontinent.

While the first arrivals of substantial numbers of black workers occasioned the usual expressions of complaint, various factors contributed to a *laissez-faire* policy by the government in this period. The immigrants were essential to the economy. Indeed, some British public services actively recruited in the Caribbean. During the 1950s, the flow of immigrants from the Caribbean closely paralleled the job vacancies in the British labour market, showing that most migrants were in touch by letter with others already here who could tell them of work opportunities (Peach 1968, p. 39). The great majority of immigrants were productive workers, who constituted a free import into the UK from developing countries whose economies had borne the social costs of their unproductive childhood years. Most left their families at home, with the option of sending for them later. Thus the migrants' contribution to the British economy was undoubtedly greater than the cost of their use of state-provided services in Britain.

The British Nationality Act 1948 reflected the post-Imperial concept of Britain as 'head of the Commonwealth', confirming the rights of citizens of the United Kingdom and Colonies and of independent Commonwealth countries to enter Britain freely, to settle and find work, and enjoy full political and social rights. The outcome of the Second World War and the establishment of the welfare state had produced a sense of optimism and confidence in the ability of the British political system to solve social problems. In the popular consciousness of the time, the British now sought their renown in something more durable than military victory, a wise, high-minded and 'tolerant' society.

Thus the new scale of industrial prosperity in Britain provided the 'pull' factor that drew in immigrants, though the desire in some quarters to see these movements 'not as a response to economic need, but as a failure of political machinery to keep them out' (Peach 1968, p. xiii) meant that much more attention has been focused on the 'push' factors of poverty and unemployment in countries of origin.

Immigration from specific areas of India and Pakistan got under way later than immigration from the Caribbean, but by the late 1950s had also reached substantial proportions, mainly composed of male workers who did not intend to settle here permanently. Migration developed in a parallel way to West Indian migration, new arrivals coming to work opportunities found for them by earlier migrants.

Black people were no longer concentrated in dockside settlements but were spread across Britain in every industrial centre. They were thus a much more noticeable section of the population. Though the statistics of actual numbers are incomplete, it seems that there were in 1958 some 210,000 black immigrants from the Commonwealth including 115,000 from the West Indies and 55,000 from India and Pakistan (Deakin 1965, p. 3). Increasing numbers of dependants came to join their menfolk and the white working class perceived them as competitors for housing and educational provision.

The leaders of both major political parties resisted parliamentary pressure to place race on the British political agenda. In 1958, however, race riots took place in Notting Hill, London, and in Nottingham. These were checked by passing examplary sentences on four white youths. White discontent with immigration had forced itself up from below. After the 1958 riots there was pressure on the government through the Conservative Party Conference, the formation of pressure groups to fight immigration, and a limited resurgence of far-right political parties (Deakin 1965, p. 4).

Immigration control reached the statute book in 1961 as the Commonwealth Immigrants Act and came into force the next year. With the introduction of legislation, political factors overtook economic ones as the main determinants of immigration, as thousands hurried to Britain to 'beat the ban'.

Establishing consensus on immigration control 1961–1964
The Commonwealth Immigrants Act 1961 was intended to restrict the immigration of coloured immigrants, though it was presented in a way that did not emphasise racial distinction. The Labour Party opposed the Bill with uneven commitment, but it was recognised that there was a broad degree of grassroots support for immigration restriction. Under the Act, persons from the Commonwealth wishing to work in the United Kingdom would require work vouchers in the same way as did alien immigrants. Category A vouchers were for applicants who had jobs to come to in this country; Category B were for applicants who had skills or qualifications; Category C were for other applicants. This last category, the Home Secretary stated, was to be used to regulate the numbers entering the country, in accordance with the needs of the economy, the pressure on housing and education services and the desire to reduce social conflict (that is, protest from the white population). Since the implementation of the Act, most of the immigrants arriving have been the wives and dependent children of those already here. By the

end of 1963 it is estimated that there were approximately 750,000 black people of Commonwealth origin in England and Wales, including 400,000 West Indians, 150,000 Indians and 90,000 Pakistanis. In the run-up to the 1964 General Election the Labour Party conceded the need for immigration control 'in principle', but the election campaign raised the issue to renewed prominence with the defeat of the Labour front-bench candidate for Smethwick, Patrick Gordon Walker. His Conservative opponent, Alderman Griffiths, endorsed the slogan 'If you want a nigger for a neighbour, vote Labour', and successfully contested the seat principally on the immigration issue. This fatally weakened remaining Labour Party opposition to control. In September 1964 the new Labour government announced the suspension of Category C vouchers. In August 1965 a White Paper (Cmnd 2739 1965) announced that the total number of vouchers issued would not exceed 8,500 per annum, which would include 1,000 from Malta. Stricter tests of eligibility would be imposed on the entry of dependents, and the Home Secretary's powers of deportation strengthened.

Anti-discrimination legislation 1965
The year 1965 saw a limited development of policies towards immigrants already here. 'Without integration, limitation is inexcusable: without limitation, integration is impossible'. (Roy Hattersley quoted in Rose 1969, p. 229). This curious syllogism introduces the convention that limiting black immigration was intended to help those black people already here. It reflects the 'melting pot' ideology of the USA, and marks a change in British politics from looking on immigration primarily as an aspect of Commonwealth relations to regarding it as a problem internal to Britain. This paralleled the declining importance, in domestic politics, of the Commonwealth ideal.

The Race Relations Act 1965 was possibly intended to help maintain Labour Party unity by balancing the stricter immigration controls with anti-discrimination measures. A weak measure, the Act made it unlawful for the proprietor or manager of a 'place of public resort' (hotels, restaurants, cafés, public houses, theatres, cinemas, dance halls and scheduled transportation services, but not shops or offices) to practise discrimination on the grounds of colour, race, or ethnic or national origins against persons seeking access. It established the Race Relations Board, in London, to obtain compliance with the law. The Board created local conciliation committees to investigate and attempt to resolve complaints of discrimination. It had no powers to subpoena witnesses and no powers to prosecute. It could refer unresolved cases to the Attorney General who could decide to bring injunction proceedings. Unsatisfied complainants could not bring proceedings themselves.

S. 6 of the Act, inserted at the request of Jewish organisations alarmed at the recrudescence of British facism, made it a criminal offence to publish or distribute written matter, or speak at a public meeting, or in public, words that are 'threatening, abusive or insulting', with intent to stir up hatred against any section of the public distinguished by colour, race, ethnic or national origin. The National Committee for Commonwealth Immigrants was established in accordance with the 1965 White Paper to advise the government, and to develop a network of local liaison committees to expedite community development and community relations.

From assimilation to integration: 1965
In December 1965 Roy Jenkins was appointed Home Secretary, and his first speech on the issue presaged a major policy initiative. Jenkins signalled the end of the period when the 'assimilation' of immigrants to British society had been the assumed aim of policy, and all the necessary accommodations were demanded of the newcomers. Jenkins redefined the ultimate aim of policy as 'integration', which was to be 'not a flattening process of assimilation but equal opportunity, accompanied by cultural diversity, in an atmosphere of mutual tolerance' (Jenkins 1966).

This introduces concepts from immigration theory (Rose 1969, Patterson 1971). *Assimilation* is now generally taken to denote a complete merging or absorption of an immigrant group into the host society, to the extent that it loses its separate identity. It almost always involves intermarriage, and usually takes several generations. It is a more likely outcome where the host society is stable and homogeneous. Assimilation has acquired negative connotations in that most of the accommodation is undertaken by the immigrants, and it can be coercive. Forced assimilation has been the policy historically employed by the English against the Celtic minorities in the British Isles, whose own languages were proscribed for long periods. Many older West Indians feel that they came to Britain with the aim of assimilating into British society, only to be rejected by the racially hostile whites. This casts doubt on the assimilationist argument that racial harmony depends upon the elimination of cultural barriers between minority and majority populations.

Integration, usually employed in the sense of cultural pluralism, can have many forms. It may denote a process whereby immigrant groups integrate economically and politically, while retaining a distinct community sub-culture based on religion, language, geographical proximity, and a residual loyalty to the country of origin. This is the normal state of affairs for first-generation immigrants. It may be more likely to remain so where the receiving society is not homogenous but made up of a number of disparate groups, as in the case of London and other British cities. Integration, unlike assimilation, aims to produce a situation in which groups of different cultural backgrounds can contribute to society on an equal footing without losing their essential distinctiveness. Thus people retain their identity whilst being accepted as equals. The onus to change and adapt is shifted from the newcomer towards a situation in which both white and black work together towards the creation of mutual acceptance (Cashmore and Troyna 1983). To be equitable, pluralism should involve adequate access to political and economic power for each group. Otherwise a policy of cultural pluralism may deny conflict by masking the continued dominance of the majority group and the subordination of other groups to its interests.

Finally, *segregation* in the sense of self-segregation is, as described, normal behaviour for the first-generation immigrants save in specific spheres of activity. Some communities display an ongoing potential for self-segregation on religious or other grounds. Or economic or territorial segregation may be forced on them by the receiving society wishing to confine immigrants to the least desirable districts or to low-status employment.

Section 11 of the Local Government Act 1966

Jenkins made a limited move to implement positive programmes to help social and housing services with particular
reference to the second generation of black settlers, whom
he referred to as 'second-generation immigrants'. S. 11 of the
Local Government Act 1966 authorised the Home Secretary
to pay a proportion of the extra expenditure incurred by
those local authorities required to make special provisions,
because of substantial numbers of Commonwealth immigrants, but only in respect of the employment of staff. The
amount of money spent was extremely small. In 1968 it was
announced that priority would be given to nursery education
and child-care.

The extent of discrimination: 1967

Jenkins intended to extend the scope of anti-discrimination
legislation, which he saw mainly in terms of civil rights, to
housing and employment. In 1967 a report commissioned by
the government (PEP 1967) was the first systematic attempt
to assess the extent of racial discrimination, which, it concludes, varied 'from the massive to the substantial'. Discriminating behaviour was found to be so widespread among the
white population that never again could it be claimed that
such incidents were untypical or characteristic of the British
people. Investigating discrimination in employment, the
survey found that over half of those refused jobs were rejected by such low-level employees as gatekeepers, and personnel or reception clerks. It disposed of the argument that
unequal treatment was due to the poor qualifications of
immigrants, as better qualified black people were equally or
more discriminated against: it revealed colour to be a major
factor in rejection both by employers and by employment
bureaux.

There were similar findings from the Report's survey of
discrimination by private landlords and by accommodation
bureaux. Even where black people were accepted, higher
rents were often demanded of them. At house agents, black
people were often denied access to properties, refused a
mortgage, or offered one on less favourable terms. In spite
of this, a proportion of black people had managed to become
owner-occupiers, often of older property in city centres.

Poorer immigrants were often concentrated in older pro-

perties where they formed a substantial proportion of those
in distressed housing conditions in multi-occupied private
lettings. Governments had repeatedly refused to help local
authorities with this problem, the scale of which was beyond
the scope of local authority housing resouces. Some authorities turned a 'Nelson's eye' to overcrowding in certain restricted areas, while relentlessly prosecuting it when it
appeared outside, thus effectively segregating most immigrants into special zones. The private letting sector was
fraught with serious abuses (Cmnd 2605 1965; Burney 1967).
Many local authorities were reluctant to allocate council
tenancies to black people for fear of provoking hostility from
white electors. Black council tenants tended to get older
properties, sometimes in areas due for demolition, instead of
properties on new estates. The residence qualification for
eligibility for council tenancies, though not directed at black
people, indirectly discriminated against them during the early
1960s. The PEP Report received wide and remarkably sympathetic press coverage. It:

> illustrated how the process of racial discrimination tended
> to push or keep immigrants in poorer housing and lower
> status jobs, reinforcing the stereotypes and preventing inte-
> gration. In this way, the conditions under which the
> coloured minorities were struggling to establish themselves
> were brought home to the policymakers and the public at
> large (Rose 1969; p. 414).

The first annual report of the Race Relations Board demonstrated that most of the complaints received fell into the
areas of employment and housing, outside the scope of the
then current legislation. A further report (Street *et al.* 1967)
examined the operation of anti-discrimination legislation in
the USA and Canada, and recommended legislation of wider
scope.

Racial panic 1968
While legislation extending anti-discrimination measures was
in preparation, the Kenya government's Africanisation policy
caused a panic in Britain over the prospect of the entry into
this country of the East African Asians who held British passports. The Commonwealth Immigrants Act 1968 removed
the right of entry from holders of British passports issued

abroad unless they had a 'close connection' with this country. It was pushed through Parliament in a week with the agreement of the leadership of both major parties, to prevent 'beat the ban' immigration. The Act breached international agreements not to create stateless persons, and also broke undertakings given to the Asian population when independence was granted to the East African countries. A 'close connection' with this country was defined as birth, adoption or naturalisation here, or in one of the Commonwealth countries independent before 1948, on the part of the immigrant, his parent or grandparent. The Act was blatantly racialist. In April 1968 Enoch Powell, then a member of the shadow cabinet, destroyed the restraint that had hitherto existed among leading elements of both parties by the impact of his 'rivers of blood' speech (Powell 1968). Powell reimposed an 'immigration' frame of reference on an issue that was moving into the area of rights of equal citizenship. Before the year's end, he was advocating a ministry of repatriation.

[Anti-discrimination legislation 1968]

The anti-discrimination legislation that emerged as the Race Relations Act 1968 extended the areas in which discrimination on the grounds of colour, race, or ethnic or national origins was unlawful to include employment, housing, credit and insurance facilities, education, and all places of public resort including shops and offices. The Race Relations Board was given the power to initiate investigations where it suspected that discrimination had occurred, instead of merely responding to complaints. It still did not have the power to subpoena witnesses.

Employment cases were to be referred to the Department of Employment and Productivity. If conciliation failed, the Board could take cases to designated county courts (that is, the Attorney-General was now excluded). The courts could act on single instances of discrimination instead of the 1965 requirement of a continuous 'course of conduct', but could only order damages and issue injunctions. They could not order 'specific performance', the provision of a job or of accommodation. While these changes were an advance on the 1965 Act, the continued weakness of the enforcement provisions showed an inability to learn from North American experience detailed in the Report by Street *et al.* (1967), which demonstrated the ineffectiveness of a neutral, referee-like-commission and favoured 'affirmative action' on enforcement.

The chairman of the National Committee for Commonwealth Immigrants (NCCI), Archbishop Ramsay, had advised the government that immigration control had a stigmatising effect on black people, which made integration supremely difficult. The Race Relations Act 1968 then abolished the NCCI and created the Community Relations Commission (CRC). The Commission had the task of securing harmonious community relations, advising the Home Secretary on relevant matters, giving advice to local authorities and other organisations, providing training and holding conferences on matters connected with community relations. It set up advisory committees for education, employment, housing and so on and established local community relations councils. Like the NCCI, the Community Relations Commission has had to balance its need for credibility with central government with its need for access to local authorities and its need of the support of immigrant groups. It has been attacked as a buffer between the black community and normal political processes, praised for its work in information and research (Dummett and Dummett 1969, Hill and Issacharoff 1971, Abbott 1971, Katznelson 1973).

The Urban Programme 1968

The year 1968 also saw the announcement of the Urban Programme as an answer to Enoch Powell's speech. It was derived from the United States War on Poverty programme, and was intended to provide a measure of 'positive discrimination' in favour of multiply deprived areas. In the first phase small sums of money were allocated to local authorities whose eligibility was determined either by the presence of extensive over-crowding in housing, or by a high proportion of 'immigrant' children on school rolls. However its relevance to immigrants was soon watered down to avoid the appearance of unduly favouring black people. The later phases of the programme were relevant to 'immigrants' only in so far as the immigrants formed part of the population of urban areas in need. The Local Government Grants (Social Needs) Act 1969 made limited funds available to local authorities to assist voluntary organisations to provide a wide variety of projects. This programme ran alongside the educational priority area programme and the community development projects. Their aim was to enhance equality of opportunity or to improve social conditions in deprived areas by changes in the characteristics of the residents, or by focusing on the extension or co-ordination of services.

Summary of the 1960s

Thus by the end of the 1960s, the four aspects of policy towards ethnic minorities were established: the strength with which they were constituted, however, reflected the extent to which they accorded with the perceived interests of the indigenous population, rather than any 'needs' of the minorities. Thus immigration policy was extensive and immigration drastically curtailed: there was only moderate progress in anti-discrimination legislation, and information and community services, and very little development of positive policy directed at the deprivation in ethnic minority areas. Roy Jenkins had briefly given policy a coherence and a rationale, but external events and his own departure from the Home Office had intervened before his ideas had come to fruition.

More immigration control 1969 and 1971

In 1969 an entry certificate system was introduced to control the entry of dependants. Entry certificates could be issued by British embassies or high commissions overseas, which investigated applicants to establish the veracity of their claim to be dependants of people already in Britain. The effect has been to 'shift the interrogation and disappointment overseas' (Moore and Wallace 1975, p. 7) and, while avoiding the risk of applicants arriving here being returned to their own country, the entry certificate system has led to long queues of applicants. The discretion placed on officials has also led to allegations that the discrepancies they uncover through interrogation are partly due to language difficulties.

In 1971 a new Immigration Act was introduced to bring the country into line with European Economic Community (EEC) membership. EEC nationals could now enter Britain for six months without a work permit. On finding employment, a five-year residence permit would normally be issued. They thus acquired a better legal status than immigrants

from the New Commonwealth and Pakistan, whose work permits were to be issued on a yearly basis, with no right to stay
in Britain. The status of new black immigrants therefore
moved closer to that of *gastarbeiter* workers in Germany,
who are admitted on temporary permits and expelled if conditions change in the labour market.

The 1971 Act extended the 'close connection' idea by con-
ferring the 'right of abode' in the United Kingdom on
'patrials'. Patrial is a rare word meaning 'of or belonging to
one's native country'. Other EEC member states were
reluctant to expose themselves to the risk of non-white immigration, so that 'patrials' are the only overseas citizens
recognised as United Kingdom 'nationals' and entitled to the
reciprocal advantages of free movement within the EEC
accorded by the Treaty of Accession in 1971.

Patrials are citizens of the United Kingdom and Colonies
who themselves are connected with the UK by birth, adoption, naturalisation, or registration here, or who have been
lawfully settled in the UK for the last five years or who have
a parent or grandparent with such a connection. Patrials also
include other Commonwealth citizens with a parent born in
the UK, their wives and former wives and widows whose
husbands would, but for their deaths, have been citizens of
the United Kingdom and Colonies. Patrials, mostly white
people living in the Old Commonwealth, are not subject to
immigration control. All others were made subject to control
according to immigration rules. Non-patrials can be deported
if the Home Secretary considers this to be 'conducive to the
public good', if another member of their family is deported,
or if they have committed a criminal offence and have not
been settled here for five years.

The Asians from Uganda 1972

The government of Kenya was co-operating with the British
government so that the Asian population of Kenya was being
admitted to Britain on a phased basis. However in 1972 the
government of Uganda expelled a very large proportion of
the Asian population from that country, and 28,000 of these
people were admitted to Britain as refugees. Camps and other
services, including a limited amount of housing, were made
available. These helping arrangements were universally
believed to have been a considerable success. Like the
similarly successful Polish Resettlement Corps set up to help

Polish forces settle in Britain after the Second World War, the help to the Ugandan Asians remains one of the few examples of a positive government initiative to help newcomers to this country with the problems of settlement. A fair proportion of the East African Asians had skills, education, capital and business experience. There could have been no reasonable opposition to their entry on social grounds, the opposition must therefore have been based on racial antipathy. By 1975 the majority of Asians from East Africa had been admitted, but a large proportion re-emigrated to North America and elsewhere. A number who 'temporarily' fled from Africa to India are 'queueing' there to this day waiting for entry to Britain (HCP 90-I 1982).

Current anti-discrimination legislation
In 1974 the PEP published the results of another national survey (PEP 1974, Smith 1977) demonstrating the continuing pervasiveness of discrimination and, with the return of Roy Jenkins as Home Secretary, new legislation was prepared. The Race Relations Act 1976 repealed all previous anti-discrimination legislation, and is still the law today. It established two main categories of discrimination. These are (s.1): *direct discrimination*, whereby on racial grounds a person treats another less favourably than he would treat others; and *indirect discrimination*, whereby a person applies a 'requirement or condition' such that the proportion of persons of the same racial group as the complainant who can comply with it is considerably smaller than the proportion of those not of his group who can satisfy it, which cannot be shown to be justifiable irrespective of the complainant's racial group, and which results in his detriment. While the direct discrimination clause deals with intentional discrimination on an individual basis, the indirect discrimination clause addresses discrimination that need not be intentional but that has the practical result of disadvantaging certain groups. In the social work field for example, the requirement of certain educational qualifications for admission to basic qualifying courses may have the result of limiting the numbers of applicants from minority groups to a greater extent than from the white population. Where there is a national discrepancy, training bodies can offer preferential training to black people.

An employer may encourage black people to apply for posts by advertising in the ethnic press, or by affording minority employees access to 'facilities for training' to qualify them for particular work. S.38 of the Act permits the granting of special assistance to minority group members alone (defined by racial, ethnic or national origins, leaving Jews and Sikhs in an ambiguous position). The employer is not held to be discriminating if he does not offer similar facilities to whites. These provisions are intended to do a limited amount to provide 'equal opportunity' and to counteract the disadvantage suffered by the black population in general. They do not go so far as 'reverse discrimination', which amounts to reserving a quota of jobs for each minority group. Compulsory job quotas or lower standards of recruitment are unlawful. For a full discussion see Lustgarten (1980, pp. 3–44).

The legal provision only extends to training the black employee so that he can compete equally with whites. However, it does provide scope for employers in multi-racial areas to influence the composition of their workforce to reflect the nature of the surrounding population. The provision also extends to the distribution of ethnic minority workers through the hierarchy of the organisation, to avoid the situation where there are few non-whites in higher level jobs, and a large number in unattractive positions. Local authorities were called upon, though not required, to implement equal opportunity policies (s.71).

Trade unions and analogous associations are also permitted under s.38 to train minority persons alone, to 'fit them for holding a post of any kind in the organisation' or encourage them to attempt to do so. Trades unions can also undertake recruitment drives directed at minority members alone.

The Race Relations Board and the Community Relations Commission were amalgamated into a new Commission for Racial Equality (CRE). For the first time an individual who felt he had suffered discrimination might bring a court action on his own behalf. A victim of discrimination may often face great practical difficulties in establishing the facts of his case, and the Commission for Racial Equality may assist him, particularly if the case raises a question of principle, or if it is unreasonable to expect the complainant to deal with it unaided. When a case is proved, damages may be awarded, though in the case of indirect discrimination, only if the complainant can prove that this was intentional. The Commission itself may also carry out 'strategic' investigations of discriminatory practices and issue non-discrimination notices, from which there is an appeal to an industrial tribunal or county court. If the notice is not complied with, the Commission may seek an injunction. The vigour with which this 'strategic' role is pursued is partly dependent on the funds available to sustain such activity, but also on the strength of political support for the Commission, and the general attitude of courts and tribunals.

The 1976 Act also re-enacted the 1965 prohibition on incitement to racial hatred, but the incitement no longer had to be intentional to warrant prosecution.

The inner area programmes 1977

Meanwhile the Conservative Secretary of State for the Environment, Peter Walker, had been deeply concerned about the problems of the inner cities and unemployment among black youth, and in 1972 commissioned three Inner Area Studies in Lambeth, Small Heath and Liverpool 8. In June 1977 the White Paper *Policy for the inner cities* (Cmnd 6845 1977), was produced, and in accordance with the findings of the Studies, the succeeding Labour administration shifted responsibility for programmes of positive help to counteract deprivation from the Home Office to the Department of the Environment (DOE) led by Labour's Environment Secretary, Peter Shore.

Seven Partnership and fifteen Inner Area Programme authorities were to link up with central government and be financed 75 per cent on the submission of acceptable programmes to the Department of the Environment. The particular needs of ethnic minorities were to be taken into account. The focus on social services co-ordination, and the assumed characteristics of the residents of the inner city areas which had characterised earlier policy, was shifted to an environmental approach that recognised the centrality of economic factors in urban decline.

More immigration control: current legislation

In 1977 the Labour government's Green Paper heralded yet more legislation on immigration, stating that 'there must be more meaningful citizenship for those who have close links with the United Kingdom'. The new leadership of the Conservative Party was also expressing a notion of Englishness which was closer to that of Enoch Powell:

The British character has done so much for democracy, for law and order and so much throughout the world that, if there was any fear that it might be swamped, people are going to be hostile to those coming in'. (Thatcher 1978, quoted in Cashmore and Troyna 1983).

In 1979, the incoming Conservative government announced new immigration legislation. In 1980 the immigration rules were tightened to stop the entry into the UK of the fiancés of black women, as a consequence of the government's belief 'that it is not right that the marriage way may ... be used as a means by which the number of adult male heads of families should increase' (HCP 90-1 1982, p. xiv).

In 1985 the European Court of Human Rights found these rules to be sexually discriminatory, and the government then introduced new rules which applied the same restrictions to women as to men.

The British Nationality Act 1981 replaced the United Kingdom and Colonies citizenship of the British Nationality Act 1948, with three separate citizenships. Intended to consolidate existing legislation, but changed in several respects during its passage through Parliament, it left several categories, including Commonwealth citizenship, outside its threefold division, so that the current nationality laws are extremely complex. The 1981 Act was principally aimed at preventing the entry into Britain of those residents of Hong Kong who might wish to come here when the colony reverts to China in 1997. Thus residents of Hong Kong and Gibraltar were granted British Dependent Territories Citizenship, while British Overseas Citizenship was accorded to certain other residual categories of those with the former United Kingdom and Colonies citizenship. People with these two new citizenships had no right of entry into the UK, and their citizenship provided them only with such rights as the help of consular services while in third countries.

Moving the second reading, the Home Secretary stated that 'We are doing nothing new in suggesting that our citizenship should give a better idea of where people actually belong'. British citizenship can no longer be acquired automatically by being born in the UK. The child will acquire it only where either of his parents is a British citizen, or is ordinarily resident in the UK. The definition of 'ordinarily resident' is difficult, and will normally be undertaken not by a court but by an immigration officer. Birth to a parent who becomes a British citizen or becomes settled in the UK enables an application for registration as a British citizen to be made when the child attains the age of ten. Meanwhile his status may remain in limbo. The application may be granted at the discretion of the Home Secretary, provided that in each of the first ten years he has spent no more than ninety days outside the UK.

While the intent of the changes in the immigration rules and the 1981 British Nationality Act was to reduce the number of black people in Britain, their effect was also to some degree assimilationist, making it more difficult for Asians for example to reduce white influences on their family life by marrying their children to spouses from their country of origin. Children might also have to be brought up here, not with grandparents, or they may in certain circumstances be prevented from rejoining their parents (Cronin 1985).

Positive programmes
The Conservative government was noticeably less keen than its predecessors on government intervention. Its programmes of positive help, such as the Docklands Development Boards in London and Liverpool, and the enterprise zones elsewhere, have reflected its ideological orientation and have been based on the need to speed up planning decisions and attract commercial and industrial development to deprived areas. The Urban Programme has been extended but is generally used only to fund capital projects which can be maintained out of revenue, leaving s.11 of the Local Government Act of 1966 as the main source of finance for developing social work with ethnic minorities.

Summary to 1981
By the beginning of the 1980s, long-term trends in British policy, whichever party was in power, had become evident. Immigration policy was unconcerned to control white immigration from the Republic of Ireland, the white Commonwealth countries or the EEC, but now excluded black immigrants. This discrimination on grounds of skin colour had been justified, however, without recourse to explicitly racist

language (Reeves 1983). At the same time fairly strong anti-discrimination legislation provided a framework for effective enforcement if the political and social will were present.

Whether these policies are consistent or inconsistent is beyond the scope of this book. Governments attempted to appease both racialists and liberals, so that arguments for consistency were 'probably more a rationalisation of what the government had done than the basis on which they had acted' (Dummett and Dummett 1969, p. 107). Attempts to alleviate the deprivation suffered by those black people already in Britain featured a similar linguistic fastidiousness — governments had seemed to try to help while trying to appear not to do so. Programmes were subsumed under the general heading of 'disadvantage', and were directed at areas rather than groups (Edwards and Batley 1978). Their aims were diffuse and the recognition of minority problems was generally avoided (Little and Robbins 1982). Concluding their detailed account of urban programmes since the 1960s, Higgins et al. (1983) point out that it was clear that the solution to our urban problems required the investment of huge resources. 'It was equally clear that urban poverty in all its aspects (not least the racial element) is low on the list of priorities in central government.'

1981 and after
The more confrontational style of the 1979 Conservative government was matched in Bristol in 1980 and in Brixton and major provincial cities the following year, by riots. In Southall the Indian community reacted to violent white skinheads, but elsewhere the riots included both black and white members of inner city communities. However these disturbances, and the Scarman Report (1981) which followed, seemed to have ended the general concealment of racial issues, at least at the level of local and metropolitan authorities with large black populations, many of which began a new, and probably more hopeful, phase of racial awareness in policy development. Criticism of the Greater London Council's and the metropolitan authorities' attempts to help black communities was one aspect of the Conservative Party's attacks on those authorities which led to their abolition in 1986. Lack of support at the highest political level was not perhaps altogether disadvantageous as authorities were free of

the restrictions that would be applied were there a minister who could be held to be directly promoting their policies. But the scope of local democracy has been reduced. Financial penalties (rate capping) contain expenditure; and the economic position of the inner cities continues to worsen. More rioting, with loss of life, occurred in 1985. Meanwhile the government has been pursuing a foreign policy favourable to South Africa, which has an unmistakable internal resonance.

3 Disadvantage and discrimination

The problem of black clients are related to the relatively recent immigration of most of their communities, the position of structured inferiority in which they now find themselves, and the ways in which both discrimination by the white majority, and the normal workings of the social system, conspire to sustain inequality. In this chapter we describe a small number of key areas of disadvantage, not just as 'background', but because the 'uniqueness' of social work has been over-stressed. The changes required in social work are also faced in other fields, and social work has much to learn from efforts to reform housing, education and employment provisions, and needs to know much about these fields in order to co-operate with agencies within them to the benefit of black clients.

Numbers and geographical distribution

The population of Great Britain is some 54 million, and in 1981 it was estimated that just over 2.2 million, or 4.1 per cent, had their origins in the New Commonwealth and Pakistan (OPCS 1982). Over four-fifths of these people have their origin in the Caribbean, the Indian subcontinent or Africa. The black population is estimated therefore to be about 3.4 per cent of the general population. Because of continuing limited immigration and natural increase (the rate of which is influenced by the younger age profile of the black compared to the white population), the numbers of black people are projected to rise to between 2.5 and 3 million by 1991, in spite of an underlying downward trend in fertility towards the level for whites. Of this black population, those of West Indian origin were the largest group until 1971, but were then overtaken by Asians, including those from East Africa (the 'African Asians'). Those of Caribbean origin now form about one-third of the total, while those originally from the Indian subcontinent comprise half (OPCS 1982).

The office of Population Censuses and Surveys (OPCS) estimates suggested that in 1976 just under 40 per cent of the black population had actually been born here, and that this proportion would rise to about half by 1991. Because of the later peak of Asian immigration, the proportion of the British-born among those of West Indian origin is higher. Thus at present there are numbers of black people in Britain who were born in the New Commonwealth or Pakistan, and numbers of younger people who were born here: but those who have lived out the whole span of a normal lifetime in this country will mostly have been from the long-established black populations in ports.

The Policy Studies Institute, successor to the PEP, recently carried out a third survey of the position of black people in Britain (Brown 1984). The black population is geographically distributed in a very clustered way, 76 per cent living in areas of 'high ethnic minority concentration'. For some years the population in general (both black and white) has been moving out of the inner city areas into the suburbs or smaller towns and rural areas, 'voting with their wheels'. The black population has not, however, shared proportionately in this movement. Thus instead of each town having a small black community making up about 3 per cent of its population, a large proportion of the black population lives in a small number of local authority areas, and within these areas tends to be concentrated in a small number of electoral wards. In most areas of the country there are very few black people indeed. Half the white population of Britain lives in towns and rural areas where black people make up less than 0.5 per cent of the local residents.

London is particularly important as the home of half the black population of Caribbean origin and a third of those of Asian origin (though, within the Asian community, the main area of Pakistani settlement is in Yorkshire). Some 60 per cent of white Londoners live in the outer boroughs, compared to 37 per cent of Caribbean Londoners and 52 per cent of Asian Londoners. There are, however, striking contrasts within the Asian community. Bangladeshis are very heavily concentrated in inner London, Pakistanis have the same inner-outer mix as the white population, while African Asians and Sikhs are concentrated in the outer boroughs.

Outside of London, the former metropolitan counties of Manchester, the West Midlands, Leicestershire, Nottinghamshire, Derbyshire, West and South Yorkshire, Lancashire, Berkshire, Bedfordshire and Hertfordshire have relatively high concentrations of black people. Within these large areas, the clustering of nearly all the black population in a set of pre-1974 local authority areas has been preserved, as has the clustering within the electoral wards originally settled by black people within these local authorities. The degree of dispersal in recent years has been limited, particularly for Asians.

Electoral implications

In 1983 there were 357,000 electors of West Indian origin (0.9 per cent of the British electorate), 47,000 of African origin (0.1 per cent), 485,000 of Indian origin (1.2 per cent), and 183,000 of Pakistani and Bangladeshi origin (0.5 per cent) (OPCS 1982, quoted in Crewe 1983).

Crewe doubts that black people make up a third of the electorate in more than a handful of seats, or constitute a majority in any. They are out-numbered nationally by those white electors who are frankly racist and produce the 'anti-ethnic vote'. The two-party system and single-member constituencies seem structurally incapable of accommodating specific group interests and there is no prospect of success for ethnic parties. However, very gradually, as more local parties are 'captured' by ethnic minority officials, officers and candidates, the likelihood increases of a very small number of black MPs being elected. There is under-registration of the black electorate compared to the white, but, if registered, the black elector is more likely to vote, and to vote Labour.

The situation at local elections is somewhat different because of the preponderance of black electors in certain wards. Crewe (1983) records about seventy local councillors from the minority communities, mainly in London. This amounts to much less than the ethnic proportion of the population warrants, particularly in provincial cities. Sometimes rivalries within and between different ethnic minority communities makes it difficult for them to find a common representation. Nevertheless the skin colour of local councillors is important for local policy, including social services policy. Young and Conelly (1981) show that white or nearly completely white councils made much less use of s.11 grants, either because they 'did not see the need' for special help for minority populations, or because they believed in a 'colour-blind' approach, which treated everyone 'equally'. The presence of black councillors appeared, at least in 1981, to be crucial in motivating social services department managements to review policy and practice for racial bias.

Housing

On arrival in this country immigrants from the Caribbean found privately rented accommodation where they could, which was usually in older property in the inner city areas. Rents were often exorbitant (well above the maximum rent allowance payable by social security), tenancies were insecure because of insufficient legal protection against harassment and illegal eviction, overcrowding was common, and basic facilities (for example, kitchen, bathroom) often shared. Entry into the council house sector was delayed, firstly because of the need to reside locally for a number of years before being considered eligible and secondly by the long waiting lists in housing stress areas. Not surprisingly, homelessness was, and still is, a more frequent route into council housing for black than for white people. Homeless families are frequently offered the least desirable council property.

The housing pattern of the black population of West Indian origin today shows clear signs of improvement over that of the desperate days of the migration. Nevertheless, it is still divergent from that of the white population. Overall, among whites there are nearly twice as many households (59 per cent) who are owner-occupiers as are council tenants (30 per cent), whereas for those of Caribbean origin there are more council tenants (46 per cent) than owners (41 per cent). West Indians also differ from the white and Asian populations in that a larger proportion (8 per cent) are tenants of housing associations (Brown 1984).

Outside of the major conurbations, the level of council tenancies is identical between the two groups at 30 per cent, though the proportion of those of West Indian origin in housing association tenancies remains higher. So it is within the conurbations that a relatively high proportion of those of West Indian origin are now found in council tenancies. The proportion sharing basic amenities with another household is now very small, and 95 per cent of both whites and West Indians have plumbed hot water, bath and inside WC for their household's sole use. In the inner city, white households are often single persons or pensioners, and these demographic differences make it difficult to compare white and West Indian housing.

Outside of the inner cities, there are indications that West Indians may generally occupy housing that is older, have more flats, which are further from the ground, and be more over-crowded than whites. However, this may partly reflect the housing stock of the areas in which they live, or the fact that more West Indians may be in growing households. Or they may be in their first council tenancy, in areas where it is the practice to get tenants to prove for some years that they are 'responsible' in less desirable accommodation before obtaining a transfer to somewhere better.

The Asian housing pattern differs markedly from both West Indian and white, in that overall the proportion buying their own homes is very high (72 per cent) while the proportion of council tenants is relatively low (19 per cent). This national picture becomes more complex when comparison is made between different Asian communities, and different areas of residence. A very high proportion of Sikhs, of whom relatively few live in the inner city, are owner-occupiers (91 per cent) and few are council tenants (6 per cent). By contrast the level of owner-occupation among Bangladeshis, most of whom live in the inner city, is low (30 per cent) and levels of council and private tenancy are high (53 per cent and 11 per cent respectively).

Dahya (1973, 1974) describes how the first substantial numbers of Asian immigrants arriving in Bradford and Birmingham obtained rented accommodation with the few existing Asian landlords. Each community, village and kinship group established itself in separate houses as soon as they were able, purchasing cheaper, older terraced housing using loans from their extended families. Dahya challenges the picture presented by Rex and Moore (1967) of black immigrants confined by white discrimination within the worst city housing. This picture might be more true of other communities, but the Pakistanis had actually made very few applications for council housing, since they had no firm intention of settling in Britain, to them a heathen country. Their idea was to work and remit home the maximum amount before themselves returning to Pakistan. From the immigrants' own perspective they had thus found in older,

terraced property, housing suited to their needs. It was
offered at prices they could afford, was close to the factories
in which they worked, thus saving on fares, and equipped
with running water and gas, facilities they had not enjoyed in
Pakistan. In this housing they could accommodate newly
arrived kinsmen and fellow-villagers, extending and reinfor-
cing the web of reciprocal obligation and mutual help under-
pinning their extended family network.

Living in council tenancies would have exposed them to
supervision by housing department officials, a concept
foreign to them, which would have limited the occupiers of
each house to the members of a 'nuclear family' on the white
model. Council housing would have been disfunctional to
their needs. They did not at that time feel deprived in comparison with white neighbours in modern houses, as their
reference groups still lay in their villages of origin.

Dahya's point is that ethnocentric factors may be present
in assumptions about comparative need, as they obviously
are in expressed need. Today Brown shows that the Pakistani
community still has a higher ratio of terraced houses than
others, and greater density of occupation than all other
groups save the Bangladeshis. The proportion lacking exclusive use of piped hot water, bathroom and inside WC reflects
the greater age of their property and is slightly higher than
all other groups save again the Bangladeshis, who are much
worse off in this as in all other respects.

As the felt needs of the Pakistani and other Asian communities change over time, council housing may appear more
attractive to them. Several writers have expressed concern
that as owner-occupiers they will be ineligible to apply for
council tenancies, and will be 'trapped' in their own sub-
standard housing. Brown (1984) shows that an increasing
proportion of Asians are now becoming council tenants, and
being housed from the waiting list. There are probably wide
variations between the different communities in the extent
to which this is taking place, but overall Brown considers
that the Asian pattern of housing tenure is moving closer to
that of the whites.

As regards expressed satisfaction or dissatisfaction about
housing needs, a striking feature of Brown's survey is the
high proportion of all groups expressing some degree of
satisfaction with their housing. All groups show an even

higher level of satisfaction with their area of residence, indicating the importance of the presence of other members of their own community, ethnic shops and organisations, and facilities for religious worship, above that which white people would regard as desirable features of a district.

Nevertheless it remains true that the black population is in general worse housed than the white population, which could be expected if only in view of the worse economic situation of blacks. However Karn (1984) also speculates on factors both within local authority housing departments and within building societies, which may tend to perpetuate this pattern of disadvantage. In the course of her survey she picks out the essence of the 'colour-blind' policy orientation which seems also, incidentally, to have been dominant in most social services departments until 1981. Essentially it is, firstly:

> the self-protective view of senior management that, if there is no specific policy to discriminate, no discrimination occurs (Karn 1984, p. 162).

Secondly, this attitude is maintained in an organisational context where there is widespread use of discretion by personnel in the lower levels of the organisational hierarchy in interpreting the rules while making day-to-day decisions. Thirdly, there is a lack of monitoring of the outcomes both of policies and of practice as regards ethnic minority clientèle. 'Colour-blind' policy has a positive function for management in that: 'it enables the liberal position voiced by the centre to remain unexplored empirically and actual practices to remain unchallenged (Karn 1984, p. 179).

The reaction of a 'colour-blind' organisation to the possibility that racial discrimination occurs within it is that, if it exists at all, it must be 'the product of the behaviour of a few racially prejudiced individuals'. This does not explain why, as research by Smith and Whalley (1975) shows, even when there are frequent changes of personnel involved in resource allocation duties, the organisation may continue to display a remarkable consistency in making racially discriminatory allocations. This is because:

> many institutional aims and rules are themselves very likely to favour dominant interests in society and are unlikely to be sacrificed in the interests of racial equality,

unless this is made an explicit and strongly stressed aim of policy (Karn 1984, p. 164).

In the case of many local authority housing departments, Karn considers that the interests of 'respectable' white tenants receive wide public support based partly on social class and race interests. These tenants are most likely to receive favourable discrimination and be offered the most desirable properties. Many white tenants are resistant to having black tenants moved into the same street, and may respond with complaints, rows between neighbours, or violent attacks, particularly upon Asians, with resulting continuing management problems for the housing departments concerned. Asians, West Indians and whites are thus most likely to have their estate preferences matched with an allocation if they request an area that is usually popular with their own group. In any case the boundaries of the local authorities in which they live often, especially in London, restrict the possibility of opting for suburbia. It is both convenient and economical in time for housing departments to make offers to black tenants which they are likely to accept, in estates of existing black settlement, rather than try to encourage them to disperse their settlement pattern by offering better housing in 'respectable' white estates. Housing departments thus probably influence the type of housing need 'felt' and 'expressed' by black people by limiting their awareness of alternatives: a complex interaction made even more so by the desire of some black communities to concentrate and segregate.

As regards the role of building societies, Karn (1984) surmises that their behaviour reflected the interests of the white owner-occupier. Brown (1984) finds that a majority of whites (77 per cent), West Indians (65 per cent) and Asians (68 per cent) who were owner-occupiers who did not own their home outright were buying their property with money borrowed from a building society. These proportions show considerable convergence when compared to the equivalent figures for 1973 of 73 per cent, 51 per cent and 40 per cent quoted by Karn (1984, p. 175). Nevertheless building societies are generally less willing to invest in older, inner-city properties. Karn (1984) also suggests that their local personnel appear to discriminate positively in favour of whites by making loans to white applicants who are not savers with the society, contrary to the rules. Black buyers, in contrast, are expected to meet the official savings requirements in full. Also blacks, even when they are savers with the society appear to be refused an advance more often than whites, who receive more help from white estate agents and solicitors in the form of pressure on building societies to make loans.

This pattern is reflected in the alternative sources of finance used by black buyers. Brown (1984) shows that West Indian mortgagors are twice as likely to have borrowed from a local authority as whites. The percentage of Asians buying with a bank loan, often from an Asian bank, is three times higher than whites, in spite of the higher interest rates. Asians are also six times more likely than whites, and three times more likely than West Indians, to have received the money for the deposit as a loan or gift from relatives.

In subsequent chapters we trace the operation of 'colour-blind' policies in social services departments. In this section we have examined how 'colour-blindness' denied ethnic minorities a commensurate share of existing housing resources. However this is only one aspect of the effects of 'colour-blindness'. The other entails a failure to examine whether existing provisions are appropriate to the special needs that ethnic minorities may have.

Because of the immense size of their operations, housing authorities tend to provide standard solutions to standard problems which may not always be appropriate to ethnic minority needs. Minority members tend to have larger house-holds, and there may be a relative scarcity of larger council properties, leading to a longer time on the waiting list. Asians may wish to preserve their extended family structure by applying for joint mortgages, such as between uncle and nephew, the reasons for which may not be understood.

A proportion of black youth, particularly those of West Indian origin, seem to be more prone to become homeless as the cumulative result of overcrowding, discrimination, unemployment and inter-generational tension (CRC 1974). A related problem is the higher level of single-parent families among Afro-Caribbean households (13 per cent) compared to the proportion in the general population (10 per cent). Afro-Caribbean single parents tend to be younger, and many of them enter council housing through homelessness, thus ending up with the worst accommodation. Ethnic minority elderly people may need accommodation near their own existing areas of settlement. Providing accommodation for extended families may reduce the pressure for sheltered housing. Battered Asian wives, or young Asian women who decide to leave home, may also need special provision. Authorities can encourage voluntary organisations and self-help groups to meet such special needs.

Recently certain local authorities have successfully improved their practice through strict ethnic monitoring of allocations, and setting 'targets' for the proportion of newer lettings to be allocated to blacks (DOE 1983, p. 20). On the negative side, the halting of new building and the sale of council housing, in so far as it is usually the newer property that is sold, is likely to limit the opportunity for black council tenants to move into better council property.

The Asian and West Indian communities still have housing patterns that diverge from those of whites and to that extent form separate sub-markets involved with different forms of tenure, different areas of settlement, different sources of finance and inferior types of property.

Education

There has been relatively little central policy response to the presence of ethnic minority children within British schools. In 1966 the Department of Education and Science (DES) set up a national system of monitoring immigrant pupils but abandoned it in the face of various objections. Such Local Education Authorities (LEAs) as collected statistics used them as the basis for claims for s.11 grants, of which the lion's share goes on education department staff. However, the extent to which LEAs actually use s.11 personnel to attend to educational needs specific to ethnic minority children is in doubt. Many LEAs have been using them to improve the teacher/pupil ratio in remedial teaching generally. New monitoring arrangements are now being introduced to ensure that the grant-aided provision actually reaches its target group.

During the 1970s DES policy was characterised as 'racially inexplicit' (Kirp 1979), subsuming the educational needs of ethnic minority children under those of the 'disadvantaged'. Towards the end of the 1970s there was movement away from the assimilationist understandings of the 1960s to the appreciation that some form of cultural pluralism is more acceptable to the ethnic minority groups themselves (Cmnd 2266 1964, DES 1977).

Initiatives and developments have come largely from LEAs, and from individual teachers, with substantial numbers of black pupils. There is still only limited agreement on what should be done. The autonomy of head teachers, and the difficulty of monitoring the attitude changes demanded of school staff, complicate policy implementation.

Reviewing the extensive literature, Tomlinson (1984) concludes that little research effort has been directed towards discovering or describing examples of the effective or succesful schooling of minority — or indeed of any — children in Britain (Tomlinson 1984, p. i). Nevertheless there are a small number of US and British studies that indicate that certain primary schools are 'effective' in teaching both poor black and poor white children. These are characterised by strong leadership from the head teacher in setting teaching objectives for the staff, and high expectations of the pupils: the schools concentrate on instruction, and have an orderly and pleasant atmosphere, and a high level of parent-initiated contact with the school. Race is not found to be important for achievement in these schools. Unfortunately there is less research on factors making for effectiveness in secondary schools.

Curriculum content causes concern in government circles anxious about national cohesion (HCP 424-I 1981). The problem reflects the dual aims of the education provided: achievement in examinations, and value transmission. The values of equality of educational opportunity demand that minority children are equipped with skills in English, mathematics and other subjects that will help them to compete in British society on a more equal footing: notwithstanding that this aspect of education is assimilationist.

The value-transmission aspect of education is more obviously in conflict with the human right to retain minority group cultural autonomy, because the values put forward are culturally determined, and tend to work themselves out in society to the advantage of the majority population. Minority children cannot be expected to feel 'whole people' without knowledge and appreciation of their own cultural background being reflected in the curriculum.

By 1981, about twenty-five LEAs had appointed an adviser for multi-cultural education funded by s.11 grants, reflecting the widespread belief that provision should go beyond teaching English as a second language. It was clear that 'the education appropriate to our imperial past cannot meet the requirements of modern Britain' (DES 1977). Links were being made between the under-performance of black pupils, and the negative presentation of black people and Eurocentric stereotypes of ex-colonial territories, presented in the curriculum. Curriculum reform is equally necessary in schools without large numbers of black children, to counteract prejudice and stereotyping by the white majority pupils. However it has proved difficult to interest such schools in these developments. Davey (1983) shows that 70 per cent of parents want schools to give more teaching about race. Some educationalists also advocate direct anti-racist teaching (Tierney 1982).

There is a low level of agreement on what 'multi-cultural education' should consist of, and how its aims of instilling respect for one's own and others' cultures can be achieved (Tomlinson 1984). Anxiety has been expressed as to how many cultures the school can be expected to reflect. Concern has also been expressed from black people as to whether the white majority may not use multi-cultural education as a means of disadvantaging black pupils even further by directing their energies away from 'basic subjects'.

These issues are being worked out in a variety of ways in the schools. There is some development of *de facto* segregated schools. Dispersing minority pupils by bus was perceived in Britain as racially oppressive, the opposite to the response in the USA. It was made illegal in 1977. Neighbourhood schools may now be all-black or nearly so, partly because of concentrated settlement patterns, and partly because a large proportion of the white inner-city population is Irish and is self-segregating in Roman Catholic schools.

The Afro-Caribbean community have set up Saturday schools, a well-established tradition in the West Indies. Temple and mosque schools have been established to preserve Asian religious and cultural values. Nevertheless Tomlinson (1984 p. 15) considers that:

up to 1980 at least, most ethnic minority parents and their children were still, by and large, seeking pluralistic incorporation into the majority society via the English state system, desiring the same kind of education and opportunities offered to white children.

Nevertheless she does note an increasing demand for education to be organised on a religious instead of a secular basis, possibly through the further establishment of private schools, or voluntary-aided schools within the state system. Muslim parents in particular may be in conflict with a secularised, co-educational Western education system (see Ahmad 1980).

Meanwhile early mother-tongue teaching — teaching very young pupils partly in their own language — is increasingly practised as it has been found to benefit achievement later. The teaching of Asian languages to 'O' and 'A' levels is also acceptable to schools and is being developed. Though statistics are lacking, it seems that about 800 black teachers may be in post, a fair proportion of them trained on special Access courses, who have a significant contribution to make in motivating black children to do well. However their organisation has complained that they have disproportionately high failure rates during training, are subject to more stringent checks during the probationary period, and tend to be denied promotion because of their colour.

Davey (1975) argues that it needs to be repeatedly emphasised that the task of the educator in a multi-ethnic society is not the elimination of difference but one of bringing about an adjustment to diversity and social change. Teacher training should be concerned with helping teachers to discover their own habitual ways of thinking about such categories as race, sex, ethnicity and social class and the manner in which their group membership has organised their perception — a delicate process that is equally valid for social work training.

Concern about the under-performance of black pupils arose in the context of complaints by white parents that their children were being 'held back' by immigrant children in class, and the resurgence of theories of innate racial differences in intelligence. Since so many whites subscribe to such theories, the political rather than 'scientific' nature of this debate needs to be emphasised:

individuals must be judged on the basis of their own personality and accomplishments, not on the basis of their race. Even if we accepted IQ differences of fifteen points

definitive, any attempts to classify people into
.nd whites on the basis of IQ alone would be right
)er cent more often than if we decided on the basis
ng a coin (Eysenck 1971, p. 34).

)n points out that IQ tests have been subjected to so
mu... :iticism that their trans-cultural validity can hardly be
accepted as unproblematic. What 'intelligence' is supposed to
be is not entirely clear. Tests of learning ability show little
difference between negro and white. Given the presumably
polygenetic basis of 'intelligence', geneticists would not be
surprised if two racial populations did not have identical
mean IQ scores. On the other hand they would not be surprised if they did, as the possible effect of a putatively higher
or lower mean endowment cannot be distinguished from the
clear effects of socio-economic differentials and language
difficulties. When the statistics are controlled for the socio-
economic background of pupils, much, but not all, of the difference between white children and black disappears.

The under-performance of minority group children is not
automatic. A small but not statistically insignificant proportion of West Indians do well, and a somewhat larger proportion of Asians. Staying on at school 'pays off' for children in
both groups in terms of examination results. Apart from the
influence of poverty, over-crowding and other factors associated with low socio-economic status, there are more specific handicaps endured by ethnic minority pupils.

> The children are being socialised into a society in which
> ethnic discrimination is widely employed. The children
> acquire their prejudice towards other groups at the same
> time and in the same way as they acquire the values and
> ideals of their own group. They see others treated with
> respect or as inferior, they hear them described in comple-
> mentary or uncomplimentary terms and they notice the
> roles assigned to them in the media and society in general.
> What they learn in one situation is likely to be confirmed
> in another (Davey and Mullin 1982, p. 92).

Davey's extensive study (1983) of the ethnic awareness of
children aged seven to ten years does not support earlier
investigations, which reported extensive self-rejection or
problems of self-identity in black children. Nearly all the
children in his study identified themselves correctly with

their own racial group. He feels that the reassertion of pride in black identities during the 1970s has contributed to this result. Nevertheless about half of the black children indicated that, if they could choose, they would prefer to be like the white group. Davey feels that this reflects the social categorisations of society, in which the whites have nearly all the power and wealth. The children 'are in no doubt as to who has the favoured place in the social pecking order'.

Research into friendship patterns revealed that children from all ethnic groups showed a considerable degree of in-group bias, but this form of ethnocentricity was most marked in the white children, who showed a greater propensity to assign favourable attributes exclusively to themselves. Neither of the minority groups, Asian or West Indian, felt that the whites were more attractive than themselves, but they reserved their dislike for the other minority. 'They concurred with the whites' damaging view of the other minority but not with the whites' image of themselves.' Disparagement of the other minority is inevitable if it functions to protect one's own in-group from an inferior status. 'How far such attitudes are implicitly encouraged within schools by their efforts to achieve some form of assimilation is difficult to say' (Davey and Norburn 1980, p. 59).

Parekh (1984) and Tomlinson (1984) point out that in the 1960s the language difficulties of Asian pupils were recognised, and met with a structured and resourced programme of English as Second Language teaching, perhaps particularly benefiting these children at a time when less structured teaching was fashionable. Research on Asian under-performance was done partly by Asian academics, who did not present Asian families in terms of intractable poverty and cultural limitation but emphasised stability and high expectation. They gave the impression that the difficulties of Asian pupils could be overcome by positive policies within the schools.

Early research and opinion on West Indian under-performance, in contrast, relied heavily on blaming factors within the family and the culture rather than the school. The language problems of West Indian children were not recognised. Coard (1971) and Tomlinson (1981) countered by suggesting that unsuitable assessment tests, low teacher expectations, teacher stereotyping, and the low self-esteem and self-concept of black children in a hostile society, could account for much over-representation of West Indians in Educationally Subnormal-Maladjusted schools, disruptive units and educational guidance centres.

Differences between Asian and West Indian under-performance may well be linked to the higher number of Asians with middle class backgrounds. In any event, West Indian parents have now become highly suspicious of explanations that locate reasons for under-achievement within the family.

Tomlinson (1984, p. 83) stresses that 'there *are* no easy answers for teachers, particularly in the 1980s, as to what exactly is required of a "good" teacher in a multi-cultural society'. A parallel situation to that in social work.

Employment

A disproportionate growth in unemployment has been the major recent development in the economic position of black people. At the end of 1982 national unemployment stood at some 3 million, or 13 per cent of the total working population. However Brown (1984) finds that the rate was twice as high among those of West Indian origin and one and a half times as high among Asians. There were also important differences within the Asian community. The unemployment rate for Pakistani and Bangladeshi men was twice the white rate, while among Hindus and Sikhs the rate was similar to that for white men.

Gender differences also emerge. The unemployment rate for West Indian women is lower than that for West Indian men. A lower proportion of Asian women, particularly Muslim women, enter the labour market, but those that do, tend to be more vulnerable to unemployment than men, partly because they work in industries such as clothing and textiles, which have suffered most in the recent recession.

Several factors contribute to or are associated with the differential between black and white unemployment levels. One is the geographical distribution of black people. The difference is reduced when they are compared to the white population in the same census enumeration districts. However, this white population is frequently itself economically disadvantaged.

Another factor is the generally lower level of jobs held by blacks. Those in less skilled work are most likely to become unemployed in a recession, a relationship that appears particularly true of males. The proportion of men who are manual workers is higher amongst blacks than whites: 83 per cent of West Indians, 73 per cent of Asians, and 58 per cent of white descent. Also, more blacks than whites, Asians particularly, do unskilled or semi-skilled work. Within the Asian community, job levels are higher for African Asians than for others, and African Asians and Hindus have an equivalent proportion to whites in the 'professional, employer, or manager' category. Only 25 per cent of African Asian employees are semi-skilled or unskilled manual workers compared to 70 per cent of Bangladeshis and 40 per cent of Indians and Pakistanis. Sikhs have a relatively high proportion of skilled manual workers. Among women there is less contrast between the employment patterns of blacks and whites, though there is still a greater proportion of manual workers among blacks.

The differential in the employment rate between blacks and whites is also associated with the fact that the black population generally hold fewer formal qualifications. Nevertheless, within each qualification level, whites tend to have better jobs than blacks. Smith (1977) finds that 79 per cent of white men with degree standard qualifications were in professional/managerial jobs, compared with 31 per cent of black men with degree standard qualifications in such jobs. Some 83 per cent of white men with 'A' levels were in non-manual jobs, compared with 55 per cent of black men with 'A' levels in such jobs. Among Asians, unemployment and low levels of employment are particularly associated with those who have a low level of fluency in English. Nevertheless, there are substantial numbers of well-qualified persons within the black community, and the overall picture of black employment patterns is one of great diversity rather than of a uniformly low economic status, so that 'average' levels are potentially misleading.

Black workers still tend to be concentrated in certain occupational sectors such as public transport, the National Health Service, motor vehicle manufacture, clothing and textiles, in which the first immigrants found jobs on arrival. They are more likely than white workers to be involved in shift working and their average earning levels tend to be lower; they still occupy the jobs abandoned by the white urban workers in the 1950s and 1960s. On the other hand there has been some limited movement by both West Indians and Asians into non-manual occupations, particularly among those recently leaving school or college here (Brown 1984, pp. 177–9).

Self-employment is becoming increasingly important to Asians, among whom a higher proportion (men 18 per cent, women 14 per cent) are now self-employed than among whites (men 14 per cent, women 7 per cent). More of these Asians employ other people than do the white self-employed. Some 11 per cent are in catering and retailing enterprises. Some of the Asians with commercial experience before coming to this country – frequently African Asians or Gujeratis – have become important elements of British commercial life and have amassed substantial wealth. According to the Inland Revenue, over one hundred of Britain's millionaires are called Patel (Patterson 1984). At the other end of the scale are the small retailers servicing their local ethnic community, part of an 'ethnic economy' (Baker 1981–2).

The proportion of self-employed West Indians (men 7 per cent, women 1 per cent) is lower than for the white population, and many of these entrepreneurs are in the construction industry. This pattern contrasts with that in the United States, where West Indian immigrants are leading elements of the black business community. Both local and central government in Britain have been concerned to assist West Indian entrepreneurship with training and advice, encouragement with which the Prime Minister has been personally associated (HCP 424–I 1981, *West Indian World* 10 October 1983).

Self-employment may act as an escape from discrimination in access to employment and promotion. Ollereanshaw (1984) reviews formal investigations and research studies by the Commission for Racial Equality (CRE) showing that, to find work, black school leavers have to make more applications and go to more interviews than their equivalently qualified white contemporaries living in the same areas. Black applicants may be turned away by lower level personnel before reaching an interviewer. Interviewers themselves may hold stereotyped assumptions about the capacity of black workers, or they may be under pressure from higher management or the white workforce not to take on black employees.

Employers may be unwilling to go against known or feared hostility to the recruitment of black staff of white employees or customers. Or action to prevent discrimination may not be seen as a priority. Recruiting blacks may, in some industries, entail overturning long-standing negotiated arrangements with trade unions, whereby the latter play a key role in recruitment, or vacancies are circulated among the existing workforce by word of mouth. When this workforce is wholly or mainly white, black applicants are unlikely to be selected or even hear of vacancies. There is a low level of awareness of the 1976 Race Relations Act among employers:

> ignorance and misunderstanding being part of an overall pattern of apathy and low priority, prejudice and hostility (Ollereanshaw 1984, p. 152).

Ollereanshaw describes the pressure and the promotional work undertaken by the CRE to modify this picture.

Central government, which reduced the CRE budget by some 23 per cent in 1980, has a crucial role in developing recruitment and promotion policies in the civil service which would demonstrate to private employers that compliance with the legislation is a serious requirement. The CRE has drawn up a draft *Code of Practice* for the elimination of discrimination and the promotion of equality of opportunity in employment (CRE 1981). This was approved by Parliament in June 1983 and came into operation on 1 April 1984. It recommends employers and trades unions to take positive measures to provide encouragement and training where there is under-representation of particular groups, in particular work in the context of the development of equal opportunity policies and systems for monitoring their effectiveness.

Local authorities also have a duty under s. 71 of the Race Relations Act 1976 to carry out their functions:

> with due regard to the need to eliminate unlawful discrimination and to promote equality of opportunity and good race relations between persons of different racial groups.

Their employment policies affect considerable numbers of employees, and they are always a major, if not the major, employer in the locality. They can influence other local employers by acting as a model, and by using the contracts they offer to suppliers of materials and services as a lever to encourage equal opportunity development in these organisations.

Ollereanshaw (1984) identifies some thirty local authorities who then had equal opportunity policy statements and stated in their job advertisement that they were 'equal opportunity employers'.

There were a smaller number who had fully developed and monitored equal opportunity policies which included positive encouragement for members of ethnic minorities to apply for jobs, and designated training for them. Some authorities have developed 'targets' for the proportion of their workforce they wish to draw from their local ethnic minorities, which are related to the ethnic composition of the local population (racial quotas are illegal under the Act). A few authorities have also adopted policies requiring their contractors to show that they are equal opportunity employers.

Racial discrimination

In the previous chapter, we described how the white consensus on immigration control infers that black people are problem people, undesirable immigrants, the fewer of whom there are here the better. This feeling became general when the numbers of black immigrants were still comparatively small, at a time of full employment, rising wages and rising expectations. Nevertheless the control and prevention of black immigration has been completed without much explicit political expression of the intention of the policy — the exclusion of persons with a darker skin colour (Reeves 1983).

This fastidiousness appears to deny strong feelings of a very long standing indeed. While it would be facile not to acknowledge that the same phenomenon — dislike of dark skins — may be caused by different factors at successive historical periods, the explusion of black people in the reign of Elizabeth I, for instance, demonstrates that the feeling predated the major slave-owning and colonial eras, whatever those experiences subsequently added to it (Jordan 1974, Walvin 1973).

It is clear that just as an inter-ethnic situation involves two or more ethnicities, an inter-racial one involves two or more races. 'The underlying fear has been not of an England no longer English but an England no longer wholly white'

(Dummett and Dummett 1969, p. 77). Nevertheless 'There is no inherent disadvantage in being black or brown. That cannot be stated too often or too loudly' (HCP 424–I 1981, p. x).

It cannot be denied that white racism is a part of the contemporary, as much as the historical, British consciousness. Dummett and Dummett (1969, p. 28) suggest that '90 per cent of British people are racialists', of which only 15 per cent are 'conscious racialists', that is people prepared to profess — in the right company — a straightforward undisguised belief in the inferiority of people of certain races or colours. The remainder they describe as 'crypto racialists', who have 'side by side within them, both deeply rooted racial prejudices and an awareness of the shamefulness of racial prejudice'.

Their opinion is, therefore, that the majority of British people are not wholeheartedly racist, and clearly the national consciousness does include a strong investment in 'fairness, balance, the rule of law, rationality and tolerance', to which appeal can be made. The slave trade and the imperialist and colonialist ethos were challenged from within British culture as well as by forces extrinsic to it. It would be a mistake to dismiss the anti-discrimination machinery as irrelevant, or to deny that the situation between the races is capable of improvement. Neverthless it must be faced that the aspects of public opinion that have hitherto had the greatest impact have been racist (Husband 1982). This is scarcely surprising, as the white British have had centuries of experience of dominating other peoples while insulating this from their conscious beliefs in fairness, tolerance, and so forth.

The black people in Britain are now in a situation where their civil rights are restricted compared to those of the white population in as much as their families may be divided, contacts between relatives made difficult and choice of marriage partner restricted, by the immigration laws, a situation that contributes to certain feelings:

The dominant consensus on immigration has had catastrophic effects on the black communities in Britain, subjecting them to insecurity and harassment from state agencies (such as immigration officials, the police, the Illegal Immigration Intelligence Unit, Health and Social Security Staff) and involving deportation, detention without trial, family separation, shuttlecocking, interminable delays, and all the associated personal sufferings and indignities of which the 'virginity tests' (*Guardian* 1 February 1970) are only the most extreme example (Ben-Tovim and Gabriel 1979, p. 146).

On a more mundane level there are reports of black people having to produce their passports before receiving certain welfare services.

We have seen how the general tendency of numerous institutional processes is to exclude black people from the mainstream of British life. This has repercussions on self-perception:

> For people to see their relatives, friends and other members of their ethnic group working in jobs which are quite different from those done by white people, and know that this has been the case for tens of years, cannot but affect their percetion of their own place in the economy (Brown 1984, p. 297).

This self-perception is reinforced in a multitude of ways. At the lowest level, there are physical attacks by whites, particularly upon Asians. These manifestations of racial hatred were the subject of a Home Office study (1981) which using incidents that were reported to and recorded by the police, indicated a rate of racial victimisation, per hundred thousand population, of 1.4 for whites, 51.2 for West Indians and Africans and 69.7 for Asians. The importance of these attacks for black people, the depth of feeling and concern that they generate, may be underestimated by whites. The assumed contribution of these attacks to black people's reputed lack of confidence in the capacity of the police to protect them makes the numbers reported to and recorded by the police all the more striking.

Short of physical violence, there are the personal experiences of rudeness and hostility from white people in everyday interactions attested by numerous black writers:

> What I found was that black people in this country are insulted day in, day out, in the normal course of social relationships (Kirby 1975, p. 196).

Husband (1975) describes how the media reflected the general denial of black participation in British life, save as 'problems':

> To be a black resident of this country is to be subject to a continuous assault on your identity and integrity. Your presence in this country is signalled to you as being unreal since the news media refuse to see you as a citizen, but as an immigrant (Husband 1975, p. 27).

While there has been some change, the introduction of special programmes on TV, for example, since Husband was writing, the media still reinforce white stereotypes of black incapacity and perpetuate the discussion of black problems without black participation.

The society portrayed by the media often appears as bizarre as the portrayal. Ceremonial state occasions are invariably all-white affairs. TV reports a service to commemorate the 150th anniversary of the death of William Wilberforce: no black priest is shown officiating; the lesson readers, one of whom is the Prime Minister, are all white, as are what we can see of the congregation, the front rows. Omission or boycott? The newscaster apparently fails to notice, and offers no comment.

Live TV coverage of the funeral of Mrs Ghandi is transmitted in the form of brief interruptions to an hilarious breakfast chat show.

Some 300 black Labour Party activists hold a meeting in Birmingham to set up a new national section of the party, for blacks only. One of them demanded to know who was advising the Labour leaders on race:

> Who is briefing them? Certainly not black people. I ask when the leadership of the party is going to talk to us, about the hopes, aspirations and concerns that we have as long-standing members of the Labour Party (*Sunday Times* 10 June 1984).

Chocolate stirs strong emotions. Rowntree Mackintosh refused to satisfy the Greater London Council that they operate an equal opportunities policy, so their contract to supply Kit-Kat was ended:

> The company have refused to answer these questions arguing, quite rightly, that they have no place in a purely commercial transaction. As it happens, Rowntree Mackintosh has a long-standing policy of offering employment to

anyone qualified, 'without discrimination by race, political view, creed or colour'. But even if it were less than exemplary on that score, the company — and any other company — should not have to satisfy the Thought Police of the race relations industry in tendering for contracts. In societies where this kind of harassment is standard, so are jackboots (*Daily Express* 4 April 1985).

Rowntree, quite rightly, have refused to bow down to such petty tyranny. The difference between the makers of Kit-Kat and Red Ken [Ken Livingstone, Leader of the GLC] is the difference between Christian charity and confounded cheek (*Daily Mail* 4 April 1985).

The chocolate faces a ban because the makers, Rowntree Mackintosh, refuse to provide details of their employment policy on 'ethnic minorities and women'. They are dead right. We hope that all companies which supply the GLC will also tell its nosey parkers to go suck a wine gum (*The Sun* 4 April 1985).

That evening on BBC-TV's 'Question Time', the Secretary for Trade and Industry, the Rt Hon. Norman Tebbitt, advised the audience to tell all their friends to buy an extra Kit-Kat.

Those opposed to anti-discrimination legislation can claim the highest motives. It is by their likely outcomes, their effects on the interests of black people, that such motives should be understood. Inequality does not have to be sustained by appeal to crudely racist arguments.

Conclusions: Marxist and Weberian analyses

The age, occupational and geographical profile of the black population entails that it is disproportionately affected by economic change and government policy with regard to the young, the cities and the working class. The principal additional disadvantage suffered by blacks over whites in similar circumstances is racial discrimination. This sustains deprivation, both directly and indirectly through the operation of long-established procedures which, while not always designed to be intentionally discriminatory, work to the disadvantage of blacks. Unless these matters are positively attended to, inequality will persist and worsen; but because of their unconscious assumptions and feelings, whites often find it difficult to give priority to this kind of change.

Sociologists have analysed the position of black people in Britain today from both Marxist and Weberian perspectives, each of which, as we show in the next chapter, has had a major influence on social work thinking.

The 'colour-blind' approach perhaps owed something to Marxist conceptualisation, which reduced racial and ethical problems to a social class analysis, calling into question the possibility that racism could be eliminated by juridical or social reform. Cox (1948), the best known proponent of this reductivist view, sees racism as an instrument of ideological control which is functional for capitalism. By creating conflict between the black and the white working class, it distracts attention and energy from the struggle against capital. Racism in the working class is thus false consciousness, which can be eliminated by a programme of political propaganda. These views have been heavily criticised on both theoretical and empirical grounds (Rex 1970). Cox paradoxically seems to have affinities with a number of theorists who have regarded racism as the product of mistaken attitudes, whereas present-day policies tend to rely on changing behaviour and resource distribution by enforcement from above.

The socialist argument that poor blacks and poor whites shared the common heritage of the working class, and that their problems were best tackled by revolutionary or other means resting on the power of the combined working class, generally has the same outcome if employed by whites, as the liberal one that to pay attention to racial and ethnic differences denies a common humanity: the neglect of existing inequalities between black and white people.

A Marxist critique from a black perspective is provided by Sivanandan (1976, 1981, Bourne and Sivanandan 1980). Sivanandan's account of black settlement in Britain stresses relations of power and exploitation and the primary role of the class struggle between capital and labour. Britain deliberately 'under-developed' its colonial territories by draining them of capital so that they threw up a 'reserve army' of labour, which waited in readiness to serve the needs of the metropolitan economy, 'reared and raised, as capitalist underdevelopment had willed it, for the labour markets of Europe'. To characterise the 'open door' period of immigration policy as a fit of absent-mindedness or British high-mindedness is thus erroneous, 'a load of bullshit', as it was the need of capital for unskilled labour that was served by the immigration of black people.

The profit from black labour did not benefit the whole of society but only sections of it, including some sections of the white working class; whereas the infrastructural 'costs' of black labour, such as over-crowded housing and schools, had been borne by those in greatest need. Having deprived one section of the working class in order to exploit the black section even more, capital 'prevented them both from coming together by intruding that other consciousness of race' and in the process exploited both race and class at once. The economic profit from immigration had gone to capital, the social cost to labour, but the resulting conflict between the two had been obscured by the common ideology of racism.

The immigrants were compelled, partly for self-defence considerations, to live in inner city ghettos, which came to be administered as 'internal colonies' of Britain. Declining demand for unskilled labour, and increasing social unrest, led to the realisation that it was more profitable to end immigration of the unskilled, while those in the developing countries with valuable qualifications continued to be 'creamed off'.

Cultural pluralism and political pluralism are accomodations made in the superstructure of the system so as to consolidate the economic base. Ethnicity is 'some kind of bootstrap' by which you are supposed to pull yourself up, and efforts to focus on cultural or ethnic differences merely divert attention from practices that perpetuate and legitimise racism. Britain's racism stems from its present position of powerlessness, 'a weakness which shores up a memory of a lost strength, an ideological surrogate for economic under-development and political subjugation to the USA'. Present policy towards the 'second generation' is designed to create a new class of 'black collaborators'. Sivanandan (1981) gives an account of black labour struggles, racist and police outrages and sometimes perverse judicial decisions, which form an alternative 'social history' to the account of government policy development presented in our previous chapter.

Other Marxist analyses have not let go of the crucial economic dimension to racism, but have also identified race as a central component of the current right-wing stress on the idea that all that is good and wholesome is under threat,

strong. Embarking on such a union was a serious step: the couple would have known each other for some time and have had sexual relations and possibly a child or two. The intention was nearly always to marry one day, when they could afford it. It might mature into a lifetime union, or one partner might leave. It then became a 'broken common-law marriage'.

Stable cohabitation might be preceded by 'extra-residential affairs'. The care of the children of such relationships and those of broken common-law marriages would be shared between the mother, grandmother and other relatives depending mainly on who was able to find work and hence provide resources. Sociologists have advanced a number of explanations for these 'matrifocal', or 'female-headed', families (Haralambos 1980 pp. 157–9, 326–7). To some they are an adaptation to poverty, the situation of unemployment, seasonal or migratory work. Fathers, it is suggested, rather than face each day their inability to support a family adequately – a 'failure' in the eyes of society – prefer the companionship of those in similar circumstances, while mothers look for financial and emotional support primarily to their indissoluble ties to their own mothers and siblings. Another view relies on a continuing influence from plantation slavery. Only the better off, whites and freemen, could live in nuclear families. Slaves were seldom kept in family units. While mothers and dependent children might be kept together, adults were sold separately and plantation staff had sexual access to female slaves. The male slave could not defend or support a family. Other sociologists look on the matrifocal family as a family 'gone wrong', the product of social disorganisation. Among Afro-Caribbeans, matrifocal families are a statistical minority and not 'the norm', and Fitzherbert's implicit comparison between their actual behaviour and the ideal of life-long egalitarian married monogamy could equally be used to make actual white behaviour seem 'different'. There is no cultural preference for matrifocality, as men and women of every social class aspire to the nuclear family as their cultural ideal. Matrifocality is common enough to be to some extent an accepted and an expected pattern among the poor but should not be seized on to distort the whole picture.

Fitzherbert (1967) considers that the father in a marriage or stable cohabitation would do his best to support children living under his own roof, including, often, step-children, but his role towards his children by broken common-law marriages and extra-residential affairs was more variable, and guided by no definite conventions. The decision whether or not to support a child of such unions might be affected by pragmatic considerations such as his financial position, and whether he felt it would be advantageous to stay on good terms with the mother, or develop his relationship with her. He might bear in mind that:

> men who have spent all their lives running away from responsibility could be left with no-one to care for them in old age, whereas the mothers are 'happy matriarchs' who undertake care of their grandchildren at certain points in their daughters' lives.

Fitzherbert insists on the importance of looking on extended families as child-care resources. Family structures were not only extended, but elastic. The behaviour of fathers and of other relatives would change if circumstances willed it, and there was no reason why previous lack of interest should not become care and concern.

She suggests that there were several aspects of the lower class West Indian cultural background which, when combined with problems of migration, 'destine many West Indian children to be in need of care'. She lists:

(i) a tradition of unstable families.

(ii) many 'single mothers'.

(iii) Victorian (then a denigratory term) child-rearing practices, involving reliance on punishment rather than reward. 'West Indians hold the view that children owe a debt to their parents, while the modern English view is that parents have obligations to their children'. (Supposedly neither culture owned the concept of reciprocal parent/child obligations.) This culture clash was difficult for adolescents to cope with, and might make them decide that their parents were 'really very odd people'.

(iv) the break-up of the extended family through migration.

(v) housing and economic problems for first-generation immigrants.

Some additional factors sometimes made West Indian parents eager to have children received into care, 'regardless of the family's need'. The 'tradition of fostering and informal adoptions' attached no stigma to a mother who let her own mother, aunt, or another relative or someone else care for her children for a time or permanently '... who has most resources takes most responsibility'. Finally some mothers were eager for education and 'culture' and had the impression that a children's home run by white housemothers was a real opportunity for their children to be upwardly socially mobile. They had no experience of the effects on children living in institutions:

> the success of the Child-Care Service relies largely on the fact that few parents apply for its help unless they are genuinely unable to cope on their own. All-out pressure from really determined parents, whatever their need, is very difficult to resist (Fitzherbert 1967, p. 42).

Fitzherbert has been criticised for an over-emphasis on the 'cultural' argument that lower class West Indians tended to use the child-care service as a substitute for their extended families. Other difficulties that might put their children at risk of reception into care could be stressed. Many West Indians came here as individuals, often with the aim of working to provide financial support for children conceived outside marriage left in the care of relatives back home.

The greater availability of regular paid employment in this country had been associated, as would be expected, with a much higher rate of marriage, in acknowledgement of improved social status. However the need to support the 'outside' children left in the West Indies, worry over these children, exhorbitant rents for poor housing, the high cost of daily minding, and low wages, obliged wives, even mothers of young children, to continue working long hours, and threatened the emotional and economic viability of many West Indian households. Adequate provision of day-care would have accomplished much to ease the situation (CRC 1975a).

Fitzherbert could also be criticised for comparing unlike phenomena: white cultural ideals with the actual behaviour of some lower class black parents. She observes that 'it was surely too much to expect people coming from such a different world' to regard the child-care services:

> in the same ambiguous way as we ourselves do, especially as our attitude is very complex, inconsistent and often

hypocritical. On the one hand we have elaborate ideas of social justice, of everybody's 'right' to health and well-being and the state's duty to provide these. On the other, we are still a competitive, *laissez-faire* society, which expects everyone to make his own arrangements. Our pity for those who fail is tinged with a good deal of contempt . . . . This ambiguous attitude is the product of centuries of English historical, religious, philosphical, and even literary traditions. It is thoroughly unrealistic to expect immigrants to share in its subtleties (Fitzherbert 1967, p. 42).

If the comparison had been with the actual behaviour of a group of poor whites applying for reception into care, would the contrasts have been so stark, or would the cultural differences have featured quite so prominently? In many areas of black settlement today, white social workers do not, for demographic reasons, have contact with many white parents applying for care, and may have similar difficulties in keeping 'cultural' factors in perspective.

Fitzherbert is conscious of the bad effects on many black children of being in care. Being brought up by white people could lead to black children avoiding other black people even though it was unlikely that they would find full acceptance among whites. They could become hostile to their own parents, which the latter found incomprehensible and deeply hurtful. 'They assumed that any child loves its mother, and is delighted to return to her at any time.' She considers that departments' 'colour-blind' policies and determination to avoid any suggestion of racial discrimination was disadvantaging black children. The conventionally permissive casework methods designed to support the inadequate family that could not cope were inappropriate when reception into care represented a convenient way out of a temporary difficulty, but by no means the only one. She advocates strongly resisting reception into care when it was clear from the applicant's 'employment record and membership of some kind of family or social group that he falls into the category of normal competent adult'. Intensive work at the initial crisis would 'nearly always' reveal an alternative solution in which some relative or neighbour would undertake care of the children. The use of financial assistance could smooth the way for such arrangements. Departments should also jettison inappropriately cumbersome professional procedures. Offers of a placement by relatives, or their desire to visit children in care, tended to be met by months of vetting which were understood by the relatives as a lack of interest in the possibility of their involvement. By the time the department had made up its mind, circumstances would have changed and lives taken a different course. Hesitating to place a child in an overcrowded family, or one where there was corporal punishment, or where ten-year-old girls were expected to be 'little mothers' and help with babysitting and household chores, also prevented many West Indian children from leaving care, though these were 'normal' conditions for West Indian children in Britain.

White social workers focused on the immediate parents; and tended to assume that single mothers would be stigmatised, isolated individuals, which was frequently far from the case. Illegitimacy was regarded by West Indians as lower class behaviour, so that the arrival of the first illegitimate child was met by parental outrage in proportion to previous social aspirations: but if the family was a common law one, outrage soon passed and the mother nearly always remained part of a functioning group of family and peers.

Fitzherbert's observation that social workers focused on the immediate parents and overlooked the potential roles of other relatives is important. Social workers' orientations derived from white family expectations and were reinforced by the psychological underpinnings of social work professional thought at the time. This tended to attribute overwhelming importance to the mother-child relationship, a perspective that has not withstood the findings of further research:

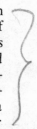

A further point of departure from Bowlby's views concerns the supposedly special importance of the mother. He has argued that the child is innately monotropic and that the bond with the mother (or mother-surrogate) is different in kind from the bonds developed with others. The evidence on this point is unsatisfactory but what there is seems not to support this view. . . . Most children develop bonds with several people and it appears likely that these bonds are basically similar . . . . Of course in most families the mother has most to do with the young child and as a consequence she is usually the person with whom the strongest bond is formed. But it should be appreicated that the chief bond need not be with the chief caretaker and it need not be with a female (Rutter 1972, pp. 128–9).

Fry (1982) points out that these findings 'make sense' in terms of care by the extended family and indicate that there is no psychological evidence for assuming that the Western isolated nuclear family, which is not the most common family structure in the world, is the only way to satisfactory emotional development and maturity. Children develop through relationships with other people, but not just with one person nor necessarily always the same person.

The policy assumptions underlying Fitzherbert's work were implicitly assimilationist. The services were to extend themselves only in so far as this assisted West Indians to fit in to British expectations. The justification was not an attempt to change the lower class West Indian family, but the upholding of a cultural value:

> it may be in the best interests of the child concerned to force (West Indian) parents to make their own arrangements for child care. If this is authoritarianism, its aim is simply to preserve individual responsibility (Fitzherbert 1967, p. 110).

Liberal pluralism

Cheetham's (1972) first major contribution to the literature endorses Roy Jenkin's 1966 replacement of assimilation by the policy aim of 'integration', 'equal opportunity accompanied by cultural diversity in an atmosphere of mutual tolerance'. If discrimination could be eradicated, equal opportunity would develop. Cheetham's work relates to this mood of consensus-based social harmony and optimism. She blends a Weberian perspective with a view of society as influenced by many élites, each relatively small numerically, operating in different spheres of life. Power is thus diffused through society and not concentrated in the hands of any one group. Black people frequently fail to gain access to sources of power owing to discriminatory practices, which also impinge on many aspects of their daily lives.

Cheetham acknowledges that most immigrants are to an extent identifiable and so can expect to experience discrimination:

In time their increasing familiarity with the life of their
new country and their adaptation to it makes many immigrants, and certainly their children, indistinguishable from
the rest of the community. However, those immigrants
who are coloured and therefore the most easily identifiable
may continue to experience discrimination and exploitation whatever their personal circumstances and however
long their stay in the new country. As a result, they and
their children can be firmly trapped in a deprived environment from which it is hard to escape both because they
are barred from superior employment and housing and
because their surroundings provide few opportunities for
advancement (Cheetham 1972, p. 5).

Special measures of positive discrimination might therefore
become necessary. However as these would be resented and
envied by poor whites and might increase tension, the emphasis was at that time on reducing actual or potential conflict
between white and 'coloured' by focusing on their common
problems. Cheetham acknowledges:

> It cannot be assumed that 'mutual tolerance' and cultural
> diversity will accompany each other if one group feels
> deeply that its own interest will thereby be threatened. It
> is probably more realistic to expect conflict between
> groups seeking some degree of acceptance and equality of
> treatment and those who are anxious for various reasons
> to exclude them from this, and to explore ways of reduc-
> ing or managing that conflict (Cheetham 1972, p. 8).

She sees the first role of social work as helping the small
minority of immigrants who have serious personal and social
problems. The understanding of circumstances surrounding
individual problems, and the development of personal relationships with those who need help, are relevant social work
strengths. The second contribution of social work was seen
as acting as a bridge between immigrants and natives, providing information on the difficulties facing immigrant
groups, the adequacy of the services that help them, and by
interpreting one to the other, working for a modification of
behaviour and attitudes.

There is at present an alarming tendency for the solution
of complex social problems to be associated with the

increased activity of social workers. If they collude with this naive assumption, they may unintentionally mislead those with whom they work by giving them the impression that social work can do more to alleviate their difficulties than is actually the case. More important, by appearing to take responsibility for solving problems not within their competence, social workers can draw attention away from the real causes and the radical measures which may be needed to solve them (Cheetham 1972, p. 31).

In spite of these reservations about the success of a neutral, consensus-based policy, she retains her optimism about the capacity of human nature to solve human problems. She advocates forms of work that would ultimately lead to black people gaining more access to their share of scarce resources and political power. She analyses three conceptual frameworks within which immigrants could be viewed either as 'strangers', as members of the poor working class, or as members of ethnic minority groups. The second was reflected in social policies of the time, which failed to recognise the extra problems of discrimination suffered by black people, and the third was becoming more important as the immigrants, having established themselves, were taking measures to preserve their own cultural identity.

The problems that immigrants shared with those of the poorer working class were to do with residence in what had been 'zones of transition' — inner-city areas whose largely transitory populations were on their way to something better, where redevelopment was planned, housing stock aging, police-community relations poor, and where professional services, particularly legal services (an important access to sources of power) were meagre. She suggests that local authorities should enhance their information and advice services in such districts.

Schools also tended to find it difficult to attract or hold teachers and their staff and careers officers might have expectations that were appropriate for local white children but unsuitable for the ambitious immigrant. The social worker's role with such problems was to mediate and enhance communication between the families and the agencies involved, and there is a sensitive case description of a family afraid that its cultural traditions will be abnegated by the school, being reassured through contact with a social worker into a more participatory and less defensive position, allowing a son to pursue higher studies (Cheetham 1972, p. 46).

With regard to employment, the social worker had a role in facilitating family discussion about parental aspirations, children's actual achievements and the state of the local labour market. While some parents had to be helped to face the outstandingly unreal nature of their expectations a more positive role was usually appropriate in promoting client's interests by accompanying children to the careers office and to job interviews, and consulting with the Race Relations Board (now Commission for Racial Equality) over examples of discrimination.

In such areas social workers tend to be presented with situations of extreme crisis and Cheetham describes outreach work with the tenants and landlords of a group of multi-occupied houses. There were severe limitations on the possible use of legal sanctions to change the situation, but greater familiarity with the social workers resulted in problems being referred at an earlier and more managable stage. Low-standard daily minding was transformed into a small nursery on site and improvements took place on a personal level: an elderly white woman teaching isolated Pakistani girls to sew in return for shopping, for instance. Cheetham recognised the time-consuming nature of this work but felt that social services should positively discriminate in the time they allotted to immigrant clients.

Problems specific to immigrants ('immigrant' and 'coloured' were then current terminology) were: shortage of money as they were expected to support families or children in their countries of origin; difficulties owing to immigration procedures; and homesickness. Depression could lead to temperamental behaviour. Social workers could play the same role as in bereavement counselling, helping the grief to be expressed. Immigrants also suffered because of the absence of the extended family and social network. Husbands and wives might be thrown on their own resources to a greater extent that they would have expected at home and need to develop more flexible domestic roles. Children might be reunited with their parents in a situation of culture shock while they grieved for their relatives and country left behind, and while at the same time their parents sought to impress on them how they should be grateful to be in Britain.

Cheetham identifies certain groups that were particularly 'at risk'. These included Asian women who previously lived in seclusion and now lacked the company and support of female relatives, and young children whose parents were frequently exhausted by work, depressed and guilty about children left behind. They might not understand the child's need for play, toys and intellectual stimulation. Social workers had a role in explaining these needs and in promoting the formation of playgroups. Cheetham differs from Fitzherbert's (1967) perception of West Indians in terms of cultural deficit and black pathology and asks how worthwhile it is to expect West Indian mothers to adopt a way of life that they regard as unnatural and not in their children's interests. 'Staying at home may involve an intolerable degree of isolation and poverty: going out to work may mean making hopelessly unsatisfactory arrangements for their children'. Cheetham (1972; pp. 139—140) suggests financial allowances for improved daily minding, or financing more day-care provision, a need that the Select Committee has recently belatedly rediscovered (HCP 424—I 1981).

The third vulnerable group identified were adolescent children with whom parents were experiencing problems of control and cultural continuity. Parents were under pressure because they felt themselves to be perpetually 'on trial' by a hostile society and were particularly concerned if their children's behaviour came to official notice. Children who transgress traditional behavioural norms may meet extreme reactions from their parents, partly for this reason and partly because their children's not valuing traditional ways represents a loss of identity and continuity for the parents also.

In a case- study, the Williamson family, the clients prefer the well-known customs of St Kitts where children 'respect their parents' to the adolescent questioning encouraged by the British education system and the habits of white neighbours. The stepfather, imbued with the pentecostal ethic, is worried about his stepson's activities with other coloured boys, and the influence of a student trying to form a black protest group. At first, angry, extreme, rigid and rejecting attitudes are expressed by everyone and it seems doubtful that the family can hang together. However the members gain more confidence in the probation officer, the parents discussing the events of their migration with her, and the children are encouraged to join a youth club where a discussion group moderates their demands for freedom. The probation officer helps negotiate compromise rules of behaviour, which allowed for the modification of demands on both sides (and presumably included a component of what a respectable white person considered reasonable).

Cheetham points out that, while white people tended to assume that all West Indians were lower class, many had been obliged to take jobs in Britain below their qualification level, or regarded themselves as lower middle or upper working class now that they had stable employment. As they associated respectability and marriage with strictness and male dominance, they could be angered, shocked and confused if they were encouraged to modify family relationships in a way that they associated with the more easy-going relationships of lower class cohabitation. This might have been an earlier stage in their own lives, which they now felt they had surpassed. Or they might feel pressured by a white stereotype that West Indians should be working class and become like the more deprived of their white neighbours, whose lack of control over their children they were experiencing at first hand.

Cheetham warns against too close an identification with adolescents in these circumstances, as the general environment was so adverse that without family support their future could be very difficult. This was perhaps even more the case in Asian families where the reputation of the women, and the arrangement of marriages for both boys and girls, is bound up not simply with the children's marriageability but with the family's honour and position in the community, so that the future of those abandoning traditional conventions without any guarantee of a secure place in white society could be bleak indeed.

Cheetham notes that the preference of the Asian communities for settling problems within their strong extended family system led to few referrals, some of these being of a kind that clients did not want known to their relatives; so that the amount of work then being done with these groups was largely dependent on the worker's initiative. She saw that with the difficulty that male heads of family have in relating to female social workers, and the unthinkability of independent access to the women of the family, Asians would prefer many services to be delivered through their own organisations.

The policy implications of Cheetham's work include elements of assimilation, integration, cultural pluralism and social mobility. Her case examples demonstrate the time necessary to form relationships with families, sometimes while only partially understanding the interactions taking place. Strictly contractual models of casework are unsuitable for this work. The clients tended to develop liking and respect for the worker on a personal level and to refer to her for advice. Cheetham warns against the temptations of this expert/dependant role, with its danger that the social worker will be unable to 'deliver' everything sought from her. She recognises the reality of culture conflict when she acknowledges that most white social workers value deeply held beliefs about individual responsibility, child-care, education and the position of women, some of them 'hardly and quite recently won', and thus rather easily threatened. She feels that this was what accounted for the 'resentment' that overtook white social workers at the demands, 'or sometimes the mere presence' of immigrant clients, asking them to assume new roles in an unfamiliar emotional climate (1972, p. 185). She thinks that the suspicion of many black clients of white workers, their feeling that they were being given an inferior service, were due to the client's experience of colonialism: she suggests 'frank discussion' of the colour question (1972, p. 190).

For Cheetham at this time the main focus was still on the problems of the interface between the black family and other agencies, rather than on departmental practices. The fundamental questions revealed by practice were the extent of the state's responsibility to help its citizens, and the degree to which social work intervention was based on personal inclinations, dominant ideas in society at the time, or cultural beliefs of the white majority.

John (1972), writing from a black point of view, carries this further, suggesting that behind the rhetoric of self-determination and equal treatment lies a set of prescriptive assumptions that are in danger of being applied in a profoundly arrogant and ethnocentric way because of unacknowledged racial feelings. He points out that the West Indians were brought up to regard themselves as British and 'sought to identify with Britain in almost every detail, only to find her a very reluctant mother', a society at once hostile, over-permissive, liberal and racist, where 'the young black can be neither West Indian nor British, so that he is forced into a new identity, where he can only be black'. The host society insulated itself from owning its racism by residential segregation of blacks in multiply deprived areas, and by instituting a new set of clichés: 'But let's face it, it's not colour, is it? It's all to do with poverty and class . . . it's all a matter of exploitation'.

John gives examples of prejudiced social work and suggests that casting the young black into the role of 'deviant' contributes to his intense personal frustration. The new social situation demands new approaches specifically related to the needs of black people and their way of defining the situation. The social worker should question the validity of the service he is offering in the light of the young black person's understanding of his situation, and his appreciation of the social worker's professional role as statutory agent of white society. John sees the question of colour being as valid for social workers as for other whites. The 'relationship' depends on the extent to which the worker brings his own values, prejudices and attitudes to bear on the situation, the degree to which he is identified with the rest of white society which the black person sees as hostile or aggressive; and whether or not the worker is concerned with making the system work in the client's favour, or offering services that are dysfunctional and could be counter-productive. John's work brings structural analysis into a de-mystified casework relationship, pointing out that racism also operates at the level of the individual social worker, and that social workers must take into account the black client's understanding of that fact, and their own understanding of their position.

> One of the peculiar functions of black people in British society is — in the process of speaking to ourselves about ourselves — to present to British society a critique of itself (John 1972, p. 88).

Cultural pluralism
The underlying view of society held by writers in this group

is basically consensus oriented but they acknowledge competition for power between different ethnic groups. The importance of cultural differences and of ethnicity is stressed above all other factors, including perhaps race, and it is the business of the cultural pluralists to show how these many ethnicities serve as a support and a buffer against the injustices and misfortunes of a racially inequitable society.

Khan (1979) and R. Ballard (1979) point out that it was no longer appropriate to speak of 'immigrants' and that the policy aim of 'assimilation' was unrealistic, as ethnic minorities were not going to assimilate. At the same time it was wrong to over-emphasise the influence of the 'traditional' cultural backgrounds of their countries or origin in isolation from the contact and influence of white society. The minorities were sustaining culturally distinctive patterns of social relations, which were the product of their experiences in Britain quite as much as of their roots overseas: they were the 'outcome of the strength of childhood socialisation, of interaction with their peer group, and of a reaction to the hostility and misunderstanding from the majority' (R. Ballard 1979, pp. 152–3). This is a long way from a straightforward process of assimilation.

R. Ballard (1979) feels that it is all too easy to slip into a perception of the cultural worlds of others as an irrational product of sheer ignorance. Rather they should be seen as 'systematic totalities'. Practitioners coming into contact with a new ethnic group for the first time step across an 'ethnic boundary' into a world with its 'internal ethnic rules and logics', which the practitioner needs to understand before he can tell whether an item of behaviour is normal or aberrant. Instead of regarding distinctive minority patterns as a pathological, bizarre, or just plain wrong, they could be more usefully seen as coherent systems, and properly tapped might even become resources for social services agencies. The provision of 'ethnically sensitive' services should be a normal part of good professional practice, and might also throw a new, and more positive, light on much that currently appears problematic.

Agencies that developed a sense of 'cultural relativity' would not judge the standards of one group by the standards of another, and would avoid making judgments about the relative merits of different cultural systems. With regard to lower class West Indian single mothers, for instance, it might be more appropriate 'to provide greater facilities for the proper exercise of grandmotherhood', than to counsel marriage or abortion.

R. Ballard and Khan are primarily concerned with the Asian communities. They feel that it is the social work ideology of self-determination for the individual that is particularly likely to be misapplied with unfortunate results in ethnic groups in which a concept of an individual's self-determination, apart from his or her kin group, is much less prominent, or in some cultures scarcely exists.

Even those Asians who share a common religion and region of origin do not necessarily form a single coherent community in any British city. It is the much smaller kinship group that is the 'primary arena for social interaction' and it is:

> to their kinsmen that they look for support in trouble, with whom they compete for and dispute about honour and prestige (*izzat*) and from whom they fear sanctions if they behave in a manner which is considered deviant.

The worst sanction is explusion, a 'highly unattractive fate in Asian terms'. The kinship group is a corporate group whose members expect mutual assistance, and who expect to sort out each other's troubles when these might affect the *izzat* of the group if they became public knowledge. Thus disputes between individuals invariably involve other members of the family, and more distant relatives, so that:

> social workers . . . need to recognise that they have to deal with a much wider body of people than they would normally expect. This may sometimes prove a frustrating and time-consuming experience but on the other hand if it proves possible to move with, rather than against, traditional procedures then some things may go more smoothly than expected (R. Ballard 1979, p. 154).

The kinship groups provide a great deal of support, but are also constricting. Individuals finding their way to the social services are likely to be those for whom the internal mechanisms of support have failed to operate, or who feel, at the time, that communal entanglement is oppressive. However this should not necessarily be taken as a wish to escape the

the minority ethnic world altogether.

An ideological foundation that stresses individual freedom and self-determination:

> may be a very poor starting-point when dealing with corporately organised communities where obligation to others is always expected to over-ride personal self interest. Paradoxically, the more South Asians move towards the values enshrined in social work theory, the more they may find themselves in need of social workers (R. Ballard 1979, p. 155).

Whites often believe South Asian family life to be too constricting. If an Indian or Pakistani woman is in conflict with her parents or husband, an outsider may assume that the subordinate role which South Asian women are expected to play towards their fathers and husbands, or the institution of the arranged marriage, is at the root of the problem. Such an interpretation may be partially correct, but the woman would be unlikely to be seeking to alter her situation fundamentally. To do so would be to reject a major part of the cultural values of her own ethnic group. Her complaint is, in practice, much more likely to be about the particular behaviour of her own husband or father, measured not in terms of her own standards, but of those of her own group. It is important that solutions should be sought within the particular cultural context, that is the values in terms of which people organise their own lives. Solutions which, unintentionally or not, have the effect of ignoring or condemning those values are likely to be unacceptable to the recipients (R. Ballard 1979, p. 151).

> cultural relativity . . . prompts a realisation that cultures must be seen as systematic totalities and that an attempt to evaluate single elements in isolation is meaningless. For instance, the possibility of parents arranging their children's marriages is inconceivable in the contemporary British cultural context, because among other things it would run quite counter to the way in which the rest of an individual's family life is organised. For South Asians, the reverse is true. Not to have an arranged marriage runs against the whole ethos of family organisation. Finally, a sense of cultural relativity can bring a realisation

that most things cut both ways. The tightly organised Asian family may limit individual freedom, but, because loyalty to the group is put before personal self-interest, no one need feel insecure. Who can judge whether liberty or security should be regarded as the higher value, or what emphasis should be given to each? Quite obviously the members of the minority should, and in any case will, choose the values they wish to follow (R. Ballard 1979, p. 151).

Catherine Ballard (1979) suggests that the basically assimilationist objectives of the white majority were revealed in the popular press portrayal of relationships between Asian parents and adolescents in terms of 'culture conflict', as though cultural values are always fixed and static and there is no possibility of accommodation. 'It is widely believed that young Asians desire all the freedom of their British peers and that they will challenge the "authoritarian repressiveness" of their parents'. They may be portrayed as a rootless generation, caught between two cultures. This formulation sets young Asians apart as a 'problem category', failing to recognise that there can be equivalent conflicts in children of any cultural background; and the focus on 'culture conflict' obscures the personal, individual elements in the situation.

She observes that in fact, although a proportion of Asian adolescents do go through a period of difficulty, these problems relatively seldom become critical, and most Asians have begun to fulfil their parents' ambitions for them when they have reached their early twenties. Very few wish to abandon their culture and their community, and most operate apparently without difficulty in the different cultural worlds of home and school or work.

Cultural autonomy is not predicated on the preservation of obsolete cultural purity: all cultures, individuals and generations adapt to new conditions. The younger generation will re-interpret traditional forms and 'however derivative, degenerate or problematic such cultural systems may seem to others, they are best understood as vigorous, vital and inherently autonomous phenomena'. Members of the younger generation are utilising their ethnic resources both to resist pressures put upon them by the majority, and to challenge the unequal position in which they find themselves.

R. Ballard (1979, p. 164) points out that ethnic aggregations are maintained in large part precisely in relation to external hostility, and many blacks are deeply suspicious of all members of the white majority. Whites tend to assume that cultural factors lie at the root of most minority problems, because such a view is the least disturbing. However he points out that discrimination is one of the most overwhelming problems with which black people have to deal, and most blacks believe that white professionals in the social services under-estimate the extent and significance of racial inequality.

He feels that the presentation of a limited amount of relatively simple cultural information could radically improve the effectiveness of practitioners, as the firm expectation of being misunderstood limited the extent that clients were prepared to confide their difficulties. Practitioners who claimed that 'I treat everyone as an individual regardless of their background' were practising a form of 'cultural imperialism', where it is the clients who have to make all the adaptations to the practitioners' unspoken cultural assumptions:

> Any practitioner who does not have a working knowledge of the way in which his clients order, or seek to order, their social worlds, the goals they are attempting to achieve, the style of behaviour they habitually adopt, and the kinds of material, cultural and social constraints under which they are operating must necessarily be professionally handicapped (R. Ballard 1979, p. 159).

He suggests that social services develop 'ethnic specialisms' large enough to attract minority group practitioners without making them feel 'ghettoised'. Ethnic specialists would be aware: of the roles of members of the ethnic minorities skilled in resolving disputes; of ethnic 'spiritual advisers' whose help is called in when problems in relationships are conceived of in terms of malevolent forces; and of practitioners of *unnani* and *ayurvedic* systems of medicine, who are consulted in addition to doctors practising Western medicine. Publication of research into whether enhanced use could be made of these 'traditional' features of Asian communities in the British context is still awaited. An alternative approach is described by Sondhi (1982), whose Asian Resource Centre has Asian staff who seem to be incorporating the need for reinterpretation of cultural norms to meet current conditions within the context of work to relieve disadvantages and injustice. They may have more relevance in taking into account the structural context within which interpersonal difficulties take place.

The structuralist position

This perspective relates to Marxist analyses in which class and racial divisions form part of a unitary state structure at the service of capital (see pp. 64–7). Structuralists locate the 'problem' in deficient material resources, in racist attitudes and practice within social work agencies, and in the current dominant ideologies of the state:

> It is the lack of resources in education, housing and employment which initially creates the need for social work intervention at the individual level in a majority of social work 'cases' involving ethnic minorities (Dominelli 1979, p. 29).

Dominelli considers that the social worker's role contained conflicting elements: job loyalty as a state employee, which entailed conservation of the *status quo* and reinforcement of society's current ideologies; and a 'liberal' helping tradition. Present conditions required pressure to be brought for shifts in resources to take place. Only success in this area could validate social work.

Dominelli dispenses with the convention that racism occurs everywhere else but not in social work. She debunks the supposed mystical, as opposed to the material, purposes of the 'relationship'. She sees that the assumption that social worker and client operate in a vacuum divorced from societal pressure and influence, and that 'the social worker/client relationship contains within itself the ingredients essential to the formation and development of that relationship', must be challenged and changed. Casework skills that 'pathologise' problems at the level of the 'immigrant' — who is placed in a humiliating dependency status in which good behaviour, defined in the white man's terms, becomes the avenue through which help is procured — are manifestly ineffective. This reinforcement of notions of inferiority or non-acceptance results in 'breakdown' in the relationship. Thus structural factors operate at the level of the social work 'relationship', and much of what passes for 'social work values' and 'social work knowledge' are expressions of the dominant ideologies of the white middle class, and work themselves out in practice to the benefit of the latter.

Dominelli suggests that a non-racist social work practice would expose the racist ideology embedded in current practice and would reveal the structural role occupied by both ethnic minority clients and social workers working with them. It would also identify the points at which both workers and clients would have to become involved in effecting change in their agencies and in government agencies 'to eradicate institutionalised racism and shift power and resources towards ethnic minorities'. She calls for more 'client-centred, community-based' provision — in which the ethnic community's organisations, resources and expertise provide the focus for the programme — and for the employment of more ethnic minority workers, reviews of departmental practices, the reorientation of normal practices and procedures, a re-allocation of personnel, and greater involvement of black community organisations, as detailed in the ADSS/CRE (1978) Report (see pp. 100—2).

The structuralist position directs attention away from the attribution of personal problems to individuals and towards meeting material needs expressed by the ethnic minorities and developing resources in their communities. In situations where resources are finite, the major difficulty with this approach is to identify the groups from whom resources are to be transferred, and to deal with the political conflicts that result. If the departmental operations that are more closely concerned with social care and control are also to have resources transferred from them, this may raise other kinds of political difficulty, for neither black nor white communities will see all social problems within an over-simplified economistic perspective.

A black professional perspective

In 1983 the Association of Black Social Workers and Allied Professionals (ABSWAP) was formed to facilitate the formulation and articulation of a coherent black perspective on social policy in Britain. This was to be done by: identifying the way in which racism, covert and overt, affects service delivery; creating avenues for the expression of the black community's views on service delivery; providing consultative and advisory services; supporting black workers and organisations; exercising influence over training; and providing information services.

In the same year ABSWAP (1983) submitted evidence to the Social Services Committee (HCP 360-I 1984), which, however, did not print this evidence in its minutes, nor ask ABSWAP to give oral evidence. ABSWAP had conducted a survey of the views of black community groups and found that, in the latter's view, social services were 'enforcement agencies', which wittingly and unwittingly broke up black families and aimed to take black children away from home. Middle class white workers were presumptuous, 'nosey', did not understand black people nor have respect for black families. They considered that black families should be like white families, and were unaware of the economic and racialist pressures on black families. They were damaging black children by taking them into care, then deliberately cutting them off from their families and the black community. Those black children who have been in care from an early age grow up thinking they are white. Most of the adolescents who come into care are there because they want to be like white children. 'Social services must distinguish between "bad parents" and conflict between parents and children'. However, 'black children dislike care', warn others off and 'would rather go home':

> Black people have a right and responsibility to help to resolve the problems of the community and they should be given the opportunity to do so.

ABSWAP (1983) points out that there was a disproportionate number of black children in care, who were not cared for in any different way from white children. Current child-care policy was 'destroying the black family as a unit' and trans-racial placements received particular condemnation as

'perpetuating racist ideologies', by disregarding the difficulties such placements caused for black children when they
grew up. ABSWAP called for the development of an 'ethnic
sensitive' service based on a 'cost-effective approach', and a
recognition of the strengths of black families and the need
for local authorities to use black families in a positive way:

> Classical social work operates within the framework of
> white middle class values. This is at variance with the
> experience of the black family.

Recognising that 'the interest of the black child is para-
mount', ABSWAP states that it should be standard policy at
reviews to check out as many members of the black child's
family network as possible to establish whether changed
circumstances would enable the child to return to its natural
family. 'Multiple mothering' had been a standard and healthy
feature of black families for centuries, a fact that was nearly
always ignored by white social workers. Black children were
disproportionately disadvantaged when taken into care
because of the racist attitudes of the white carers, and
because they were at risk of being separated from, and growing up apart from, their own culture and community. The
racism of the wider society would be certain, later, to drive
them back to the black community for the support that only
the black identity and culture could give.

While the document does record the findings of a survey
of the views of the black community, the ideas are 'professional' in that they recognise the paramountcy of the interests
of the child, and embody a conception of the black family's
'best interests' rather than merely advocating that expressed
needs should all be met, and children taken into care whenever the parents or children felt like it. The document emphasises the importance and potential of the extended black
family, and the need to be 'ethnically sensitive'. It describes
separation from black community and culture as 'deliberate'
effects of receiving children into care; most white social
workers would regard these as unfortunate but unintentional.
It compels the recognition that, in so far as insufficient
action is taken to recruit black substitute families or locate
residential facilities in black areas, the effects are deliberate.
The ABSWAP document is sympathetic to poor black families throughout, and does not distance itself from them. It

embodies an assertion of black ethnic identities and of black self-respect:

> The essential ingredient of any substitute home for black children should be the ability of the placement in:
>
> Enhancing positive black identity.
> Providing the child with the techniques or 'survival skills' necessary for living in a racist society.
> Developing cultural and linguistic attributes necessary for living in a racist society.
> Equipping the child with a balanced bi-cultural experience thus enhancing the healthy integration of his personality.

Many of the ideas in the ABSWAP document parallel those for community work expressed by Ohri *et al.* (1982).

Conclusions

The five perspectives are set out in Table 4.1 overleaf. They differ on a number of crucial dimensions.

The first is *the location of the problem*. Fitzherbert's (1967) approach focuses on the assumed cultural deficit of the client, who was meant to adjust to society as it was, irrespective of its racism. The model relates to various case-work formulations, notably Hollis (1964), in which the worker's perception of social reality is superior to that of the client because of her detachment, maturity, insight and ability to function in society as it exists at present.

The liberal pluralist approach, guided by a belief in British fairmindedness, while to some extent also concentrating on the difficulties of the black family, understands these more as problems on the interface between the family and the outside world. This parallels the 'integrated methods' approach to social work intervention of Pincus and Minahan (1973), which focuses on the 'interactions between people and their social environment'. The intention is to give black people more access to power and resources, but casework, group-work and community work all play an integral part. Liberal pluralists risk being led into a neutral stance in support of the *status quo,* and there is a problem in sustaining the black clients' faith in their effectiveness. Whether racialist attitudes exist within social work does not seem to have been considered by white liberal pluralists at the time.

Table 4.1: Five perspectives in multi-racial

Perspective	Related political ideology	Location of the problem
Cultural deficit	*Laissez-faire.* Emphasis on individual responsibility.	In lower class West Indian families who use services inappropriately because of black pathology and cultural deficit.
Liberal pluralist	Fabian. Policy should be designed to reduce inequality.	Interface between the black family and other agencies. Multiple deprivation. Inter-generational tensions.
Cultural pluralist	None. Lacks a vision of political change.	Idiosyncratic individuals who fail to carry out cultural reinterpretation. Racism in wider society. Lack of cultural information among social services providers
Structuralist position	Socialist/Marxist	Material disadvantage. Racialist policy and practice. Dominant ideologies of the state.
Black professional perspective	Creation of a black Black community to be allowed to assume some responsibility for its own problems.	Black people have insufficient power and influence over policy and service delivery. Racism and multiple disadvantage.

practice and their differences

Related social work method	Race relations goal	Social work practice
Worker's perceptions are superior, as she can function better in society as it exists now cf Hollis (1964).	Assimilation	Services to have residual role. Resist the use of services that seem inappropriate to white cultural ideals.
Systems approach. Casework, group work, community work, cf Pincus and Minahan (1973).	Blend of assimilation, integration, pluralism.	Enable black people to use other services better. Ensure full entitlement is provided.
Uncertain. Relates to structural-functional concepts in social anthropology according to which each culture forms a coherent self-sufficient system.	Pluralism. Protection of ethnic minority cultures.	Social Services Departments (SSDs) to form specialist sections staffed by ethnic minority personnel to work through 'traditional' conflict resolution mechanisms, healers etc.
'client-centred, community-based' practice.	Removal of racially 'structured subordination'.	Provide black clients and black community with more material resources. Work through black community organisations. Review policies for racial bias.
All methods but incorporating a stress on ethnic identity and employing mainly black workers.	Power to be shared with black people, leading to the elimination of racism. Celebration of ethnic identity and diversity.	Practice under black direction supporting the strengths in black communities and families and carrying out policies designed to meet needs in ways considered appropriate by black people.

For the cultural pluralists the problems, in so far as they exist at all, are located, firstly, in a small number of families with individualistic idiosyncracies that interrupt cultural redevelopment and reinterpretation, and, secondly, in the social services with their damaging devaluation and ignorance of Asian family and cultural forms, the assimilationist context, and their under-estimation of the mistrust that clients hold of them because of the daily experience of racial discrimination. Both Fitzherbert and the cultural pluralists agree that the operation of social services across community boundaries embody a cultural threat, but differ as to whether the threat is to the white culture or from it.

The structuralist position directs attention away from the attribution of personal problems to individuals and locates the 'problem' in deficient material resources, in racist attitudes and practice within social work agencies, and in the current dominant ideologies of the state. In so far as the economistic rhetoric of this approach relates to wider aims for society as a whole, these are often far from the objectives of black people, who will themselves choose the issues on which they wish to struggle (see pp. 7–8).

To the proponents of a black professional perspective, the most important problem might well be that black people do not have commensurate power and influence over policy formation and service delivery.

The second dimension of difference between these perspectives is *their treatment of the issue of power* and, related to this, the fastidiousness with which they choose the social work activities they wish to describe. The black professional perspective aims to create a power base for black people in social work agencies. Black people would define the needs of black clients and the ways of meeting them. Fitzherbert (1967) bravely tackles an actual activity of social workers involving a major decision, reception into care. However Dominelli (1979) concentrates on the 'good' use of power – to obtain material resources. A knowledge of welfare rights, and the ability to relate to and bring pressure on housing departments, are indeed a central part of social work activity in all housing stress areas. What a non-racist practice is in this or any of the other operations of social work agencies is left undescribed as yet.

The other writers perpetuate a view of social work activity

as time-consuming consensus-based discussion, often of an 'outreach' nature. This derives from American casework literature about practice in private agencies. Hopefully, social workers in inner city areas are still able to spend some of their time in this way, in spite of legislative changes that have given them far greater powers to intervene in families without parental agreement, in spite of time obstacles, the fashion for clear-cut 'contract' work, cutbacks in services, and the constant 'rationalising' pressure of management. Perhaps this is still the most personally rewarding and productive part of their work.

Nevertheless it must be faced that many of the most stressful social work activities, often with far-reaching and long-lasting effects, are not like this at all and are centrally concerned with the operation of power. They involve the allocation of scarce resources: limiting individuals' legal rights in the interests of third parties; and attempting to influence judicial and medical sources of power. While some of the provisions of social work agencies, such as day-care, or aids and adaptations, may seem largely unalloyed 'good' to the recipients, the others certainly do not appear like that to all, sometimes to any, of those involved. They may be stressful to social workers, to some extent, precisely because the rhetoric of self-determination and consensus gives no guidance as to their operation.

The third dimension of difference between the four perspectives is the degree to which the writers believe that a social worker is insulated from racism, and *that racism occurs everywhere else but not in social work.* The major components of racism are prejudice plus power. As the American casework literature to which the liberal pluralist perspective relates does not acknowledge power as a component of social worker/client relationships, liberal pluralists did not acknowledge racism within social work. Dominelli (1979) is the most clearsighted in debunking the supposed mystical, as distinct from the material, purposes of the 'relationship'. However the liberal and the cultural pluralists are also aware that much of what currently passes for 'social work values' and 'social work knowledge' are expressions of the dominant ideologies of the white middle class. While this does not seem to us to be an adequate ground for rejecting them entirely, the racial issue does clarify their limitations. Behind the rhetoric of self-determination and equal treatment lies a set of prescriptive assumptions that are in danger of being applied in a profoundly arrogant and ethnocentric way. A black professional perspective would most likely see the elimination of racism in social work as being directly related to the acquisition of power by black social workers and black people generally.

5 The managerial response

Research attempting to ascertain how ethnic minority clients fare within social work usually compares their use of provision with the use expected of a white population of similar demographic characteristics. More sophisticated calculations of 'proportional justice' are not conceptually impossible, but do not seem to have been made. During the 1970s and 1980s a number of small local surveys of ethnic minority client groups began to reveal a predictable state of affairs, in that patterns of discrimination and disadvantage seemed to be reproduced and reinforced within the operations of social work rather than being compensated for by its provision.

The emerging picture was generally one of disproportionate numbers of children of West Indian origin with one black and one white parent and in care, remaining in care longer, and with a higher proportion in residential placement. The numbers of Asian children did not always seem so high but once in care their position was similar, with a lack of provision for sustaining ethnic or racial identity, for appropriate diets or physical care. It was not usual for children of either community to be fostered or adopted by families of their own race or cultural group and placements with white families or children's homes were not infrequently some distance away from areas of black settlement (RSG 1980).

Disproportionately few black juveniles were said to be subject to supervision or probation orders and disproportionately high numbers were in custody and in CH(E)s (Community Homes with Education on the premises) with shorter criminal records than their white peers in the same institutions (Husband 1980).

In the mental health field, disproportionate numbers of black patients were subject to compulsory orders, and concern was felt at mistaken diagnosis.

With regard to the elderly the picture was one of under-use of the services. Fewer were in receipt of domiciliary help, meals-on-wheels, or were in sheltered accommodation or Part III[1] residential care than would have been expected from the demographic projections (RSG 1980).

However there was generally a shortage of relevant statistical information and of systems for monitoring the cumulative effects of innumerable day-to-day discretionary decisions by lower-level staff. Social work is generally no better, though no worse, in this respect than other local and central government services. One task of this book is to convince social workers that it is the same.

Social services departments

The emerging pattern was addressed by the Association of Directors of Social Services and the CRE in a joint report (ADSS/CRE 1978), which, though much criticised, contains recommendations that have stood the test of time. The Report suggests that the focus in social work on individualised needs might have obscured awareness of the extra dimension of the group needs of ethnic minorities. These were due in some cases to newness of arrival and hence unfamiliarity with the services available, cultural differences, which must be taken into account if services are to be sensitively and appropriately provided, and racial prejudice and discrimination, which enhance the 'exposure' and 'vulnerability' of ethnic minorities and may increase their need of support from public services.

The response of social service departments to the existence of multi-racial communities was characterised as 'patchy, piecemeal and lacking in strategy' and like other departments they had failed to grasp the scale or work through the implications of the multi-racial situation. The resources needed to tackle the causes of problems would have to be provided, if they were to be provided at all, through other departments. However, it was alleged that the social services were peculiarly suited to giving a lead and influencing such departments, and it was suggested that race relations units for whole authorities should be set up within SSDs. This assumption of moral authority was not supported by any argument, and the rest of the Report was sensibly devoted to recommendations that would help social service departments put their own houses in order.

The Report recommends that each department should carry out a review of each of its operations, which would examine the relevance of current priorities and practices to the changing needs of multi-racial communities. Because of the different social and ethnic characteristics of each area, these reviews would be at a local level. They were to involve ethnic community organisations through their representatives.

There should be more *ethnic minority community involvement* through 'professionally participating in current service delivery, and as communities in the actual provision of services'. The Report gives several examples of ethnic voluntary organisations providing services to members of their own communities, with the financial support of the social services. The communities themselves were to be seen as an effective channel for delivering services. Ethnic minorities were to be further involved by the *recruitment* and training of members of the same communities to work in social services departments 'at all levels'. While ethnic minority personnel could be validly deployed on special projects directed at their own communities, they should also be working in the mainstream of the department's operations. Ethnic minority staff were needed to demonstrate commitment to an equal opportunities policy, to help white social workers communicate better with ethnic minority clients, and advise on cultural patterns and the understanding of specific situations. They could also act as 'role models', for children in care, for instance.

Because 'ignorance is no basis for policy development', departments should *monitor* staff and clients to provide information about recruitment and the use of services, on which policy development could be based.

Additional *training* was needed for staff at all levels: this included the giving of information on cultural and social background, child-rearing patterns, the social situation of ethnic minorities in this country, and the economic reasons for migration. Consideration also needed to be given to the operation of social work techniques: 'should the preference of some minorities for having a worker of a certain sex or age be disregarded as manipulation on their part, or are there valid grounds for this?' Staff should also be made aware of how their own attitudes contributed to the problems of the local situation through discussions in small groups with ethnic minority members, using films, and inviting speakers from local organisations. A larger component of this teaching should be included in basic qualifying training.

Laudable as these objectives were, the ADSS/CRE Report does not feel that local authorities should do anything, not even conduct policy reviews, unless extra central government funding was made available to do it, because 'race relations is a tense issue' and 'fears of how the majority community will react inhibits policy initiatives'. The needs of ethnic minorities were described as 'extra' and 'special' rather than an ordinary part of services to the population of the authority, which should be financed in the ordinary way. It is hardly surprising therefore that the Policy Studies Institute (Young and Conelly 1981), researching a sample of authorities immediately prior to the 1981 riots, tends to show that only where black councillors had been active had there been substantial progress. There was a wide variation in the progress made. *Changes in services* were categorised by Young and Conelly (1981, pp. 84—6) in the following eight ways:

1   *Do something negative* A social worker expressed concern at the willingness of the local Asian population to make use of such practical benefits as bus passes, telephones and aids, and said that consequently her team exercised more rigour in approving applications than they did for indigenous applicants. This contrasted with views expressed in other offices that, although overall use of social services by ethnic minorities might be relatively low, their use of practical services was more in line with estimated proportions of the total population: they welcomed this as an indication that they were able to provide at least some acceptable help, whatever their ability to meet more complex needs.

2   *Do nothing: go on providing the standard service* This could be justified on the grounds that services should be uniform, or should respond to individual need only. Or that to meet differing needs of differing groups is impracticable because of the number of groups involved, the number of other 'priority' groups or because of shortage of resources. Or that the standard service has been tried, and failed, but attempts at adaptation would be too difficult or time-consuming, or that information and guidance on which to base more effective measures are not available.

3   *Provide the standard service on a separate basis* For example, mother and toddler groups formed specially

for Asians.

4 *Make some specific but relatively minor adjustments to the standard service* Examples are the provision of vegetarian meals in a variety of day-care settings, providing care staff with information about hair and skin care, and changing children into play clothes for their day at the nursery, thus meeting the desire of West Indian mothers to take home tidy children.

5 *Make some adjustments to the way in which standard services are administered or delivered* Examples were attempts to recruit black foster parents and trying harder not to take black children into care and 'increasing flexibility' so that children in care could be placed with grandparents.

6 *Provide additions to the standard service, or new services, to meet needs seen as specific to some of those from ethnic minorities* Examples were the provision of Asian meals-on-wheels, or setting up an Asian childminder group with training sessions in Gujerati on diet, health care and child development.

7 *Provide additions to the standard service, or new services, aimed at reducing general problems, but with some explicit or implicit policy aim of helping those from ethnic minorities or such an effect in practice* Childminding development services aimed at getting across to parents the value of play may be of this type.

8 *Include an ethnic dimension in considering current and future use of resources* Most policy development tended in practice to be incremental responses to particular situations, though there were some moves to review wider groups of provisions from the ethnic aspect, a more 'strategic' approach.

Young and Conelly comment that it seemed ironical that paying attention to group needs enabled practice to approach more closely to the social work ideal of service attuned to the individual's needs.

The disturbances of 1980 and 1981 gave rise to a number of fresh initiatives or gave new point to those already in train. In spite of long-standing fears of a 'white backlash', a large number of those in the local authority field became convinced that facing the race issue squarely now would lead to less trouble in the medium term than to continue to ignore it.

The Home Affairs Committee published a report *Racial Disadvantage* (HCP 424-I 1981) recommending that local authorities should examine all their services to identify areas where s.11 funding would be of value. Those with a significant ethnic minority population should institute ethnic monitoring of the services they provide. They should take a joint initiative with government to ensure that provision of facilities for the under-fives comes closer to meeting the demand for it, among ethnic minorities in particular, and should seek s.11 funding for such provision. They should explore the possibility of employing hostel staff through s.11. They should review their arrangements for consultation with ethnic minorities and should rid themselves of the notion that Community Relations Councils (CRCs) can represent ethnic minorities. They should keep the needs of the ethnic minority elderly under review; and local authority associations should regard it as part of their function to disseminate good practice in a range of issues connected with race relations and racial disadvantage.

In reply to the Report, the government stated:

> Where the needs of the ethnic minorities are different from or greater than those of the majority population, special measures may be called for. In public discussion of such special measures, concern is frequently expressed that to follow this course would be to give members of the ethnic minority communities an unfair advantage over the majority population. The Government accepts that measures that had this effect would be undesirable . . . . The Government believes, however, that if the aim of equality of opportunity for all members of society is to be achieved, special help will often be needed for those who start from a position of comparative disadvantage. The ethnic minorities are one group for whom there is a need to redress existing imbalances (Cmnd 8476 1981).

A joint government/local authority working group report (DOE 1983) devoted itself to the practical problems facing any local authority contemplating policies to combat racial disadvantage. It warned that:

> any attempt to introduce measures aimed at benefiting the ethnic minorities will almost certainly lead to some

degree of conflict. This may be with existing staff who feel that their career opportunities are prejudiced by an equal opportunity policy that leads to more appointments from outside the authority. It may equally be with the public or the media, or there may be disagreement among elected members. It is important that attempts are made to minimise conflict by way of consultation, discussions, education and training but it is unlikely to be completely eliminated. Authorities which understand this are less likely to be diverted when conflict does occur and more likely to tackle the problem constructively. It is far better to face this kind of conflict than the confrontations which could result if the need for positive action is dismissed . . . race relations issues . . . will not go away unresolved and by avoiding these issues, policy-makers and managers are actually creating the conditions for greater conflict in the future by way of grievances, industrial tribunal cases, industrial relations problems, and community disharmony.

Local authorities need to consider member arrangements, officer arrangements, ethnic records, relations with trades unions, and liaison with the community. The aim is fully to integrate positive action in race relations and equal opportunity policies and initiatives into the local authority's general practices, procedures and systems. 'They should not exist as a peripheral development which can be easily ignored.'

The working group suggested that, instead of seconding members to CRCs, each local authority should have a permanent race relations committee or sub-committee involving the leader or his/her deputy. This would meet regularly to review the work of other committees, and refer issues to them where action was needed. It would co-ordinate the council's policies and programmes in line with s.71 of the Race Relations Act 1976: by reviewing all existing policies to determine their impact on ethnic minorities, with a view to removing all forms of direct and indirect discrimination; by taking steps to develop policies and programmes to overcome racial disadvantage; and by developing positive action programmes in line with ss.35, 37 and 38 of the Race Relations Act 1976 (recruitment and training). It would co-ordinate the council's race relations work through its publicity, publications and information services, secure the compliance of contractors, suppliers and grant-aided voluntary organisations with the

council's equal opportunity objectives, and provide assistance
and support to voluntary and self-help organisations that are
working for racial equality, good race relations and the alle-
viation of racial disadvantage. Co-options from the local
community should be 'seriously considered'.

'Officer arrangements should reflect member arrangements' and it was suggested that a principal race relations
adviser, responsible to the chief executive, could support
specialist advisory staff in other departments.

Consultation with local ethnic minority communities
should be direct rather than through the CRC though the
CRC should play a part. Young and Conelly (1981) show
that the structures for consultations in some local authorities
actually divorced ethnic minorities from the policy-making
process. Consultation:

> must involve a wide range of methods but above all it must
> be sustained even though the early results are likely to be
> disappointing and even though there may always be a
> degree of tension and conflict between the local authority
> and the community it serves.

By means of consultation, the authority should carry out a
review of each of its services 'from the ethnic viewpoint'.

A national survey of social service departments' practices
(ADSS 1983), with regard to specialist services, specialist
staff, expertise, staff training, and working with ethnic
groups, concluded that some authorities with clear policies
had already developed a wide range of services as a direct
response to identified needs. A number were in the more
formative stage, while a few had 'opted for a more traditional
approach'. It is important that social services are not seen as
integrationist:

> It is important that the ethnic minority problem is not
> viewed in the same way as the middle class practitioner
> working class client issue, in that Social Services Depart-
> ments are seen by some as attempting to 'integrate' ethnic
> minorities to the values and lifestyles of the indigenous
> population. Only by recognising cultural differences, and
> by identifying and meeting different needs, will it be
> possible to provide an effective response (ADSS 1983,
> p. 15).

Funding: urban aid and s.11

The 1978 ADSS/CRE Report notes that s.11 and urban aid money was 'not entirely successful' in reaching its target group: only about 10 per cent of urban aid funds seemed to go to multi-racial areas. A report (Stewart and Whitting 1983) for the DOE points to the need for greater access by black groups to the decision-making process for urban programme applications. Authorities should produce explicit local strategies for race relations, which would form the basis of their bid for Urban Programme funding, and which should be used by the DOE in their allocation decisions.

Few social services departments made use of s.11, a failure for which the ADSS/CRE Report notes that they had to accept responsibility. The working group (DOE 1983) considers that 'the temptation to see s.11 as the primary resource for meeting ethnic minority needs should be avoided but there is little doubt that it could play a greater role than at present'. It urged more rigorous monitoring to ensure that the posts funded were used for work with ethnic minorities. Bradford (1982) had conducted a survey of the use made of s.11. The working group notes the uneven take-up: in 1981 88.5 per cent of the total of £56 million was spent on education; 6.3 per cent on social services, and 5.2 per cent in other areas such as housing and central advisory staff. The eligibility criteria were subsequently widened (HOC 1982) and Home Office monitoring improved. It has been alleged (Sharron 1985) that many authorities are using the money as part of their general budget rather than for specialist posts, a situation which parallels that discovered long ago in education, and which can have been known only to a few hundred social services managers across the country. However efforts to transfer established posts to s.11 funding may represent attempts to avoid rate-capping or transfer staff to time-limited contracts. Whether using s.11 marginalises or safeguards provision for ethnic minorities is thus a complex issue.

Ethnic monitoring

The working group (DOE 1983) considers that, because ethnic monitoring was a sensitive and difficult issue, rather than get bogged down in fruitless debates about monitoring, authorities were well advised to start race relations policies with other initiatives, and to raise the monitoring question only after the trust of the local ethnic minority communities has been gained. In 1985 Enoch Powell (15 March) drew attention to the importance of ethnic monitoring by describing it as evidence of 'a manic obsession with race'.

Cheetham (1981), in an influential DHSS-funded study, compares social work services for ethnic minorities in Britain and the USA. Much of this was subsequently published in a reader of examples of good practice (Cheetham 1982). Most British social workers interviewed 'had no difficulty in grasping the arguments for monitoring of services to clients'. However:

> some respondents said they did not know which of their clients were black. They were then asked if they knew which were men and women, a question which some thought silly . . . it is almost certainly a well-meaning self-deception, meant to imply that colour and ethnicity are not the most important facts about an individual, and will not entail discriminatory treatment. The motives for maintaining a colour-blind approach, which may be absolutely sincere, deserve further examination . . . (Cheetham 1981, p. 26).

It seems unreal to continue with the convention that the strength of the adherence to a colour-blind individualised approach is invariably, in social workers, drawn from some rational error or deficiency in training. Nevertheless, Cheetham recognises, opposition to monitoring is not necessarily associated with prejudiced views. There was a general fear of the use to which the information might be put. Young and Conelly find the same thing:

> Without an assessment of need in ethnic minority groups, a low take-up of services could indicate that there was little need, that the community was self-sufficient, that services were not available or not appropriate or that there was discrimination. A high take-up could indicate that the group was particularly unable to cope with its own problems, created a disproportionately high number of problems, was particularly effective in seeking out resources and making demands on them, or that there were adequate services, easily available and there was no discrimination. The interpretation is clearly so open to being influenced by prejudice that I do not consider it advisable

to become involved in such an exercise (quoted in Young and Conelly 1981, p. 73).

On the other hand in almost all departments there were some people who felt very strongly that systematic record keeping was a necessary basis for any discussion about the meeting of current needs, let alone for revealing gaps in services. Cheetham (1981) finds, however, that commitment to the principle and logic of monitoring was matched by an almost total absence of appropriate action. Some departments had take-it-or-leave-it attitudes. In the words of one respondent, 'if you found ethnic minorities didn't use the meals-on-wheels services, so what?' Cheetham admits that there was naturally a prevailing but unspoken intention to reduce demand for shrinking services as far as possible. It seems that it may also be an obvious way of excluding black elderly people from a share of the service. As this would have disproportionate effects on one group, it would be racially discriminatory.

The working group (DOE 1983) considers that three kinds of ethnic data were particularly relevant for local authorities:

General demographic data for the authority, that is, the size and composition of ethnic minority communities, location and quality of their housing and the level of unemployment experienced in the various age groups.

Ethnic data on the clients of local authority services, for example, children in care, homeless families, leisure centre users, number of students going on to further education.

Ethnic data on job applicants to an authority, the staff employed by an authority, their promotion record, transfer and training.

Such information would enable an authority to be factually informed in order to accept or refute allegations of racial discrimination; provide a basis for policy formulation and programme planning; highlight patterns of discrimination that might have occurred unintentionally but nevertheless leave particular racial groups disadvantaged; assist in the identification of particular needs that might require different responses in service provision; and enable an authority to monitor the effects of its policies on different racial groups and assess whether its race relations policies are being successfully implemented (DOE 1983, pp. 19–20, quoting Ouseley *et al.* 1981).

Cheetham (1981, p. 31) suggests that, while the information that may be useful varies with the situation and ethnic background of the client, clients might be asked their religion, nationality and cultural background (with the options including those of Black British, British Asian), language spoken and colour. Various classifications are suggested in the appendices to her report.

Access
Black clients may well be deterred from using social services if they have to travel to an office in a white area, face a white receptionist and white social worker. Asian clients may be further disadvantaged by signs and information material in English only, and by communication difficulties with white staff.

In a study comparing a central SSD office with a local CRC, Jackson (1981) finds that most referrals for help concerned housing and pre-school day-care. Afro-Caribbeans did not perceive central office as offering a relevant service, and it was only used as a last resort because its physical remoteness led to a lack of contact and familiarity with the services, plus the risk of seeing a different social worker on each visit. The low rate of Asian referrals might reflect a process whereby they were 'not so much organised into their own welfare system, as organised out of the social services'.

Ethnic minority staff
Cheetham (1981) finds that, in the USA, ethnic differences were everywhere celebrated in a positive, indeed an exuberant, way, and the client's ethnicity was taken into account in assessment and in policy as a matter of routine. The USA is an example of a society with 'a long and sorry history of gross racial discrimination', which moved quite rapidly in significant attempts to redress the wrongs suffered by minorities. This change is ultimately connected with the assertion of the strengths of ethnic identity (Cheetham 1981, p. 34). In contrast, the attitudes of white British social workers have seemed to Cheetham to be characterised by 'squeamishness' and 'embarrassment'. Young and Conelly (1981) find that personnel varied between those who saw the ethnic dimension as 'a taken-for-granted, inexplicable part of the social

services task' to one — in a city whose population he estimated as 50 per cent Asian — who was at pains to make clear
that, as only about 15 per cent of the cases that came to
their attention concerned Asians, ethnic minority considerations were 'of little significance for staff', and the 15 per cent
were handled 'on an *ad hoc* basis'.

Cheetham describes a residential home where the staff,
'who in other respects showed a great deal of sensitivity',
were vague as to whether the children were Muslim or Hindu.
'After some discussion in front of but not including the
children (who were old enough to respond) they concluded
that several were Hindu: and then served them beefburgers'
(Cheetham 1981, p. 47).

A study by Derbyshire County Council (1984) concludes
that 'ignorance in itself is sufficient to cause discrimination',
but knowledge of ethnic cultural values and dietary laws is,
in itself, insufficient to motivate white staff to take them
seriously enough for actions to ensure:

> The rarity with which social workers seem to recognise
> *strengths* in ethnic minority cultures and lifestyles has
> been noted by a number of writers in this field. Certainly
> lip service is paid to the strength of Asian family support,
> but many social workers may be hampered by the fact
> that their most frequent contact is with those in trouble,
> or at crisis points: they thus have little opportunity to
> judge the strengths of 'ordinary' lives, and how difficulties
> are overcome within them. An extreme example of this
> was an area officer who stated that it was not possible for
> children to cope with two cultures.
>
> Finally, a somewhat different aspect of the ethnic di-
> mension is recognition of the experience of being black
> in a white society, the experience of racism, and the
> associated need for maintaining feelings of ethnic identity,
> particularly in the case of black children growing up in
> largely white environments. Concerned white staff, and
> most of the black staff interviewed, mentioned the diffi-
> culty of getting over this aspect to white workers (Young
> and Conelly 1981, p. 71).

The inevitable conclusion to these observations is that an
'ethnically sensitive service' cannot be provided unless black
social workers are involved. The provision of this kind of

service, and the employment of black staff, are inseparable. The reasons are not merely to do with racial feelings, experience of what it is like to be black in a racialist society, and knowledge of a different culture. Nor are they merely that the white workers need the help and advice of black workers on specific cases, that white and black workers tend to give different priorities to racial and ethnic issues and that, although white workers may intellectually assent to 'cultural pluralism' and understand that other ways of defining situations may be as valid and held' with a conviction equal to their own, they generally find it hard to put into practice — for example, with some West Indian parents' use of corporal punishment, or the position of women in some Asian communities. The main reason for black involvement is that the contribution of black workers seems to be essential at the next stage of the development of a multi-racial practice, when departments move towards rethinking strategies and practice, in consultation with black communities, in order to provide services that are specially attuned to and appropriate for ethnic minorities. Such developments essentially require a degree of trust in the black community, and an appreciation of the strengths of black cultures and lifestyles. These are in the nature of things more likely to be found in staff who are members of the black community themselves and in frequent contact with black families who are not in crisis. This again indicates the need for a department's black staff to be from the ethnic groups from which substantial parts of the authority's black population are drawn.

The development of ethnic sensitivity in service delivery is therefore dependent on the development of an equal opportunities policy in the department (Conelly 1984). This entails ethnic monitoring of staff, careful recruitment policies to avoid disproportionate black representation at the lowest levels, and clearly thought out staff development and promotion policies. It will be extremely difficult for departments to do this unless it is the policy of the authority as a whole.

As regards a local authority's equal opportunity employment policies, the working group (DOE 1983) considers that a policy statement alone would achieve little without some supporting structure, practices and procedures. Equal opportunities policies needed to be clear to avoid accusations of reverse discrimination, and to obtain full union co-operation and the confidence of ethnic minorities. Advertisements can be placed in the ethnic minority press. Ahmed (1982) gives extensive practical advice on how application scrutineers and interviewers can avoid placing applicants in double bind positions, such as requiring prior experience of a type that might not be available to them. Continuation of the practice of first advertising vacancies internally will reduce the impact of an equal opportunities policy and changes may require the renegotiation of existing agreements with trade unions: 'negotiations may be difficult and no one should underestimate the strength of feeling which may be expressed against change'.

The working group also points to the importance of training on relevant race relations matters for those involved in selection and recruitment, and training for ethnic minority staff to enable them to make progress within the authority. Additionally there is a need for all staff to undergo training related to service provision. 'Race awareness', concerned with attitude change, can only be effective in a context of training about policies and practices. Students and staff from more encapsulated sections of black communities may also benefit from training in white cultural expectations if they are to be involved in caring for whites.

Cheetham (1981) comments that social work training courses in the USA would regard a failure to recruit students from disadvantaged communities as unusual, if not positively immoral. Black students in training have the same requirements as other social work students. If they have come from relatively comfortable backgrounds, these sometimes include a need to be helped to understand better the predicament of poorer members of their own communities.

Black staff and policy change

Departments employing black staff need to be committed to changing policies and practices if they are to make adequate use of them. Change in organisations is nearly always accompanied by conflict: Rooney (1981) shows how one department avoided change by appointing black workers who did not share the same ethnic background as local black communities, and had no connections with them, and then dispersed these workers across the organisation in jobs restricted to mainstream service delivery. Later, a new initiative formed a black team with local connections (Rooney 1982), which had the specific remit to research and recommend policy changes. Cheetham argues for a clear differentiation in job descriptions between posts with advisory and innovative functions and those without. Nevertheless, all black social workers are likely, at the moment, to be drawn into an advisory role by their white colleagues for specific clients and situations, and also within the department, since they rapidly become aware of situations in which service to ethnic minorities is either not being offered, or is being offered in an inappropriate form. It seems best to link black staff to the policy-making process formally through regular meetings convened by a development officer with a defined remit, as well as providing such staff with 'support groups'. Sympathetic white staff also need 'support groups' run by black staff.

Job descriptions for some 'ethnic specialists' and 'ethnic advisers' entail impossible tasks such as carrying out all the normal duties of a social worker and, in addition, conducting individual, group and community work with ethnic minority clientèle, and advising the director on matters concerning ethnic minorities (with no formal arrangements for doing this). The Local Government Training Board, the DOE, Home Office and CRE have established the Local Authorities' Race Relations Information Exchange (LARRIE 1984) to provide free access for local authority personnel to committee reports, working papers, job descriptions, action plans and work programmes from a wide range of authorities, to suggest contacts who have experience of implementation, and to indicate the current situation in respect of particular issues. Specimen job descriptions available through LARRIE demonstrate that some authorities now provide clear and practical job descriptions in the ethnic field, and have constructed appropriate structures both to support such specialist workers and to enable them to make a full contribution to policy. Liverpool (1982), Rashid (1982) and Thomas (1984) have all written good subjective accounts of what it felt like to be a black social worker in a white department, which taken together are a salutary reminder of the variations in individual and group experience within ethnic communities, and the impression that whites make as a group. Black social workers suffer the same stresses as whites, but also extra pressures to over-identify either with white-oriented policies or with the black client.

The development of 'separate' services or sections or voluntary agencies must also be envisaged as a possibility where minorities are numerous or well organised. Jewish and Roman Catholic voluntary agencies have existed in Britain for decades. The working group (DOE 1983) states that it was a mistake to see 'service delivery' entirely in terms of local authority services, and to under-estimate the potential contribution of the non-statutory sector and the community itself. Ethnic minority communities often desired to provide for their own needs and could often do so more effectively than the local authority. There was, however, a danger in over-emphasising the role and responsibilities of community organisations as the major providers of services for ethnic minority groups in a way that was different from white groups. This might give the impression that the statutory sector had less responsibility for the ethnic minority community and therefore had less need to change the way in which its services were provided.

'Separatism' in local authority services would seem to be mainly dependent on three factors: the size of local ethnic minority communities and the strength of their desire to be provided for separately; the size of each specific task (for example, residential provision) and the staff it requires; and the availability of willing and suitable staff from the appropriate ethnic group. Separatism is most practicable in specialist units and least likely in generic functions such as intake, which requires wide-ranging cross-referrals. In Britain a few departments now have black people in very senior positions, and have announced policies for localising and racially matching child-care provisions.

Cheetham (1981) comments that the greater use of voluntary agencies for service delivery in the USA made comparisons with Britain difficult. Nevertheless there was only somewhat ambivalent support for 'separatist' services among ethnic minority staff. Although Cheetham notes the enthusiasm and infectious exhuberance of 'ethnic commitment' compared to 'the attempted alliance of groups whose discomfort undermines their weak belief in common interests', the idea that only black staff should see black clients had a mixed reception, and underlying black and white staff attitudes may lie a recognition that career prospects may be limited by separatism.

The issue is further complicated by inadequate terminology. It seems wrong to speak of 'special' or 'extra' provision for ethnic minorities, when the aim can be merely to provide them with a service which is as 'ethnically sensitive' to their needs as the existing services are to whites, or to provide a service to them where the service was previously provided only to whites.

Current pressures for progress

The Race Relations Act 1976 s.71 laid a duty on local authorities to carry out their functions with regard to the need both to eliminate unlawful discrimination and to promote equality of opportunity and good relations between persons of different ethnic groups. This gave local authorities the responsibility not merely to eliminate any racial discrimination there may be in the services they provide, but to work more generally towards its elimination in the wider community, including the responsibility of promoting equality of opportunity and good relations between racial groups.

The Working Group (DOE 1983) recognises that this raised a number of questions about objectives. Did equal opportunity merely mean eliminating the worst excesses of discrimination, or achieving a proportionately equal share of jobs, resources, access to services, and involvement in decision-making? Were they simply seeking to assist ethnic minorities to overcome the cultural and language handicaps that they suffer in an unfamiliar society, or were they attempting to go further 'and tackle the different and deeper problems posed by racial discrimination and multiple deprivation'? The issue was the extent to which they were 'prepared to adopt positive policies to change the existing position'.

Much exciting change is now taking place. In many authorities, the hesitation about being specific about race has been overcome, and meetings are now held about it. Since the 1981 disturbances there has been more interest from councillors, and less 'colour-blindness'. There are more black councillors, and the specific needs of black clients may be raised in social services committees, which sometimes have a black person in the chair. Race relations committees may call for action plans from social service departments. Apart from their long-standing interest in black children in care, black communities now show more concern about other client groups, and provide a third source of information about black needs, after black clients and black staff, for departments who have begun the difficult and often painful process of consultation. Departments issue policy statements, collect ethnic statistics, review current needs, involve ethnic organisations, issue action plans.

It is relatively simple for those committed to change to attempt to eliminate direct discrimination and obvious inequalities in both equal opportunity and the provision of services. Dealing with indirect discrimination raises more fundamental issues, such as whether to provide services through specialist black staff or by funding an ethnic minority organisation, which arouse trades union and ideological interest. Indirect discrimination is also sometimes more difficult to quantify. For instance, while factors making for equal access are location, knowledge of services, language provisions and ethnic minority staff, those making for equal shares in the department's resources, or equal treatment in its operations, are far more complex. Some concept of proportionality is implied, but proportionality to what is a matter of the specific circumstance. At the moment there seems no agreed way ahead and departments have to negotiate their progress through conflict situations as they go. It seems probable that the DHSS will establish a development group for ethnic minority services (Conelly 1984).

Bradford (1984a) — an authority that has developed further than most — states that 'we prefer to think in terms of what we have achieved in changing our services, rather than focusing on the client groups as though their needs were special'. This reflects the recognition that everyone is 'ethnic', including whites, so that before changes were made, services served primarily white interests:

> There are many examples of multi-cultural societies where there are no differences in physical appearances. However, it is an established fact that colour and race do affect people's social opportunities and the options that are open to them.
>
> It is in family life that differences in cultural values and expectations are most striking. How people expect to bring up their children, to get married, to care for their elderly and handicapped varies enormously. Other people's ways of doing things often seem very strange —

yet everyone thinks their own way of doing things is normal, reasonable and — naturally — the best . . . .

Shared cultural values are a very effective basis for organising networks of mutual support: new arrivals in any situation have a great need to develop such support which is why they concentrate in particular areas. Adverse economic or social conditions similarly emphasise the importance of such communal resources.

Culture is a matter of deeply held values and beliefs. Parents feel that it is very important to pass them on to their children because they are a binding element in family life. A people's culture is part of the way in which they see the world and see themselves — it is an important aspect of their pride and confidence.

It is for these reasons that we believe children of ethnic minority groups will continue to have a distinctive and a significant set of religious values and will also sustain a sense of identity and community spirit.

From an outsider's standpoint, the distinctive lifestyles and cultural practices of minority groups can often appear to be problematic, but as far as members of these groups are concerned their own beliefs and values make perfect sense.

The more people feel misunderstood, the more tenacious they are likely to be in defence of their own cultural values.

Now, faced with the facts of the last twenty years, we accept that assimilation is not a realistic basis for planning and providing services. Rather, services should be equally available to everyone who needs them. If however, the services are uniform in style, then those sections of the population which do not conform to that uniformity will be at a disadvantage. This means that Social Services will have to meet different needs in different ways, or meet similar needs in different ways according to cultural group. Moreover, cultural differences are most striking in family life — the very basis of the services we offer. We believe that ideally the services we offer should build on the varied strengths and support the varied weaknesses of Bradford's many cultures . . . . In accepting the continuation of many different ways of life, we are accepting that services must be oriented to relate to these ways of life — and that action will be needed to achieve this — the ethnic element should be quite explicitly recognised in policy-making.

However there is no simple way forward:

It is a fact that the provision of services to ethnic minorities is raising many issues which are not only peculiar to the ethnic minorities but also raise questions about the work we have traditionally done . . . . Many unresolved issues in the services we provide and the comments we make now will probably seem to be wrong in two or three years' time. It is, therefore, not possible to present an internally consistent long-term package, since there are too many issues of which we have too little experience (Bradford 1984a).

The probation service

Early in 1976 a review by the Home Office Probation and After-Care Department concluded that:

there was a need for the Service generally to promote a professional approach to the racial dimensions of its task and that, in some areas, this represented an urgent priority.

A wider understanding of the cultural background of the ethnic groups was essential to the development of a greater awareness of the racial dimensions and, thereby, to a more sensitive and effective relationship with individual clients.

Such knowledge should be provided in staff development programmes, and there was a further need for basic information about race relations legislation. The service could benefit from liaison with local ethnic groups and other agencies with experience in developing new professional approaches to clients from ethnic minority groups. All probation and after-care committees were invited to examine the needs of their own areas in this context and develop appropriate in-service training. Each area with a significant ethnic minority population should appoint an officer to have a liaison, information and development role in race relations matters (HOC 1977).

In November 1979 the Home Officer race relations adviser commented that after this initiative a few services had become active but the overall approach had been one of ambivalence:

> The service in general — possibly without realising it — has neglected this area of work, overlooking group inter-action in the community because of the traditional focus of one-to-one case work (quoted in Taylor 1981, p. 16).

In the West Midlands, a comprehensive review of policy and practice was carried out with the support of the Home Office Research Unit, and published by the CRE (Taylor 1981). The exercise reveals some successful development of specialised services, but other officers advocate a policy of 'inaction and containment':

> There are also views expressed that a focus upon black ethnic groups is an admission of a separatist approach which mitigates against a policy of integration. However, others point out that until such problems as the black people are experiencing within society are recognised and acted upon by those who *are* in a position to instigate changes, however slow this process may be, there will be no possibility of harmonious long term co-existence within society (Taylor 1981, p. 22).

Ethnic monitoring aroused the usual resistance. 'Some members of staff took the view that even asking about the ethnic origin of clients was itself a racist act. For others, however, it represented but another aspect of the work . . . and not a very important one at that' (WMPS 1985, p. 43). Monitoring revealed, however, that adult black people of both West Indian and Asian groups were over-represented on all forms of licence after custodial sentences, and under-represented on probation orders, community service orders, as hostel residents, and on pre-release schemes from custody. They were however over-represented on voluntary after-care after custody. Juveniles of both major ethnic minority groups were over-represented on both supervision orders and on detention centre and borstal licences.

The CRE (Taylor 1981) recommends that the service nationally should undertake surveys to discover the extent, location and nature of their work with minority ethnic groups, and initiate a separate study of their work at the social enquiry report stage. They should develop new professional approaches to clients from ethnic minority groups (as suggested in HOC 1977), develop public education about the service among ethnic minority communities, and enter into partnership with these communities so that the service builds on their caring strengths and networks. They should recruit more ethnic minority probation staff, as well as black volunteers, ancillaries and interpreters. They should set up projects to assist young black offenders and provide relevant training for all staff, who should be encouraged to expand their experiences and methods to provide a more relevant and sensitive service.

Taylor (1981) concludes that, by indicating the ways in which black offenders were dealt with differently from the majority, monitoring provided the basis for reviews of what changes in policy or practice were needed:

> The provision of equal opportunities for all ethnic minorities requires working towards winning general approval and acceptance of positive discrimination as a means of offering compensatory support to meet special needs (Taylor 1981, p. 84).

After the 1981 riots, a report from the Central Council of Probation Committees (CCPC 1983) again recommends a more active role.

> Irrespective of the apparent size of the problem locally, we invite Probation Committees to enquire how well their officers are equipped to deal properly with the needs of black offenders, however few in number, and how they might be prepared or trained to perform their tasks more effectively and realistically (CCPC 1983, p. 1).

The work of area ethnic liaison officers had, with notable exceptions, been 'unobtrusive to the point of non-existence', and committees were invited to review their functions and give consideration as to how their role could be effectively implemented. There should be clear training policies designed to raise the level of consciousness of course members, and managers should be 'more assertive' in directing officers to them, and should themselves acquire the necessary knowledge and expertise.

Probation services interviewers of white applicants to basic qualifying courses should attempt to screen out those with prejudiced attitudes. As the service is unwilling to use unqualified officers, it is dependent on basic qualifying courses for recruitment of black probation staff, and the Report notes that the numbers of applications from black people for Home Office sponsored places on such courses was disproportionately low. It was suggested that the service should draw the attention of the careers service in schools to the opportunities available and provide information and publicity.

Access to the service could be improved by relocating offices in black areas, by publicising the service among ethnic minority groups, and by developing information and interpreting services. The recruitment of competent black reception, administrative and clerical staff, who are 'most significant in their day-to-day dealings with the public', was encouraged.

As well as monitoring the use of its provisions by black people, each service should establish the basic demographic facts, location and socio-economic position of each ethnic minority community in its area, as a basis for consultation, a platform for people to express views on current service delivery, and about new areas that needed to be considered. The Report notes that:

> a spectrum of viewpoints exists within an ethnic minority community in exactly the same way as it exists within any white group . . . in the same way, many of the views expressed by their appointed representatives may be extremely personal.

Channels of communication could include CRCs, religious bodies, black professionals and semi-professionals, black hostels, community resource centres and community group associations, self-help groups, cultural centres and alternative schemes, and black volunteers.

Noting that the content of probation work was flexible, the committee hoped that, with the help of consultations and by using black officers, the service might discover how to adapt and use 'the concept of the probation service' within their own communities, so that:

> there might gradually evolve a sort of 'alternative service', a modification of the white probation service rooted . . . which will have meaning and relevance for the minority communities, yet which can be organically linked with the traditional service . . . . Such a process might well entail the development of facilities

and services which are not immediately recognisable as duties of the Probation Service as at present constituted (CCPC 1983, pp. 23–4).

In order to become seen as useful by ethnic minority groups, the service would have to 'trespass' into areas hitherto reserved for the local authority, with a preventive rather than a remedied emphasis. The service would have to become involved with the mainstream elements in communities as well as the deviant fringe. For instance, a survey of the work of ethnic minority liaison officers (ILPAS 1982) finds several who had helped to set up day-centres for the ethnic minority elderly, and were quite satisfied of the trade-off to the service.

The committee saw that these changes would require a commitment to change, a shift in attitudes and diversion of resources. A probation service that withdrew behind its passive role of 'servant of the court' would not be assisting the course of 'justice'. The service should actively seek to identify the areas in which its services to black clients were inferior to those given to white clients, and seek means of remedying the situation. It should establish what needs of black communities were relevant to its work and divert resources appropriately. 'Traditional' methods of working (presumably office-based interviews) were 'not solely to be used', and the service should provide schemes and projects centred within black communities and relevant to their needs. It should engage with local authority education and housing departments to attempt to improve facilities for black people. Though the service was expected to help courts process those involved in riots (CCPC 1983, p. 38), it should also be prepared to liaise with the police in a mediating role, 'taking note of warning signs of conflict'. 'Although there is some risk attached, it might be thought better to face the risks of realistic engagement' (CCPC 1983, p. 37). Probation committees themselves had a role in supporting the establishment of community resources centres and work not usually undertaken by the probation service, and 'may find it necessary to speak out in support of the work of their staff with deprived and under-privileged minorities'. Committees could also adopt policy statements on problems of race as they affect the criminal justice system (CCPC 1984, p. 4).

A further report (ACOP 1985) suggests that the service

could fulfil a 'crucial mediating role between ethnic youth, police and courts', but emphasises that this would only be possible if it was a multi-racial service. The hostility between the criminal justice system and black people makes this projected mediating role an improbable proposition in general terms. A multi-racial service seems years away. Black applicants who are already, or likely to become, alienated from their own communities should be avoided; and the need to write court reports in good English is a further obstacle to recruitment. In 1984 1.38 per cent of probation officers were black. No black person was in post beyond the grade of senior, of whom there were four (0.4 per cent). The Association of Black Probation Officers has limited scope for recruitment. Of ancillary grades 4.74 per cent were black. The report gives no figures for the numbers in clerical and administrative grades. The service's recruitment material hardly acknowledged that it operated in a multi-racial society, 'It clearly portrays a white probation service'. The Report suggests positive discrimination in reserving a number of places on basic qualifying courses for ethnic minority applicants.

There was a need to highlight racism as a pervasive phenomenon as otherwise a concentration on the victims of racism as a phenomenon of study to improve understanding 'reduced racism to racial disadvantage and equated the victims with the problems'. The Report gives very detailed attention to race training within basic qualifying and in-service courses, 'race training to be a continuous process which is never completed'. Some city areas had developed active policies but it was emphasised that it was equally necessary for officers in areas with relatively few black people to raise their consciousness of racism in order to avoid future disagreements within the service nationally. Additionally, the regionalised structure of the prison service brings all prison probation officers into contact with black prisoners.

Notes

1 Residential accomodation which Part III of the National Assistance Act 1948 empowers local authorities to provide.

6 Face-to-face issues

The disadvantage suffered by black clients indicates that obtaining resources will be the most frequently appropriate form of social work help. While demonstrated concern can generate useful relationships, racial and cultural differences limit the white worker's understanding and ability to work 'through' relationships. In this chapter we have eschewed the conventional appeal to social work values and description of consensus-based client-centred casework in favour of showing some of the complex ways in which the ordinary transactions of everyday social work can operate to discriminate against and disadvantage the black client, even though there is no policy to do so. We have therefore focused mainly on situations in which power is a self-evident component of the social work task, and social workers are acting either as gate-keepers of scarce resources, or as agents empowered by statute to investigate and intervene. A 'damage limitation' objective seems more appropriate to many of these situations than the usual more ambitious aims.

Language issues

White social workers cannot assume that all clients of West Indian origin can understand or speak standard English particularly those from rural backgrounds or from French-speaking islands. Raising the voice, or verbal bombardment, is usually unhelpful, as is constantly correcting the clients' grammar. The help of another person from a similar background is sometimes necessary. When clients have a command of both standard English and dialect, the circumstances in which each tends to be used is a matter of dispute (Edwards 1979). However there may be more use of dialect in stressful situations, as illustrated in this taped conversation on the vexed issue of missed appointments:

> Probation Officer: but that means me waiting around for a long time.
> Client: (Long pause). . . so
> Probation Officer: What do you mean . . . so?
> Client: So I couldn't get 'ere.

Probation Officer: If you make an arrangement to meet someone, I think you should do your best to get here on time, don't you?

Client: So mi decide fetak a walk down a Brixton.

A cooling-off period may be indicated if the client retreats into a dialect. In other circumstances a client may use a symbolic word to disengage. A Rastafarian interviewed in a remand centre may volunteer nothing, or respond to any question with the symbolic word 'Babylon', which represents all that is bad in the white world, the place of his exile, and emphasises the perceived incongruity of the white social worker's concern in such circumstances.

When Asian clients do not have much English, it seems generally agreed that it is better to use interpreters than to communicate through the children of the family. The parents may not wish the children to know everything about the problem and to communicate through the children is humiliating for parents from cultures where respect for parents requires that, in the home, communication to the children is through the parents, not vice versa. The most common difficulties in using interpreters are that clients may fear that communication will not be kept confidential, or may find that the interpreter is from an unacceptable part of their community. Interpreters may wish to give more help than merely interpreting words, and offer advice to clients and explanations of culturally specific material to social workers. They may not wish to pass on information they feel is discreditable to their community. Whether social workers want simple answers to standard questions, or general descriptions of areas of difficulty, they may find either that their original perspective seems increasingly irrelevant, or that their control of the interview, and participation in it, is slipping away. Effective interpreting for social work requires training (BASW 1982, pp. 59—63). In some authorities interpreter posts are occupied preliminary to social work training. There is force in the argument that to have a worker who can speak to the client is more important than to have a trained worker. Shackman (1985) provides a comprehensive handbook on organising, funding, training and working with interpreters in statutory agencies.

It is a well-established linguistic fact that certain features of a person's native language are carried over into their use of a second language. Thus even when the client with standard English as a second language speaks it well, different emphasis in words, or putting the key message in the sentence at the end instead of the beginning, can create irritability and misapprehension in white listeners, an issue explored helpfully by Gumperz *et al.* (1979).

Who is who in the family
The social worker has to make assessments that bear on the allocation of scarce resources, and write reports for outside sources of power such as courts and psychiatrists. These specify the names and relationships of those in the family group, and, since systems of naming persons and relationships reflect systems of cultural preferences and family structures, misunderstanding can occur with profound consequences for the client.

Afro-Caribbean names
Some accounts of West Indian family forms were described on pp. 70–8. They involve the same system of naming persons and relationships as whites use save that children born to unmarried parents are quite frequently registered in one parent's surname, but are known by and use the surname of the other. This suggests, correctly, that West Indians tend to have a strong consciousness of biological relationships no matter who is bringing up the child. The practice is relevant to the writing of social enquiry reports for courts unfamiliar with Afro-Caribbean defendants. To avoid confusion, the name of the report should be the same as that on the charge sheet. If it seems likely that the use of both names will become known to the Bench, a few words of explanation in the report may be appropriate, since to English ears being 'known as' something different to one's 'real' name has sinister Dickensian connotations.

Asian family relationships
Asian relationship and naming systems commonly have widely different emphases to the white systems and this can lead to feelings that 'each time you ask it's a different story', and suspicions of bad faith. The difficulty of translation for the client or interpreter is not just a matter of accent, and of literal or idiomatic forms, but of trying to make a framework

of ideas comprehensible in a language (English) that has no equivalent terms. If the client has a fair understanding of English family systems, he may distort his account of his family relationships in order to convey what he thinks will be comprehensible to a white person, or fit in with the latter's expectations. Or he may omit what he thinks will be misunderstood.

Relationships within Asian families are influenced by the existence of what are known to anthropologists as 'marriage classes' — individuals expect to find a spouse in the group within which their family intermarries. The composition of this group is determined by religious and ethnic identification, descent and economic status, and Asian communities vary widely to the extent that their cultural preferences stress endogamy or exogamy (marriage within or outside close kin).

Muslim marriage preferences and names

The Muslim system stresses an endogamous preference — for marriage within a group of closely related people. Instead of each married couple forming a separate household, the preference is for joint households to be established between closely related males and their wives and children, to which unmarried adult males will be attached. Anwar (1979) shows that in Rochdale a quarter of Pakistani households were of this 'joint-extended' type, in spite of the small size of local houses and some relatives remaining in the homeland. Many had other close relatives in the same street or nearby.

Less westernised Muslim males often refer to what anthropologists term their 'patrilateral parallel cousins' as their 'brothers' (*bhai*), or 'cousin-brothers'. There is no everyday English term for patrilateral parallel cousins, as the category has no functional significance in a white family. A diagram (Figure 6.1) is therefore necessary. A and B are patrilateral parallel cousins, as they are descended from fathers who are siblings of the same sex. A and C, A and D, B and C, B and D are pairs of cross cousins, as they are children of siblings of different sexes. C and D are matrilateral parallel cousins as their mothers are same-sex siblings.

The closeness and importance of the patrilateral parallel cousin relationship rests on a number of considerations. The preferred household composition is a group of male kin (agnates), their wives and descendants. So A and B, their

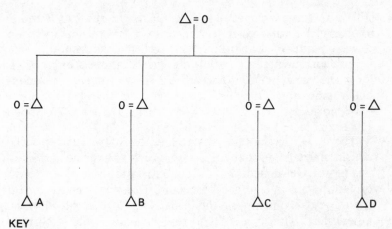

KEY
Δ male
0 female
= marriage
Figure 6.1 Patrilateral parallel cousins

parents and their paternal grandparents may form one household and one economic unit, pooling their resources under
the leadership of the grandfather. This is probably how they
would be organised if they were still farming together in Pakistan. When the grandfather dies, under Islamic law property
descends through the male line: each brother receives an
equal portion of the inheritance, whereas each daughter
should receive a share which is one-half of that of a brother.
In practice, however, the dowry accompanying the bride at
her marriage may be counted as her share ('anticipatory
inheritance'). So the fathers of A and B could divide the
inheritance between them and go their separate financial
ways. However there would be a cultural preference not to
do this. Relatives and fellow-villagers both in Britain and in
the homeland will be linked to the deceased by a network of
reciprocal financial obligations, usually translated as 'loans'
or 'debts' in English though the connotations are different
(Dahya 1974). If the inheritors continue as one economic
unit it sustains the network of relationships of which these
are the financial manifestations. They therefore may prefer
to continue as one household under the leadership of the
older or more capable brother. In this way A and B will be
as close as young white 'brothers' in terms of economic
support. When they reach an age when their fathers think
it appropriate for them to marry, there is a strong cultural
preference for the fathers to strengthen their relationship

still further by arranging for A to marry the sister of B and B to marry the sister of A (marriage to 'first cousins' in white terms). White social workers may well misunderstand if they hear their clients are going to marry the sister of their 'brothers' and perhaps this is one source of the erroneous belief among some white social workers that black people have 'no incest prohibitions' (Cheetham 1982, p. 27, Ahmed 1983, p. 22).

There are economic advantages to patrilateral parallel cousin marriage, in that fixed assets such as housing and small businesses are difficult to divide, and farming land, the basis of family prestige in the homeland, is not fragmented. Also the dowry accompanying the bride is not lost to the common inheritance. The women, who tend to play a role in 'sifting' potential marriage partners in any family, can also benefit from and support this form of marriage. In Asian families wives are under the authority of their mothers-in-law, and the predictable in life can have its attractions, particularly if 'anticipatory socialisation' has taken place as the girl has been thinking of her father's brother's wife as her future mother-in-law as she grows up. Close agnatic (male line) relationships between affines (relations by marriage) may help avoid nasty problems between the young wife and her mother-in-law. The bride will also remain close to her own mother and within her circle of close relatives, and does not fundamentally change her domestic world on marriage. In cultures where there is a preference for the seclusion of women (*purdah*, that is, avoiding contact with unrelated males) this is a crucial consideration. When families are divided by immigration or immigration legislation, the stress felt by women is greater since future mothers-in-law are less well known, and the young wife's close circle of female kin is less likely to be in one locality in Britain, so that wives are more isolated.

If we now include one more ascending generation in the diagram (Figure 6.2), it will be evident that if the mothers of A's and B's cross-cousins, C and D, had married in the preferred fashion then C and D are closely allied to A and B. Should the patrilateral parallel cousin union not be necessary or available to A or B, then marriage with a cross-cousin, sister of C or D would renew an existing alliance and have favourable connotations.

This Muslim marriage system is preferential not prescriptive and obviously deaths and births and the balance between

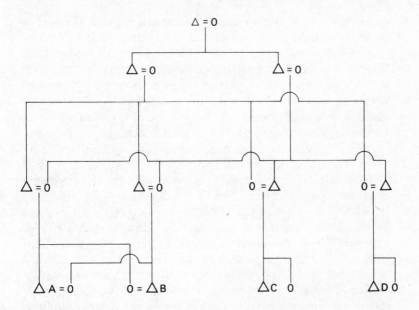

Figure 6.2 Preferred Muslim Marriages

the sexes will not so arrange themselves that in each generation every individual will marry in this endogamous way.
Families also need to seek spouses for some children further
afield, using marriages to create or reinforce wider alliances
and relationship networks. Nevertheless such marriages will
be arranged with an eye to the honour (*izzat*) of the family,
and will be with partners who will sustain the prestige of the
family group. They will tend to be endogamous to the local
sub-caste status group. Though Islam does not recognise
caste, caste-like endogamous groups persist among Asian
Muslims and can be ranked in prestige.

White social workers need to appreciate that, because of
the preferential marriage system, each relative tends to be
related to the client in two different ways in English terms:
your wife is also your cousin, your uncle (father's brother)
is also your father-in-law. Which term is used may depend on
the circumstances. In the domestic domain, at a home visit
for instance, a man would tend to introduce his relative
through the affinal (marriage) link, for instance as his father-
in-law. However, encountered in the political or community
domain, the office, community centre or mosque, the same
person would tend to be introduced through the agnatic

(male line) link, as his uncle. A married woman adopts her husband's terminology, an unmarried girl, her father's.

There is also a simple problem over names of persons. Each Muslim has three or four names or titles, which may be used in different circumstances. Your client may be referring to someone you already know, but using one of his names or titles with which you are unfamiliar. Or in some groups there may be no name that corresponds to a 'surname' so that biological full siblings may have completely different sets of names (Hawkins, undated).

In Asian families generally members of the older generation may be accorded the honorary title of 'father' or 'mother', and the younger, 'son', or 'daughter', while those in the same generation may also be loosely referred to as 'brother' or 'sister'. It may often be better to lead your client into delineating the precise line of relationship, for instance by asking 'your father's brother's son?' when 'brother' or 'cousin-brother' is mentioned, or similarly 'your son?' 'brother's son?', each time 'son' is referred to. This will also have the effect of revealing the presence of 'honorary kin'. These are males who have no close male relatives in the locality, for whatever reason. Such people, provided that they are from sufficiently prestigious families, are readily included in the kinship terminology of the families with whom they are staying and the preference is to plan things so that these alliances are gradually strengthened by marriages (Anwar 1979). In these and other ways, the kinship terminology used reflects actual social relationships rather than biological connections. It is the culturally preferred idiom or ideology through which various relationships are described and discussed (Fox 1967).

Hindu marriage preferences and naming systems

The Hindu family, while sharing a preference for marriage endogamous to (that is, within) the local sub-caste, emphasises exogamy (marriage out) with regard to both agnatic (male line) kin and one's village of origin. Patterns of marriage preference vary considerably between different Hindu communities, but overall they tend to be integral to elaborated caste and status distinctions. There are four major divisions (*varna*) in the caste hierarchy: the Brahmans, or priests, are the highest; the Kshatriyas, or rulers, come next;

below them the Vaishyas, cultivators and later merchants; and then Shudras, or servants (Dumont 1970). Finally the untouchables have no caste status: they perform important ceremonies for other castes on occasions considered ritually polluting (for example, at funerals), and they monopolise polluting occupational roles concerned with animal products or human waste (Khare 1985). The caste hierarchy is ranked within an ideology of religious and ritual purity and impurity, and relations requiring contact (pollution) between members of different castes are limited by caste endogamy and other probitions. Those most relevant for social work relate to the food that can be eaten, by whom it can be prepared and served, and with whom it can be eaten. The religious structure obliges the Hindu frequently to purify himself from polluting influences by appropriate ritual observances.

Within each major caste, local sub-castes compete for wealth, power and influence, split into new sub-castes, or merge with old ones. However 'the politico-economic domain is encompassed in an overall religious setting' (Dumont 1970, p. 275), which has an existence independent from it. The idiom in which higher or lower status is expressed is the idiom of purity, so that successful groups will seek recognition for aspirations to higher status by 'Sanskritisation', adjusting their ritual observances to conform to those of the superior groups with whom they are seeking parity.

Tambs-Lyche (1980) describes, in London, the Patidars, part of a sub-caste of Gujeratis who usually have the surname Patel, although not all Patels are Patidars. The Patidars are former farmers and landowners who have now adopted a 'merchant ethic'. 'The most striking aspect of the kinship system of the Patidars is their hypergamy', that is to say, women marry upwards in the social hierarchy. The villiages are exogamous, and some of them are organised into marriage circles. These are known by the number of villages in them, for instance the six-village circle, the five-village circle, the twenty-one and twenty-seven village circles:

> Marriage is allowed (between different villages) within the circle, but it is also possible for men in a certain circle to marry women from lower circles. For the father of the girl concerned, this would mean having to pay a higher dowry, but it also meant establishing a relation with a more prestigious family which reflected on the prestige of his own,

as descent is patrilineal. Further, it meant that other daughters might be married upwards at slightly smaller cost. To give a girl in marriage outside the marriage circle, however, entails the father having to pay a fine laid down by the local caste council. This is much smaller when she is married upwards than when she is affianced to a man from below (Tambs-Lyche 1980, p. 42, from Morris 1968, Pocock 1973).

There is a preference for 'patrilocal' residence (with the husband's male kin). If the husband moves in with his father-in-law, he is accorded less respect. This pattern takes the bride away from her own kin and, even if she is living in a joint family household, her mother-in-law, under whose authority she comes, is unlikely to be a close relative as men may not marry brides with whom they share a common grandparent — for instance, not their mother's sister's daughter or their mother's brother's daughter (Kapadia 1966). Tambs-Lyche shows that in Britain, household composition is flexible and, depending partly on economic considerations, can include relatives of the wife as well as the husband, which would tend to provide wives with added companionship. Husbands appear to use affines (relatives by marriage) as well as agnatic (male line) kin in business contacts. People from the same village are also used and if roughly the same age as the speaker are referred to as 'brothers' (*bhai*) or 'sisters' (*bahen*). The relationship between biological brothers is a very important one and, notwithstanding the dispersed and flexible residence patterns of Gujeratis in Britain, males continue to be responsible for the honour, chastity and reputation of unmarried female relatives, particularly their sisters. This is an aspect of family honour (*izzat*) common to the major Asian groups.

The Hindu system of naming individuals consists of one or more personal names followed by the sub-caste name. 'Shri' and 'Shrimati' are titles roughly equivalent to 'Mr' and 'Mrs', so that letters should *not* be addressed to 'Mr Shri Patel'.

Sikh marriage preferences and naming systems
Sikhism is an egalitarian religion. The communal meals at Sikh temples intentionally contravene Hindu caste regulations. Nevertheless Sikhs are divided into endogamous (in-marrying) groups of different historical origins, each at one

time broadly associated with an economic category: for example, Jats (landowners and farmers); Ramgarhias (craftsmen); Aroras and Khatris (urban merchants); Mazbhis (labourers); and Bhantras (pedlars). Within each of these large endogamous divisions are a number of mostly exogamous clans of equal status, whose members may use the clan name as their family name, for instance Garewal, Sidhu, Gill, Maan, Chahel and Bhullar. But since the existence of such names signifies a falling short of the ideal unity to which Sikhs aspire, many prefer, for religious reasons, not to use them, and younger people may not even be aware of them. Sikhs prefer to marry out of the clans of both their father and their mother, out of their own village, and often out of their mother's village. A strongly egalitarian ideology of relationships between families facilitates the ramification of very extensive kinship networks within the endogamous group. All lines of relationship are potential sources of reciprocal help or influence, whether through the mother, the wife, or the affines of married sons or daughters. Sikhs also adhere to political 'factions' (Pettigrew 1975) engaged in a bitter struggle for power and economic privilege within the Punjab. These factional allegiances enmesh the first generation of Sikhs in Britain, preoccupy their organisations, and are likely to influence the choice of their children's marriage partners.

In the Punjab, the preference for patrilocal residence (with husband's male relatives), together with village exogamy, separate the Sikh bride from her own kin and domestic background. She commonly forms close relationships with her sisters-in-law, whom she then calls 'sisters'. A strong relationship with her own growing sons will be one foundation of her future authority over their wives. (Pettigrew 1975). Women cannot usually inherit property nor can it be transmitted through them. Nevertheless in spite of male predominance Sikh women are manifestly influential and are accorded a full part in religious organisation and observance. The observation of *purdah* restrictions is a matter for family choice, a Punjabi tradition not a religious preference, and where followed, operates only in contacts with relatives by marriage, and strangers. Female influence may be enhanced by migration, as the Sikh wife's own kin are often living in adjacent streets of the same English town, while mothers-in-law may be in the Punjab (Helweg 1979, Werner 1981).

James (1974) provided a vivid description of the Sikhs in one British town and the conflicting influences on the children from white and Sikh expectations. Bhachu (1985) describes Sikhs who have come here from East Africa.

It is a matter of personal choice for individual Sikhs to confirm their faith and adopt the outward manifestation of Sikhism in dress and hairstyle, but later to abandon these attracts considerable stigma: hence the reluctance to wear motorcycle crash helmets. Respect for their hair is crucial to Sikhs. To avoid threatening their religious identity, it should be uncut, clean, tidy, and dressed in the traditional style.

To orthodox Sikhs, the Granth Sahib, their one sacred text, reflects, consolidates and continues the teaching of the ten historical gurus. But certain smaller groups would admit later or modern religious teachers to guru status. For brief accounts of the religion see Beetham (1970) and Cheetham (1972).

Sikh personal names may cause difficulty to an English social worker in that most are common to men and to women, so that the sex must be indicated by the religious titles which follow, Singh (warrior) or Kaur (princess). If the family does not use the clan name which follows this title, which is not infrequently the case, the English social worker can leap to the erroneous conclusion that the man (called Singh) and the woman (called Kaur) cannot 'really' be married to one another, as they have different 'surnames'.

Will distinctive family systems disappear from Britain?

The extra effort white social workers sometimes require to tell one black client from another may compound their difficulty in understanding either who people are, or their culturally ideal model of family relationships. The latter is one aspect of the meaning to the client of the actual relationships. Even when this lack of information has been remedied, the belief may persist that within a few years the different systems will disappear in favour of the white model of the nuclear family.

The opposite view has been taken by many writers. Foner (1977) notes that, while lower class parents of Jamaican origin tended to marry earlier in Britain, spend more time together and share a few household tasks, this might reflect not 'assimilation' but a temporary response to circumstances. As time goes on, the older generation will tend to be found living nearby, and might well be willing to share in the up-bringing of their grandchildren, in which case the Jamaican pattern of later marriage might well come to be followed again. Whitehouse (1983) points out that in a largely unem-ployed young black community, income is maximised by partners claiming state benefits apart.

Asian parents may be driven to supervise their adolescent children even more strictly here than in India, partly because in exogamous Hindu and Sikh villages all young people are 'brother' and 'sister' which allows for respectful conversation between them; partly because in Asian eyes Britain has a reputation for moral depravity, so that their slightest misde-meanours may confirm the worst suspicions of their fellow villagers about the effects on children of being brought up here, and have a disproportionate effect on the family's stand-ing and the children's marriage prospects. Prohibition of the entry of male fiancés by the Immigration Rules 1980 put up the dowries demanded of girls brought up in Britian to com-pensate for the Western influence they are assumed to have absorbed, and make them more acceptable in competition with fiancées from the homeland, who could still come here. There has been talk of 'cross-caste' marriages, but these almost invariably turn out to involve the most minor adjust-ments to previous marriage patterns, which widen the range of partners to a very limited extent. The Asian preferential marriage system is a flexible system for survival, which will probably itself survive, with minor adjustments, just as it did in East Africa before the African Asians came here.

The most obvious threat to continuity is the financial inde-pendence which young Asians might gain from working in the British economy (CRC 1976a). The recession has dimi-nished this possibility. The importance of opportunities for waged work with fellow-Asians, or for joining close relatives in self-employment ventures, is correspondingly greater, and likely to strengthen family control.

The interaction between English family law and ethnic minority customs is described in Poulter (1986).

The power to intervene

To Max Weber (1954) power resided in the probability that an 'actor' would be able to realise his own objectives even against the opposition of others with whom he had a social relationship. Power is usually accompanied by, but is not the same as, authority, which Weber defines as the legitimate right to issue commands to certain others. In the literature, social workers seem most likely to derive power from what Weber termed legal-rational authority, whereby obedience is secured because the subject has an essential belief in the norms and values underlying that authority. It is in the nature of work across racial boundaries that worker and client may adhere to different but equally well-established systems of norms and values. Or even if this is not the case, they may well envisage common values being realised in different ways. There is also a strong possibility that they will have only a limited or distorted idea of the other's purposes.

During the 1970s and 1980s legislation greatly enhanced the statutory powers available to social work agencies, while the area of political and social consensus conspicuously narrowed. Conceptualising client-social worker interaction around legal-rational authority is of increasingly limited use.

Some conceptual framework that includes the interests of the agency itself, as a social control agent, seems to be required instead. Intervention on an 'involuntary' basis (that is, not at the client's behest) usually has a mixed outcome in terms of advantage to the client. Whether to intervene or not has to be decided on the basis of whether the foreseen consequences of not intervening would be more deleterious than the foreseen consequences of intervening. In this calculation, reality requires that the social worker takes into account the apprehended consequences to his agency, as well as to his client, of each possible course of action. In so far as unfamiliarity with different cultural preferences will limit the extent to which social workers can foresee the likely consequences of their interventions, black clients will be relatively disadvantaged by social work activity. A white social worker's account of a Sikh family provides an example:

> The social service department first became involved one night when the father was taken into hospital with a heart attack and the ambulance crew noticed there was no one to care for the children, boys of fifteen and twelve, a girl aged ten and younger children aged seven and eight. The department put someone in to stay that night, and next

day found a relative, the mother's brother, who agreed to put them all up in his house with the exception of the eldest boy, whom he alleged was out of control and had been for some months past, going missing for several nights at a time, sleeping rough, and mixing with the wrong crowd. If the boy had been willing to 'knuckle under' he would have been quite happy to take him in as well. As his wife already had three children of her own, the department paid him a small allowance so that he could reduce his overtime work to give more assistance in the home, and also arranged for the family allowances to be transferred.

It appeared that the maternal grandparents of the children lived nearby and owned the family's house. The children's father did not get on with them too well as they were critical of his heavy drinking, and the mother's brothers had been round in a group several times to advise him to mend his ways. The father had been looking after the children by himself because the mother had gone to India with her own father, partly to find a fiancée for her eldest boy.

The boy told the social workers that he was unhappy about this arranged marriage, and he offered this as the reason for his bad behaviour. He was received into care on a voluntary basis and placed in a children's home some twenty-five miles distant. He said he did not wish to return home, he 'felt white inside', and would not have minded if he had been married off to a white girl. By the time his mother and grandfather returned to Britain he was awaiting a court appearance for several offences committed before his reception into care.

The mother appeared to be very depressed and spent her time sitting cross-legged on a cushion on the floor of their front room. The second son and eldest daughter did the cooking and laundry. The eldest son had been supposed to do odd jobs about the house, but he had opted out of this as he had become aware through visiting white families that it was not expected that children should do the housework. The mother applied for him to be returned home from care explaining that she had borrowed the money for the visit to India from her father against the 'security' of her eldest son's anticipated earnings when he left school and started work. But because he was beyond her control and because he did not wish to return home, the department resisted her request, threatening to make him a Ward of Court if she persisted, this being a fashionable practice at the time.

The court made a care order and the boy returned to the children's home. An attempt was made to foster him with the family of a white school friend who lived in the next street to his parents. This seemed to work until his parents accosted the friend's parents in the street and expressed their sense of insult in no uncertain terms. They felt it was less disgraceful for him to be in a children's home, than living with white neighbours. The department was told that the reception of the boy into care had disgraced the whole family in the eyes of the community. Up to then the husband had been held in little respect, but the wife had apparently been held in considerable respect.

After eighteen months the case was passed to an ardent feminist in the long-term team. She considered that the wife's problems were due to the husband and encouraged her to put him out, which she eventually did, without the help of any court order. This seemed a pity in some ways as because of the wife's deadness of reaction the children looked to the husband, their father, for comfort, and they were very fond of him in spite of his drunkenness. He was not violent to his wife and would bring drink home rather than go out drinking. At night time they would bring down their bedding to the floor of the front room. He would lie there with the children leant up against him in a row. He went to live with his brother's family in another area. His father had died when he was a child, he felt this was the cause of his troubles.

The only member of the family whom the boy would visit from care was his father. The boy continues to offend while in the children's home.

Our responsibility as a department was difficult to evade once we had been told of the original situation. Nevertheless our intervention had several unforeseen consequences: the mother going into debt; the disgrace making it more difficult to marry off the boy; and also more difficult to marry off the other children, according to the maternal grandfather, because the parents had been shown to be incompetent parents. And the breakup of the family, for which we must also bear some responsibility. If we had not been involved, the boy might have lived rough and stolen milk off doorsteps and the like. The Sikh community would not have reported it because of the disgrace and the whites would not have known about it. Presumably the police may have caught up with him eventually. Or perhaps the white friend's family would have looked after him for a bit. In any case it is difficult to know whether the outcome would have been better or worse.

The course of events had also further distanced the boy from his community. The informant probably over-estimated the influence of his feminist colleague on the wife and both social workers may have projected on to the family different white interpretations of the husband/wife conflict. The decision to get rid of the husband is unlikely to have been made by the wife alone, as it would be relevant to the reputation of her wider circle of relations.

The family was more matrilocal than patrilocal, contravening Sikh cultural preferences, and this diminished the husband's position. The whereabouts of the husband's mother, who would normally be at hand to give him support, is not mentioned. One would like to have known the relative standing of the partners before the marriage and whether the personal pathology of either or both was already evident. If it was, this would probably affect the kind of partner they could secure; as well as their relationship with their children, their influence over the next generation.

The scope for further discussion is considerable, but we have already seen how far-reaching the unforeseen effects of intervention can be.

Competing for scarce resources
Midgley (1982) draws attention to the failure of social work philosophy to recognise that the exercise of self-determination by different individuals is interdependent, in that the way one person exercises self-determination may limit the extent to which others can be self-determining. For instance, in a clash of interests between family members which has resource implications for the welfare services, there are no professional guidelines as to whose need should be met. Resources are then allocated for three main reasons: because

they happen to be available; because the issue is forced by
the family ejecting or refusing to continue caring for one
member; or because the case is deserving on some 'moral'
ground, that is, it conforms to some cultural ideal or preference. Black people are thus disadvantaged in the struggle for
scarce welfare resources when their cultural preferences differ
from those of the white resource-holders:

Sharmila was a twenty-two-year-old Hindu girl of East
African Asian parents, the second of five children who
lived with their mother in council rented accommodation.
Of slight physique, she was severely mentally handicapped,
had no speech and was doubly incontinent. But she
could recognise people and places and perform simple
tasks, including feeding herself. The previous year, she had
spent some months in the local mental handicap hospital
while her mother underwent surgery. On her return home
the social worker arranged a place at the social education
centre, and then ceased contact.

There was a crisis in October when she was knocked
down and badly bruised by the bus which took her to the
social education centre. The driver was reluctant to leave
his vehicle in the charge of its occupants to knock at the
doors of the handicapped people he had to collect. Thus
they were involved in waiting on the pavement in all
weathers, sometimes for long periods. Sharmila could not
tell the time and was too handicapped to be left in the
street on her own. Her mother therefore had to wait with
her. When the bus appeared Sharmila would recognise it
and joyfully run straight into its path.

The driver now refused to collect Sharmila, because of
the risk involved, unless her mother would forcibly res-
train her. This the mother was unable to do. She spent
most of the day lying on her back resting. She had under-
gone several major operations for cancer of the throat and
much of her tongue had been removed. She was becoming
progressively more disabled and less able to care for Sharmila. As the driver with the support of his supervisor refused to change his attitude, and as the mother was in no
shape to hold Sharmila back, she stopped taking Sharmila
to wait for the bus and threatened to keep her out in the
garden most of the day.

At this point the white social worker involved left, and

the opportunity was taken to re-assess the case using a male Asian social worker and a female East African Asian occupational therapist. They reported that the family were isolated from their relatives because of some stigma or shame concerning the father, which they did not care to explain precisely. The father seemed to have deserted the family: he may have been in prison in the past: there seems to have been a quarrel over inheritance with other members of his own family. The mother's illness also seemed to have special significance in that a major curse in the family's first language was 'May your tongue rot in your mouth' — which appeared to becoming literally true.

Because of all this no aunt or other female relative was available to care for Sharmila and give the mother a rest. The Asian staff reported that 'the problem' was that Sharmila was 'extremely unpopular with her family because she was preventing the mother being cared for at home by stopping her brothers and sisters from getting married'. Feelings had reached such a pitch that they recommended a residential placement for Sharmila, in her own interests.

They tried to explain to the white team leader that the brothers and sisters were approaching the usual age of marriage, and, for a Hindu family, an unmarried woman who has reached physical maturity is an 'abomination' for which the family's reputation is likely to suffer severely. Such a person faces a marginal future.' All four siblings were therefore working and saving as hard as they could for the sisters' dowries, to which their father would evidently not be contributing. But because of the mother's failing health it would be obligatory for her eldest son to marry first, to bring a wife into the home to care for his mother 'as though for her own mother', as the cultural ideal has it. The dowry she would bring might also form an important component of the sisters' dowries. Because of the father's bad reputation the family had approached a semi-professional 'marriage broker' to find the eldest brother a spouse from more distant circles than usual. But they had discovered that their chances were poor, because prospective parents-in-law were discouraged not only by their stigma, but because the bride would have a double burden in caring for both the ill mother and for Sharmila, who additionally tended to spoil the accommodation. If

Sharmila were not there, the bride's prospects would be quite attractive: she would be caring for the mother at first, but on the latter's demise, would be mistress of her own home. Sharmila's presence was jeopardising the whole family's attempts to rehabilitate themselves as members of their own community. The mother could not be cared for by a daughter-in-law in her last months or years, and the girls would soon be too old for a good marriage.

The team leader was unaware of an eldest son's wife's obligation to care for her mother-in-law, and thought that the eldest son would seek separate accommodation after marriage. He knew that the white cultural ideal would be for one or both of the daughters to leave work to care for their mother and Sharmila and that if an application for a residential placement were to be made some reason or excuse would have to be offered for why this preference was not being followed. Since the Asian staff were unable to make him understand the wider picture, they eventually suggested that none of the siblings could help the mother to care for Sharmila because, after the age of puberty, one's sibling's bodily products are ritually polluting, and one must avoid contact with them. The family was disadvantaged as in Britain it was unable to hire persons of servant caste or of other religions to carry out caring task for incontinent persons.

As the authority had no accommodation available, a case review was arranged with the hospital, and the case for admission made out on the grounds that Sharmila's sisters could not help their mother because of ritual pollution. Intent on keeping down the numbers of patients in their nineteenth century hospital, the consultants dismissed this as 'superstition'. The team leader could not think of an effective reply, either because he felt out of his depth, shared the same racist assumption that difference equals inferiority, or felt guilty because he had not found a community-based solution. Or because the higher the status of a contributor to a discussion, the greater the likelihood that their contribution will be seen as 'objective' and 'value-free'; that is to say, in accordance with Weber's rational-legal mode of authority based on shared internalised values between superior and subordinate. The superior thus has a potential for shaping the perceptions of the subordinate (Janis 1968). Power seems to have a decisive role as to which competing perceptions of a problem will form the basis for action. 'He who has the biggest stick has the better chance of imposing his definition of reality' (Berger and Luckman 1972).

In this case the clients were not cut off from the political process. A social worker married to an Asian solicitor asked the team leader whether an enquiry from the appropriate Member of Parliament to the hospital would be helpful. Another letter was sent to the hospital and in a few weeks a reply was received that they were fortunately able to offer Sharmila a bed in a small local unit.

The English clerical worker dealing with the case records commented 'They got away with it then', meaning, presumably, that the resource had been obtained without an adequate excuse for not following white cultural preferences.

Saying 'no'

Rack (1982, p. 131–2) offers a useful guide for the worker entangled in a situation where a black client makes a request, and it is refused, and the client assumes that the request would have been granted had he been white;

Check that you have correctly understood the request.
Ask yourself why it is impossible to grant the request: is there any element of choice or not? If there is any element of choice, would it be exercised differently in any way for a different applicant? If so, has the difference got anything at all to do with the applicant's ethnicity? If these questions are faced with complete honesty and the answers are 'no' then it is possible to proceed with a degree of detachment.
Ask yourself why the refusal is not being accepted.
What is the applicant's view of the situation? There may be some factor that is so blindingly obvious to you that you take it for granted, but of which the client is unaware. What assumptions is the client making, and what previous experience leads him to make these assumptions?

The client may be making the assumption that the worker is racially prejudiced, based, one hopes, only on his experience with other people. Clients brought up here are likely to voice this assumption. The client who is less 'fluent' in British culture may be making the assumption that the worker possesses more power or discretion than is actually the case. He is 'one of them' — an establishment figure with influence over other establishment figures and access to resources and sanctions out of reach of ordinary people. If he refuses, it is because he chooses to refuse, and it is therefore quite reasonable to plead with him instead of taking no for an answer at the first time of asking. It may sometimes be difficult, for instance, for an Asian to understand why a worker says he has no influence with the Home Office over an immigration appeal, and may interpret this refusal as a personal rebuff, because there is less conception of limited and clear-cut functions. Helpful individuals tend to be seen as family allies and hence obliged to use their influence to its furthest assumed extent. Or alternatively the client may be making the assumption that the worker is motivated by self-interest, and will not make a move unless there is something in it for him.

Writing court reports

Bean (1976) describes at considerable length how in its court reports the social work profession calls routinely upon a rather restricted number of factors thought to be relevant to the client's problems in order to interpret the 'facts' and produce an 'assessment' of what is best for the client's future welfare on terms that do not trouble existing social arrangements. It is difficult for the 'set of home circumstances and psychic features' (Bean 1976, p. 91) to be described without imputing to them some measure of blame for the process that brought the individual to notice. Society generally wishes to see something different about those identified as deviant by the relevant control agencies, courts are involved in judgement, guilt and penalty, and social work is influenced by psychoanalysis, with its explanation of present behaviour in terms of the pathology and the 'problems' of the past. The tendency is for whatever is or has been the 'story' of the client's life to be perceived and presented as the pathological cause of present difficulties.

Ethnic minority defendants provide report writers with opportunities to extend the range of relevant factors, but the general tendency described has produced explanations of current situations that 'pathologise' whole communities and cultures. The Asian family head may be described as 'authoritarian' because of his influence over the family's marriages. Contradictory West Indian stereotypes emerge: for some it is the absence of a father and the presence of a 'dominating' mother that is the problem; for others, the presence of a forceful, 'authoritarian' father and a weak, anxious mother is the contributory situation. Parents feel it is always they who are held to blame, never the pressures they are under, the discrimination they face or the problems of bringing up children in an inner-city neighbourhood.

Supposing the following to be about a family of West Indian origin, what five 'background' factors would you consider most relevant for the social enquiry report?

T aged thirteen was taken to the police station by his father after an incident of stealing in the home. The police gave the boy a ticking off and referred them to the social services department.

My aims on the initial visit were to speak with the parents about T's difficulties . . . and focus on T himself and show him that unlike the police I was not there merely to castigate him or tell him what might happen if he got into trouble again. Only T and his mother were present. She was tired and anxious. There had been many arguments with her husband about T, which had not resolved anything. T had always been a difficult child. Her husband was working long hours to sustain their recent move to a new housing estate, where it seemed important to keep up a respectable image. This caused a conflict between his role as breadwinner and his role as husband and father and head of the family, and left his wife to cope with the three children. T seemed gloomy, reticent and unwilling to talk.

I decided to focus my initial intervention on T, to get him to open up, and encourage him in activities that would raise his self-confidence and enable him to get attention through acts that did not increase his isolation within the family. But shortly after my visit T stole some money from a neighbour and his father again took him to the police station and told the officer that, if he did not remove T from home, he would not be answerable for his safety. So T was taken to a local children's home.

I considered that the father's reaction to T's behaviour

was out of all proportion . . . . I would need to look more
closely at the reasons for it. My aim was to get the parents
to accept T back home, and with my help to look at the
reasons why they found themselves in their present situation. They already held firm ideas about how the situation
should be resolved, and what my circumscribed role and
purpose was to be. They felt that if T stayed at the children's home he would learn his lesson, and realise that
stealing was wholly unacceptable. They did not want to
look at the reasons that had contributed to their crisis . . .
I felt that the father should do less overtime, encourage
his wife to go out to work, share responsibilities and
decisions with her. He tended to see T's actions as a
personal attack.

The father realised how strongly I felt that T should
return home forthwith and the family sit down and discuss
what was happening and analyse the difficulties they had
in communicating. But he remained adamant, and threatened that T would be at risk of physical violence if he
returned now. I felt that this was an attempt at manipulation, although he had severely punished T in the past.
But my team leader felt that the agency could not take
the risk of involving itself in possible child abuse. I felt
helpless . . . .

Suppose that one reason for violence may be a feeling of lack
of control over one's own life. The social worker's failure
to see the father (who was doing overtime or shift work) at
the first interview can hardly have helped, nor his careful
distancing of himself from the apparent reason for his intervention and from any attempt to support the parents in
discouraging the boy from further stealing. His adherence to
the supposedly 'non-judgemental' approach of social work
theory masks some very firm expectations about how parents
should behave towards children, and towards social workers.
He perceives the father's behaviour as a personal attack.
Social workers tend to experience the kind of situation described here as an attack on their child-care values — it looks
like something wrong, rejection. However perhaps it is best
to try to hang on to the idea that the parents may not want
to reject the child, but feel that the situation has become so
complex that they no longer feel able to cope. Did what the
social worker say add to, or detract from, this complexity?

To return to the five points you felt were important for the report: using Chapter 3, you could have listed more than fifteen lines of enquiry as to how racism could be adversely affecting the parent's *employment*, the family's *housing* situation, and T's position in *education*. What is the effect of the move on links with the *extended family*, and friends? Could it be that his actions have struck at some central value of his parent's *ethnic identity*, their support in the long years of hostility from whites?

T is exacerbating relationships with new neighbours, and the social worker should have recognised this as a 'last straw' incident (Fisher *et al.* 1986) and learned the history of the difficult behaviour. If the father is to be persuaded to take his son back home, then some investigation of the strength of his violent feelings is a necessary preliminary. If they do not turn out to pose too great a risk, then the father could be told that in care his son would be cared for by white people, away from the black community (though this would come better from a black social worker), and is likely to mix with more disturbed children and to re-offend. The son also requires some advice on the disadvantages of being in care. In reality, however, this was a white family in Sussex. It may be useful to re-read the case material with this in mind, and rewrite the five background factors you would now consider most important, for comparative purposes.

The assumption that social workers deserve credit for doing good cannot be far from the surface of most of us. If this is questioned, implicitly as in the last case, or explicitly, this is uncomfortable. Do we really need this information for the client's benefit? How, precisely, can we help? Suppose the client has every reason to resist the further intrusion of official agencies into his own family and community? Or that the worker is honest enough to recognise that his difficulty in describing just what he can offer may reflect a lack of relevance, or appropriateness?

Rastafarianism offers a particularly comprehensive critique of the racist assumptions underlying white society and is likely to be uncomfortable to social workers. It is a social and religious movement, originating in Jamaica in the 1930s. Commentators such as Smith *et al.* 1967, Nettleford 1970, Barrett 1977 and Cashmore 1979 have stressed Rastafarian belief in the divinity of the late Haile Selassie, Ras Tafari,

Emperor of Ethiopia, and the wish for the physical repatriation of black people to Africa as the way of redemption from 'Babylon' — white countries that are their place of captivity and exile.

Gilroy (1980), however, describes Rastafarianism as a 'mass cultural nationalist and unrelentingly anti-imperialist movement — a popular ideology'. Campbell (1980) argues that stressing its idealistic and spiritual aspects was the way the Jamaican ruling class accommodated to it in the 1960s (after the state visit of Haile Selassie to Jamaica), without acknowledging it as a movement of social criticism. Campbell shows that Marcus Garvey, founder of black nationalism in Jamaica (Garvey 1967), criticised Haile Selassie for failing to educate his people, and for apeing white ways, in the late 1930s. Campbell questions whether, taking into account the unstructured diversity of the movement, being a Rasta did necessitate a belief in the divinity of Haile Selassie. In white-dominated colonial Jamaica, limited educational provision excluded blacks from access to any set of systematic ideas save those in the Bible, and:

> in the established churches God the Father was white, God the Son, Jesus, was white, the angels were white, the Holy Ghost was white — and Lucifer, of course, was black, being the embodiment of evil. Those who preached the religion of Ras Tafari were rejecting the link between Christianity and whiteness (Campbell 1980, p. 12).

The glorification of Ras Tafari, ruler of the last remaining independent state in Africa, was a reaction to the photographs of white King George, which were reverentially displayed everywhere.

In Britain wearing the Ethiopian national colours and other Rastafarian practices are both a declaration of independence from, and a way of contesting, a disadvantaged and deprived status. They represent a social and political parody of white ideology and society.

Carrington and Denney (1981) examine the way that some thirty probation officers understood the Rastafarian phenomenon. The content of Rastafarian beliefs was not mentioned in social enquiry reports, and, while this could indeed have been because magistrates would not be sympathetic, the effect was to restrict the explanation of the defendants' lifestyle. When interviewed, only two probation officers recognised that Rastafarianism was a sub-cultural response to racism. Eight saw it as a reaction by black youth to the 'suppression' (that is 'unintentional stifling') of West Indian culture in Britain, but this suppression was not associated with racism. Three suggested that Rastafarianism might be a reaction to their unequal position in employment, housing and education, but none seemed willing to attribute this to racial discrimination. The remaining seventeen viewed Rastafarianism as an individual, psychologically determined phenomenon. Some saw it as the result of an 'identity crisis' due to living in an alien and hostile society. 'Unable to cope', and 'incapable of adjusting' to life in Britain, the West Indian youth, in a state of desperation and ontological insecurity, turned to Rastafarianism as a means of achieving a sense of self. Others alluded to the 'generation gap', presenting Rastafarians as rebelling against the work ethic and values of the parent culture, or against authoritarian father figures, or their absence as the case may be.

The probation officers assigned Rastas to categories: the 'true Rasta' based their lifestyle on a system of religious beliefs and ritual including the smoking of ganga. These were amenable to probation supervision, in contrast to the 'untrue Rastas'. Some of these were 'bandwagon Rastas', who adopted the outward forms without, allegedly, any real cognisance of the Rastafarian world view, and they were perceived as particularly vulnerable to manipulation by the other 'untrue Rastas' who were politically not religiously motivated. 'If Rastafarians could overcome their personal problems, which are preventing them from accepting the dominant value system, then life would be easier for everyone', seemed to be the argument.

These results are very much in line with Khan's (1982) account of the white view of ethnic minority cultures described on pp. 12–13. It regards them as dispensable, as it divorces them from their economic and political context. The underlying philosophy of this interpretation of Rastafarianism in terms of personal pathology is assimilationist.

7 Client groups

To the many readers whom we sadly anticipate will start this book here, the following sections are not intended to be self-contained but merely draw together some material not yet dealt with, but which cannot be understood apart from the earlier chapters. Readers may also wish to consult the index for our earlier references to specific topics.

Children

Day-care provision for under-fives
The difficulty experienced by ethnic minority working mothers in finding satisfactory day-care for their children is part of the difficulty of all working mothers in finding such provision. There is limited official responsibility for provision, and what there is mostly tends to be seen as part of the social services departments' 'preventive' work, reserved for children considered 'at risk', mainly those of unsupported mothers, but classified into priority groups according to the different policies of local authorities. Provision is made only for exceptional cases and the needs of the remainder are left to 'market forces'. The resulting unsatisfactory arrangements have been harrowingly described by Jackson and Jackson (1979).

Reports by the CRC (1975a) and CRE (1977a) suggest that market forces may disproportionately disadvantage ethnic minority mothers because of the greater likelihood that they work for long hours and low wages. Afro-Caribbeans may have a particular need because of the greater number of lone parents among them and because these are more likely to be in full-time work (DHSS 1984). The greater likelihood that ethnic minority fathers will be on shift working or permanent night shifts is also relevant. Policies restricting provision to children of unsupported parents do not recognise this and may particularly disadvantage Asians.

CRC (1975a) points out that the main reason for mothers working was financial need. Whatever the rights and wrongs of the hundred-year-old debate about working mothers, their wages might not infrequently be 'preventing' the break-up of a family through poverty. Secondary reasons for working were boredom and isolation at home, often relieved at work by mixing with women from the same group.

CRC (1975a) describes 'day fostering' provision for those children in priority groups who did not respond to group care in day nurseries, using childminders recruited and paid for by the local authority. CRE (1977a) points out that staff need to understand that not only are ethnic minority children disproportionately disadvantaged through poverty, over-crowded housing and general urban deprivation, but they also have special needs relating to language, health, culture and identity. It advocates the recruitment of more staff of nurseries and nursery schools from ethnic minority groups. If there is someone around who speaks their language or even just looked like them, this increases the children's security and helps them to settle down, Other staff can go to them for advice on children's behaviour, attitudes, language or dietary needs. Staff from the same background can communicate more easily with ethnic minority parents, ease their worries, reassure them about what goes on and encourage them to get involved. Training for staff should include ethnic minority child-rearing practices (CRC 1976d), understanding a child's need to establish his or her racial identity by providing suitable toys, etc, practical problems of skin and hair care, handling racial prejudice among children or their parents, and what stories to read that present different cultures and ethnic groups. Staff also need an insight into different cultural backgrounds.

The report of the Home Affairs Committee (HCP 424—I 1981) draws particular attention to the importance of services for the under-fives in preventing family breakdown and reception into care. An inter-departmental consultative group has correspondingly produced a comprehensive guide (DHSS 1984) for local authority policy and practice. It suggests that local authorities should conduct a review of the numbers of ethnic minority under-fives in their area, to assess their needs for day-care. Training of health visitors, social workers, nursery nurses, and so on should pay more attention to ethnic minority issues, and recruitment of ethnic minority staff encouraged even if they do not have the traditional qualifications, as their knowledge and experience is equally valuable. There should be co-operation and partnership with ethnic minority communities in making provision.

It is suggested that family centres could provide a drop-in service for childminders, be a training and information resource, a contact point with professional staff and a link to other pre-school provision. Recruitment of childminders of and for ethnic minorities can be encouraged by use of the media, better support services and training. Guidance could be given to parents on how to choose a childminder. Day nurseries could work more closely with nursery schools. There are suggestions as to how play groups could be made more welcoming. The local authority should encourage local ethnic minority voluntary groups to set up community nurseries and playgroups. Close attention is given to possible sources of funding. It is suggested that NHS premises may be suitable for these purposes and NHS clinics conveniently provided where mothers visit. S.11 money can be used to fund posts of special adviser for under-fives from ethnic minorities. However all these recommendations are made against the general drift of central government fiscal policy, which has severely restricted local authority provision, and which is now proposing, for instance, to tax mothers for using nurseries provided by their employer.

Reception into care

As described on p. 73, many working class Afro-Caribbeans of both sexes migrated here as individuals, sometimes leaving children conceived outside marriage in the care of relatives back home. Children 'sent for' later arrived to a strange and hostile environment, and perhaps a new step-parent, particularly difficult if they were already teenagers. Today fewer children are caught up in the migration process, and the numbers of younger children of West Indian descent coming into care may well have declined, with improvements in housing, and greater numbers of grandparents in Britain to offer help. It is still sometimes suggested (Roys 1984) that the cultural expectation that child-care will be shared with other relatives may play a part in inclining working class Afro-Caribbean mothers to seek reception into care for their children if no willing relative is available. It is mistaken of mothers to do so, for the British child-care system does not reliably provide the same care as does a loving relative: the child in it is likely to be exposed to very negative perceptions of his mother's action and grow up to resent being in care — and, no matter what the intentions of social worker or parent, the working of the system tends permanently to separate natural parents from their children.

The very young children in need of care today are not infrequently those of teenage mothers too young for a council or other tenancy. The destiny of such babies is bound up, among other things, with the mother's future eligibility for housing, no mean consideration in housing stress areas, and clearly thought through policies are required as a basis for individual decision-making.

[Perhaps the problems of adolescence now account for a higher proportion of child-care problems, and grievances over social workers' handling of conflicts between parents and adolescents featured in the ABSWAP (1983) survey (see pp. 91—3). In small towns and villages in the West Indies everyone would be well known to everyone else, and parents could generally rely on the help of all adults to support them in maintaining their customary control over their children's behaviour. Children would be expected to maintain a respectful attitude, assist with household duties, attend school or seek work, keep away from disreputable people and places, and be indoors early at night (often at nightfall). In inner city environments in Britain these cultural preferences were undermined because working hours interfered with parents' own supervision of their children. Other adults cannot generally be relied on to control the children of people who may not be well known to them. A fair proportion of white parents have 'lax' parenting styles and allow their children to roam at will from an early age. An important group of studies by Wilson (1974, 1980) shows that styles of parenting are partly independent of social disadvantage. Lax parenting in areas with high offender rates does not make delinquency inevitable, but does make it probable. She suggests that strict parenting is the truly child-centred method of parenting for the inner-city environment, and shows that strict parents had children who were better behaved in school and were much less likely to commit offences later.]

[In approaching inner-city families, therefore, social workers need to take account, in their assessment, of social class differences between their own experience and that of their clients, and beware of trying to apply models of parenting derived from more affluent, relaxed circumstances.]

> I would guess that higher incomes, smaller families, better health, more resources provide a fuller life and parents need not function as guard dogs for their children (Wilson 1974, p. 449).

The personal experience of many social workers may ill equip them to support parents trying to get children to attend school instead of truanting, stop associating with known delinquents, or stop going out all night or until the early hours — behaviour that threatens the ability of the parents to get up for work, and hence the family's economic survival. Middle class aspirations towards family consensus and self-determination for their children operate within limits that exclude these behaviours. To assume they are universally relevant inevitably entails racially stereotyping the parents.

[Black parents who expect their adolescent daughter to be home by a certain time can be assessed as 'rigid' whereas prospective white foster-parents, who insist on a similar time, 'offer a firm structure' (NBF 1983).]

Sometimes the social worker may be first presented not with the 'problem', but with the 'solution' in that one or the other party wants reception into care. Each case requires an individualised assessment, but if it is the parents who say they want this, as indicated on pp. 147—9, it may be best to try to hang on to the idea that they may not want to reject the child, but their moral values, standing in the community, and often their financial viability may be at risk, and if they do not get the support they expect they may lose the sense of understanding the situation and may feel that things are too complicated for them to cope, or that white society, represented by the social worker, has defeated them. If it is the adolescent who wants to be received into care, it may be that he or she envisages leading there the life of their laxly parented white contemporaries. The DHSS (1982) survey of children's homes in London shows that a worrying proportion of children in care stayed out very late, or all night, and generally did much as they pleased.

Each case requires an individual assessment, but social services 'must distinguish between "bad parents" and conflict between parents and children' (ABSWAP 1983). Instead of thinking about self-determination, the social worker might try to involve parents and children in negotiating the exercise of reciprocity in their relationships, including the duty of the child to develop a responsible attitude towards others (Wilson 1980, p. 234). If self-determination is to evolve eventually, it has to incorporate order rather than chaos.

Though social work cannot always be effective in the immediate crisis, very few children will benefit from reception into care: perhaps only if this 'prevents' something worse, or allows a temporary respite. Departmental procedures involving management authorisation of reception into care decisions can reinforce social worker's reluctance to receive children into care. Or 'pre-care conferences' involving the parents can set the framework for 'shared caring' (Thoburn 1980) with them, and continuing negotiation.

Cheetham's (1972) method of family negotiations (see pp. 80—1) centring around the practicalities of agreeing the times when children were to be in, and letting parents know where they are going out to and with whom, may make sense to clients, though extreme positions may well be voiced at the outset. It is normal for children and parents to use the cultural differences between the generations as ammunition, and in order to win the support of the social worker, as well as to resist the pressure of negative white perceptions. The worker needs to beware of an over-reliance on 'cultural' explanations that disparage the West Indian culture and obscure the need for understanding class, race, financial and individual aspects of both nuclear and extended family.

Most of the Asian migration pattern has been different, in that the men arrived first, only sending for their wives and families when these could join a settled and established community. Immigration procedures now impose many years' delay on this process, so that children arrive at varying ages. Relatively few younger Asian children seem to come into care, the most frequently reported circumstances being the temporary inability of one parent to cope when the other parent has returned to the sub-continent on inescapable family business (for example, a funeral), or when the husband has deserted.

The problems of Asian women and girls are another area in which denigratory 'cultural' explanations can mask the need for detailed individualised assessments. Ahmed (1983) points out that some women may feel 'trapped', but, before blaming traditional culture, social workers should consider whether their isolation is not more often due to migration, with loss of family, group and country. If they have arrived from an urban background, they may even have had to accept less skilled work than previously.

Ahmed (1983) suggests that Asian girls may present social workers with their unwillingness to face an arranged marriage, and desire for a 'love match' because they know this will meet with a sympathetic response. Underlying this apparent problem may be difficulties owing to the girl's class and race position in society, so that it is dangerous to fall for a 'victim' approach. Though living in working class areas, Asians seldom share working class aspirations or culture. While social workers may regard the position of white women as unconditionally superior, it may be that the model of 'freedom' idealised by the girl needs to be explored. Is it that of her low achieving white school fellows, 'whose lives are more or less entirely given over to the pursuit of boys — catching boys, going to discos to meet boys, following pop music to fantasise about boys, invariably with hopes of marrying early . . . . Can such dependence be called genuine freedom or genuine liberation?' Such models could not be further from the aspirations of their parents. Ironically, the high aspirations expressed by Asian parents for their children, including their daughters, may be discredited as unrealistic:

> seen as an unhelpful cultural value rather than an adverse commentary on the British class structure and the stratified educational system which seems, on the whole, to 'cool-out' the aspirations of English working class parents.

While 'many young Asians may pass through a stage when they uncritically accept the English way of life as superior and desirable', the 'cultural conflict' and need to ally with a white social worker may mask a crisis of racial identity and self-image:

> Sometimes the reaction is resentment towards one's own group which has been devalued by the outside world and a lashing out at the values held most dearly by that group (Ahmed 1983).

In exploring the implications of various courses of action

with such clients, individual factors must be seen from a perspective that recognises that the structures of relationships within the family, and their cultural values, are sources of considerable strength, while the destiny of an Asian woman severed from her family in Britain is problematic indeed. If the boy is an Asian, she may not be in his 'marriage class' (p. 128), and, if his parents took the view that the involvement was proof of the girl's unfitness to be his wife, she would be left in an invidious position.

Departments establishing residential accommodation for Asian girls at odds with their parents have become aware of the need for provision to be controlled by Asian staff and be within areas of Asian settlement, so that the girls' reputation suffers as little as possible and the possibility of reconciliation may perhaps be kept open — though some girls will be at physical risk from their families. Such provision will probably always be contentious, both because of the effect on the girls' future of leaving their families, and because the complement to conformity to the Asian system is the exclusion of deviants. From this perspective, some will see such provision as a deliberate attempt to undermine the Asian family.

Non-accidental injury

The discussion of statutory intervention on pp. 137–41 is relevant to these circumstances in which the usual difficulties may be exacerbated when work is across ethnic or racial lines. It may be more difficult to establish the legitimacy of the intervention, because of communication and language difficulties, and because the legislative framework, and the concepts of child-care policy and public child-care itself, may be distant or unknown to some of the participants:

> S was made the subject of a Place of Safety Order over a bank holiday. She was two-and-a-half years old, the third of five children of a Moslem family, of whom four were daughters. She had a fractured skull and was severely underweight for her age. Father was away, and so mother had to be interviewed concerning the injuries. The only available interpreter was an eight-year-old cousin who gave three different accounts of the injuries, all apparently directly from the mother. The assessment culminated in care proceedings which had to be conducted entirely

through an interpreter for the benefit of both parents and relations of theirs who had offered themselves as foster-parents. Cultural/language misunderstandings made assessment difficult as it was unclear whether the assault had been occasioned by resentment against this one child because of her sex, her position in the family or father's special attention to her. Family interpreters had all judged mother guilty and written her off as 'bad' — and mother would not communicate directly with an unknown interpreter (Derbyshire 1984, p. 8).

The exaggerated 'cultural' explanation that Asian girls are subject to NAI because of Asian resentment of female children has also been reported by Ahmed (1983), and should not mask the need for an individualised assessment.

'Cultural' explanations impinge in a different way on NAI in Afro-Caribbean families, where the procedural manuals of some authorities may stress the 'normality' of severe corporal punishment. When such punishment is causing real physical damage to the child, the department may need to intervene for its own sake as much as that of the child, so that balancing the likely costs of intervention against the likely gains (Cheetham 1981) is more than a two-column calculation.

Offers by relatives to look after the victims or their siblings may avoid traumatic moves and would accord with cultural assumptions that, even when their parents are incapable of fulfilling their proper role, children still belong to the wider family. Fry (1982) provides case material showing how requests by grandparents in countries of origin to assume the care of even quite young children tended to be discounted by social workers, who assumed that substitute care in Europe must be superior. On the other hand social workers can be justifiably anxious about the security that placement with close relatives in Britain can afford to children who have been subject to NAI. The assessment has to take into account the relative's understanding of the department's duties and its purposes, and anticipate that many parents of any group — no matter what their admissions on first contact — come to believe that no injury was involved and wish to re-assert their rights over the child. The relative's attitude to monitoring by the department is thus a crucial factor, and the use of detailed written contracts may clarify the expectation that the family dynamics will not brush aside the department's intentions. Perhaps in a small way, what seems practicable in the particular case may be influenced by the extent of the other links between the department and the community involved.

An ethnocentric policy?

During the past three decades developments have taken place within the British child-care system intended to provide better protection for dependent children. Powers to remove neglected or ill-treated children have been enhanced, and the pressure to exercise them is considerable. The possibility that children may remain in care indefinitely, in default of practical plans for them to return home, has been reduced by limiting parental rights after the expiry of statutorily determined time periods. A preference for clear-cut alternative arrangements of a legally 'permanent' nature has emerged.

During the past decade shrinking financial resources have reduced the provision of 'preventive' resources and rehabilitative help. The convergence of 'permanence' ideology, bureaucratic practicality, economic stringency and the paramouncy of the interests of the child has enhanced the powers of social work agencies and the importance of their interpretation of the child's best interests, at the expense of the 'rights' of the parents. In so far as present practice is justified by psychological theories that children develop through relationships with one person, subsequent research has not supported such beliefs (see pp. 75–6). In a review of current policy developments Roys (1984) suggests that, whereas the work of Holman (1975, 1980) and Thorpe (1980) support the idea that continued contact between foster-children and their parents was beneficial to the child and the placement, present-day developments have conspired to influence the system, over which neither social workers nor parents have much control, to regard the parents, if they are not offering the child a home, as an unwelcome complication in the lives of their children. The parents may require as much social work help with their feelings and in all other respects as the child and the foster-parents, if they are to continue to participate constructively in the child's life.

Within the white community, current practice tends, through adoption and to a lesser extent through long-term fostering, to move children from the poorest to the better off. This may be resisted by white parents but mainly on an individual basis. Ethnic minority parents have similar fundamental feelings towards their children and may be equally unimpressed by current professional interpretations of children's needs. Some may additionally feel that current policy goes against their cultural expectations. In every culture, there is some inevitable need for substitute care for children whose parents are unable or unwilling to care for them personally. This is generally arranged on a mutually selecting basis between parents and foster-parents without statutory intervention, and may often involve members of the extended family, or close friends. The British concept of creating a fictional change of parentage by legal ruling may seem, from their perspective, to be contrary to common sense. Ethnic minority parents may additionally feel that current policy is penalising them in particular not only because of their disproportionate poverty but because white social workers tend to make ethnocentric assumptions about their families and their children's best interests. Unless positive measures are taken, current practice will tend to move children from the black communities to the white. Black politicians have become actively interested in child-care issues, and may well feel that, in spite of the high numbers of black children in care, the current system is the outcome of pressure-group activity that did not involve many black people.

Ethnic minority parents may need particular help if their legal rights are to be safeguarded. Asian parents may need translations of forms and documents, and the help of a specialist interpreter who is knowledgeable about child-care legislation. They may well not be able to receive such assistance from their own community on a confidential basis. Parents of children who have been newly received into care particularly require personal explanations of the financial assessment forms, and clear information about visiting arrangements (CRE 1977b suggests issuing cards similar to hospital visiting cards), if they are not to be confused, alarmed or alienated at an early stage.

Substitute care
There are a fair number of black residential staff in some authorities, so that it is not now correct to assume that the black child in a children's home will always be isolated

among whites, or be among black children with overwhelmingly white staff. In some authorities a white child may sometimes be cared for by black staff. However in many authorities and institutions, the proportion of black staff to black children remains inadequate.

Proportionate matching of staff to children, which presupposes monitoring, is important, and not only to reduce the strangeness felt on first arrival in care. Without special training, white staff may not be competent at the basic level of physical care. They may not be aware of the need to avoid dry skin by the use of moisturising creams or oils. They may not be able to carry out specialised hair care for younger children (CRC 1976e), and, depending on the ethnic group, they may not be able to produce acceptable food. They may find it more difficult to communicate with parents, or to understand how black children and parents are feeling. It may also be more difficult for them to act as role models for the children. This disproportionately disadvantages the black child in care, and to follow an 'integrationist' policy of objecting to ethnic matching in residential homes on the grounds that children in care should be 'integrated' racially and culturally to provide a proper preparation for life in society 'demands for children in care a quite different set of expectations that would be considered desirable for children in their own homes' (Cheetham 1982, p. 77). Only too often the outcome is not the kind of fluency in two cultures that can be developed by children with one black and one white parent, or by black children attending British schools from their own homes; but of children who have lost the capacity to identify, feel with and communicate readily with members of their community of origin. A black British social worker thus recalls a visit in the Home Counties:

> When I first met Winston he exemplified everything that care could do to mess up a black child. He had dyed his hair ginger and was wearing a kilt and when he saw me he said 'I ain't talking to no nigger' and he cycled off (Brown 1985).

Any children in care have a particular need to sustain a strong identity, and, if they are placed in an environment where people who look like them are held in low esteem, or rarely encountered at all, the outcome will probably not be bi-culturality but a marginal identity within the white community. Rejection by whites is frequently encountered at the stage of adolescence or young adulthood, leaving an isolated and confused individual.

Alternatively children may try to resist the negative projections of the majority both about blackness and about being in care by determinedly defiant behaviour that puts them at risk either of sanctions or of exploitation by others. Pinder (1981) describes how older children can turn their marginality into a psychological resource, using race in a self-assured way to threaten workers' competence, and set their own terms for their stay in care. While this might be interpreted as a successful adaptation to the lack of competent adults in their family life, the appropriate response is one of management rather than therapy. The DHSS (1982) study suggests that many children's homes had not established an adequate framework of expectations about reasonable behaviour from their residents, and their staff cannot do this without management support and fieldworkers' co-operation.

Black children in care may also be disproportionately disadvantaged by the location of residential provision, which is often outside of areas of black settlement, in the suburbs or in the country. This is relevant to 'matching' difficulties, but may also geographically distance the child from other black people. It is important for the child's feelings of wellbeing as well as for his behaviour that he is afforded relief from the pressure of pervasive whiteness and the CRE (1977b) suggests that efforts be made to 'involve the black community in the running of the home', recruit black social aunts and uncles, take ethnic minority newspapers, and so on. However this can only be a poor substitute to being cared for by people from the same background.

If the child has feelings of resentment towards and rejection by his own community because of being in care he needs to be able to express and get these into proportion with somebody, most appropriately someone from the same background. While in care he needs the opportunity for continuity of ethnic identity. Some homes may need to develop a 'multi-racial ethos', with links to the appropriate communities, and appropriate staffing, while elsewhere certain homes may appropriately meet local needs by having both staff and children from one ethnic minority group.

Fostering provides another situation in which a child already undergoing the stress of an unpreventable separation may be subjected to the additional stress of adaptation to a culture that is alien to his own. The greater the cultural difference the greater the potential of normal procedures to add to stress:

> Considerable input of work with the natural parents led to plans being made for the child to return home. The familiar pattern of gradual re-introduction was arranged. The little girl went home to her natural parents for a day and back to foster-parents. This was repeated a week later and the intention was to allow a gradual acclimatisation to the change while assessing the mother's ability to cope.

> The cultural confusion that this child was going through emerged later. When with her mother she was dressed in Moslem clothes, hair plaited and oiled, her skin treated with customary oil and special dust applied to her eyelids. The food was traditional spiced dishes and the language spoken, Urdu. When she was returned to her foster-parents she was taken out of the Asian clothes, given a bath, hair washed, all traces of Moslem culture removed, presented with English food and surrounded by English people who spoke only English . . . the child received a standard of care which physically and even emotionally was good, but . . . there is a need for more sensitive approaches (Derbyshire 1984, pp. 62–3).[1]

The difficulties that arise for a black child returning home after a period of long-term care in a white family are similar to those faced by a white child in similar circumstances, but the difficulties are compounded by those of culture and race, and a successful return is much less likely unless positive measures have been taken to sustain the continuity of the child's racial and cultural identity. Thus placing a black child in long-term fostering with a white family should be seen as a decision with implications as to the ultimate likelihood of return home:

> It is crucial that, in fostering, a special effort is made to provide an environment for minority group children which does not perpetuate the under-rating of black achievement and the rejection of blackness which is so typical of the

wider society (CRC 1975b, p. 12).

Unless positive measures are taken, black foster-parents will be proportionately under-represented among those recruited, and this may not be unconnected to the statistical indications that, once in care, black children tend to stay longer, with a higher proportion of residential provision and a lower proportion in foster-care than white children.

Payne (1983) lists the factors that make for the under-representation of black families as adoption resource for the black child in care. Adoption agencies, faced with an historical glut of white applicants for white children, applied arbitrary criteria such as age, marital status, religion, health, no proof of infertility, housing, education and income, to screen out applicants at an early stage: these criteria are precisely those that would tend to eliminate black applicants. Offices were seldom based within black areas. As many black adults follow manual occupations it is difficult for them to take time off work to keep daytime appointments, which is easy to misinterpret as lack of interest and commitment rather than attention to economic necessity. If offices are predominantly staffed by white workers, racial and cultural differences can lead to misunderstandings, particularly if the social workers have black clients as their primary source of reference on black families. Black families may also be deterred by the alien legal ideas of terminating parental rights, official oversight, placing children with strangers, and so on.

Research suggests that there is a lack of information about adoption within the black community, and suspicion and anger directed at social work agencies, who represent the power to remove children rather than to restore them. General disadvantage also places economic constraints on the ability of black families to adopt or foster. They may be preoccupied with daily problems, both partners may be working, and members of the extended family may not be in this country (Payne 1983, pp. 26–8).

Payne's review of the research is primarily directed at applicants for adoption, but most of these factors are equally relevant to fostering. The stress on adoption may itself be somewhat ethnocentric, and Bagley and Young (1982) and Fletchman-Smith (1984) suggest that long-term fostering may be both more appropriate to cultural expectations and

more economically practicable for many potential black substitute families. Policy developments towards 'shared care',
with parents, and the reconciliation of 'permanence' with
measures short of adoption, are indicated.

Arnold (1982) gives an account of the lessons learned from
projects to recruit substitute families from the West Indian
community. She concludes that projects were successful if
they used social workers of West Indian origin, involved prominent organisations in the West Indian community, and
made use of ethnic media such as *West Indian World.* In the
New Black Families project, vetting procedures were not
shortened or jettisoned, and established procedures were
followed in full; but the initial response to an enquiry was
rapid, and subsequent delays anticipated and fully explained.
Forms were personally presented and explained to overcome
the distaste for vetting, long forms and long waits. Applicants
anticipated rejection by adoption panels and required reas-
surance. Panels had 50 per cent black members.

It had been anticipated that preferences for children of
a particular island or religious background would be expressed, but these did not materialise. Where successful applicants requested children of a particular racial appearance so
that they would look as like them as possible, these preferences were met, though this was not an aim of the project.
Suitable stable and well-established single women were
accepted as both adoptive and foster-mothers. Some 20 per
cent of female enquiries were women aged between forty-
eight and fifty-nine, who had successfully raised their own
families in Britain and were now prepared to accept the West
Indian grandparent's role:

> It is relevant to ask how much money agencies will be
> prepared to spend on finding black families when there
> appear to be waiting white families. It is important not to
> sacrifice the long-term goal of finding black families for
> the short-term expediency of placing children with avai-
> lable white families (Payne 1983, p. 32).

The recruitment of black foster or adoptive families requires
a policy decision to do so, as a precondition for the allocation of appropriate resources. Thus authorities who have
made no such policy decision have, in effect, made a deliberate policy decision to place black children with white foster

and adoptive parents:

> the very fact that a case has to be made for placing black children in black families is quite telling. It should not be necessary (Fletchman-Smith 1984, p. 125).

Nevertheless it has been necessary. Directing resources towards recruiting black families threatens vested interests by changing policy and practice, personnel and resource allocation. In addition black children were placed with white parents during the 1970s as an aspect of helping 'children who wait' in residential care indefinitely, and was part of the 'no child is unadoptable' movement. Blackness might then have been presented in the same light as physical or mental handicap. Changing policy arouses anxiety that there may be a return to bad child-care practice in leaving children in residential homes unnecessarily. There is also an emotional investment in past work, and a desire to defend white adoptive parents who were pioneering at the time and had no reason to believe that their families would become controversial.

While the need for change inevitably arouses resistance, this is articulated on two other levels. The suggestion that a 'colour-blind' policy represents 'integration' can be dismissed, as the 'mixing' is always of black children with white foster and adoptive parents, and never the reverse, supposedly because of anticipated objections from natural parents or white councillors. Pursuing a truly 'integrated' fostering policy would have the effect of reducing still further the numbers of black families available to black children (Cheetham 1982, pp. 75–82). Claims that successful trans-racial adoption demonstrate that love is stronger than racial tension seem similarly muddled. The best available evidence (Gill and Jackson 1983) suggests that a naive reliance on (white) parental love will be unlikely to protect many black children from severe difficulties in coping with racism, and that carefully thought out compensating measures will also be needed for these children. From the black perspective, trans-racial adoption has come to symbolise white denial that racism exists, that it needs to be acknowledged or changed, or that it is very much connected to the reasons why black children come into care in the first place. The white defence of trans-racial adoption can be bound up with a complacent belief in white paternalism and the failure to take discrimination as a serious problem:

> the implications of child-care policy and practice based on white ethnocentric thinking must feel like a sick joke to black families who hear about them or experience them.

> Is the liberal tradition of rescuing so strong that it is to provide the counter attack against 'black parents for black children' in the context of a society that is racist? Do liberals who see same race placement for black children as racist really understand what racism is? (Fletchman-Smith 1984, pp. 122–3).

Gill and Jackson (1983) argue that black families suffer from material hardship likely to produce tensions in child-care, and from the stigmatising views of white welfare agencies. The latter has partly created the large number of black children in care. The black community becomes a 'donor' of children for white couples. This system of 'benign neglect' results in a one-way traffic of children away from black homes into white. Trans-racial adoption becomes one of the issues in the distribution of resources and of opportunities. The mechanism of the 'adoption market' has resulted in the 'servicing' of whites by blacks. Trans-racial placements take from the black community their most valuable resource, their children. Black people cannot maintain pride and dignity if advantage is defined for them as being brought up by white families.

At the child-centred level, the reasons why black children needing a permanent substitute home should be placed in black rather than white families are not whether 'identity' is more important to the child than 'love' — a fallacious dispute that is supposedly to be solved by research on the model of the biological sciences. It is rather that a black child in a loving white family is faced with particular difficulties that he or she would not be facing in a loving black family:

> the difficulty for the black child [is] of developing a sense of racial identity in the white family. The reasons for this . . . are, first, the tensions between making the child fully part of the family and at the same time highlighting his or her differences. Second, they are that because of their class and related factors in the housing market the families seem unlikely to have significant contacts with

the black community (Gill and Jackson 1983, p. 137).

The trans-racially adopted children studied by Gill and Jackson had been 'made white in all but skin colour', had no contact with the black community, and their coping mechanisms were based on denying their racial background. However Small (1984), in a detailed analysis of trans-racial placements suggests that these outcomes would tend to result from the ways in which most white families construe black people, part of the internalisation of the parental 'super-ego' which is a normal part of childhood development. A small proportion of young black children are overtly damaged by such placements, trying to wash off or scratch off their skin, as first recorded in Britain more than twenty years ago (Jenkins 1963, Antrobus 1964). Nevertheless it is anticipated that the majority will face their most severe difficulties in late adolescence and early adulthood when they meet prejudice and hostility at work, in leisure activity and in trying to find a partner to set up their own families. The fear is that the children will not have internalised feelings of pride in their racial identity, which will enable them to resist the negative projections of the majority, and will not have acquired the ability or the inclination to communicate readily with other black people to obtain reinforcement and support for that self-respect.

Small (1984) also doubts that the majority of well-intentioned white caretakers, be they residential staff, foster or adoptive parents, can 'understand the pain of apparently small hurts that come through racially prejudiced behaviour towards the child by others, and offer comfort, 'the ultimate survival tool', rather than tension or rage. Not having internalised these survival mechanisms, the child grows up without needed defences or learned coping behaviours.

In order to try to compensate, the white family will have to form strong contacts with black people to reduce the child's feeling of isolation, provide the child with the skills of communicating with black people, and provide black role models. The family will have to see itself as somewhat apart from the white community, as a 'racially mixed family', which few will comfortably be able to do.

Some authorities doubt whether the black community can produce enough substitute families to provide for all the black children coming into care, and regard a continuing limited placement with white families as necessary, while others like the Select Committee (HCP 424–I 1981) believe that 'where black families are looked for, they will be found'. This issue is inextricably bound up with doubts that the 'passive racism' of many agencies will allow them to make a serious effort in the required direction.

A further area of difficulty is the correct foster placement of children of 'mixed parentage' (one black parent and one white) and of black children who have lost or not acquired any black culture through spending many years in white institutions or placements in white families. Small (1984) is surely right in saying that the white majority will regard these children as 'black' and that after leaving care nearly all will face rejection and need to seek support from within the black community.

On the other hand the children themselves (BIC 1985) seem to wish to preserve the widest freedom of choice among black, mixed and white foster-parents. The reasons could be the lack of a black identity; a wish for continuity with the familiar cultural background; higher achievers educationally may feel they will get more facilities in white areas (a clash between racial and class identification); or merely that the provision of a home may seem the first priority. Different weight may be given to individual compatability to racial and to ethnic matching. Some children of mixed parentage may not see themselves as black or feel able to 'just push away the white part of ourselves' (BIC 1985). BIC suggests that a black worker should be involved in the decisions made with these children.

A small number of local authorities have now approved new child-care policies designed to relocate residential provision in black areas, recruit black social workers, foster and adoptive parents, and make it necessary to obtain the approval of higher management before placing a black child in a white family. The most important aspect of these 'revolutions' is that they are overwhelmingly being introduced by black councillors and managers. During the past twenty years whites have generally adhered to other priorities.

Mentally ill people

Black people appear to make proportionately less use of 'preventive' aspects of psychiatric help than the white population; and when in hospital they are more likely to have been detained involuntarily, to see relatively junior psychiatrists, and to receive phenothiazine[2] drug treatment or electroconvulsive therapy (Littlewood and Lipsedge 1982, pp. 65, 81). Referral is commonly delayed until a crisis is reached, though this may be less likely when the general practitioner is from the same ethnic group (CRC 1976b). It has been suggested (Rack 1982, CRC 1976b) that the attitude of the 'first generation' to mental illness contributes to this state of affairs. In countries of origin, psychiatric hospitals are primarily custodial. Violent behaviour is usually a factor leading to hospitalisation and hence tends to be seen as an integral part of madness. Mental illness reflects on the patients' upbringing, and the possibility of genetic stigma readily appeals to rural people. Hospitals are places of last resort, and mental illness may not be generally seen as a condition that doctors can treat.

The CRC (1976b) recommends the provision of better information about available services, the training of psychiatric interpreters, additional training for mental health professionals in ethnic minority issues, and the recruitment of more black professionals. Hospitals should make special provision in terms of language and diet. To reduce the isolation of individual black clients, and make appropriate provision for them, different cultural groupings should be recognised and catered for in hospitals, day-centres, hostels and group homes. Contact between hospitals, social services, community psychiatric nursing services, community relations councils and ethnic minority organisations could facilitate the development of appropriate provision and set up support networks for preventive activity. Francis (1982) describes a project established with joint funding, which offers 'ethnically sensitive' informal advice and psychotherapy in an accessible and non-stigmatising setting, and acts as an information and training resource.

The reasons for immigration can have significant consequences for mental equilibrium years later. The special problems of refugees have generated an extensive literature (Rack 1982, pp. 150—9). Immigrants may regard themselves as exiles, *gastarbeiter* (here to work and save for return home), or settlers, sustain these self-images as the years pass, or undergo painful readjustments from one to another (Rack 1982, pp. 34—9).

'Culture shock' distresses those arriving here from the Third World, and entering an urban from a rural environment, through the absence of the familiar psychological cues that help them function in society, the loss of role identity because of the irrelevance of much traditional knowledge and authority, the pressure to succeed in order to give some point to the move, and because linguistic isolation can give rise to suspicion and misinterpretation. 'Culture shock' can lead to several months of inappropriately intense emotional reactions of anger, despair or homesickness and condemnation of the new country. Insulation by living within the ethnic enclave can scarcely be sustained indefinitely in the face of every new need or difficulty, and relapse is possible at any time that the old feelings are reactivated by a new stimulus:

> any white person who engages in conversation with any black person in Britain today should appreciate that blacks receive from white people a hundred snubs and belittlements daily. Not only the obviously disadvantaged immigrant but also the most articulate, self-possessed and confident-seeming black person has had to cope with the stereotyping and scapegoating which white society inflicts indiscriminately on those with coloured skins (Rack 1982, p. 246).

Perhaps reactivated 'culture shock' contributed to the situation of:

> a black pensioner who was placed by the housing department in condemned property, as a result of which he was bitten by vermin. Because of the manner of his presentation at council offices when he sought to complain he was brought to the attention of social services and eventually sectioned under mental health legislation. But in fact, as his ability to marshall support in order to confront the authorities about his housing problem showed, his mental state did not warrant sectioning (Murray 1984).

In general, 'the question is not whether a patient is "orientated to reality" but to which reality and why' (Littlewood and Lipsedge 1982, p. 10). There is a danger, for instance, of labelling 'paranoid' someone who has a legitimate grievance. Rack (1982, pp. 134—8) points out that it is normal for people who feel themselves to be oppressed to have detailed historical and social knowledge that they utilise in stressful conversations. Rack (1982, p. 116) also warns that behaviour that in a white patient would correctly lead to the diagnosis of mania, may be reactive excitation in a West Indian. White stereotypes of wildness, violence, aggression may contribute to provoke an over-reaction that aggravates matters further.

> The white practitioner who is confronted by an angry, emotionally disturbed black person may do what he can to avoid confrontation, and create an atmosphere in which communication can occur and understanding become possible, just as with a white patient.

Rack points out that 'colour is the greatest single factor which governs society's attitude to members of minority groups, and it is inescapable' (1982, p. 63). Furthermore:

> we must never under-estimate the extent of injustice suffered by minority groups, nor the sheer unpleasantness of a life of rejection (1982, p. 63)

> at the very least we have a responsibility to ensure that our own actions and those of our professions and departments do not add to the inequalities or the exploitation (1982, p. 68).

Language and communication difficulties, and different cultural backgrounds, are also important sources of disadvantage for the ethnic minority patient (CRC 1976b). Language is crucial for diagnosis, and a mis-diagnosis can either overlook a developing psychiatric condition, or unnecessarily stigmatise a patient when no condition is present. Rack (1982) considers that a linguistically varied pyschiatric team is ideal, necessarily supplemented, given the diversity of groups represented here, by specialist interpreters. Translating psychiatric material requires training, it is unethical to use a patient's children as interpreters, and it can be difficult to find an *ad hoc* interpreter who does not know the patient already, or who can be impressed with the code of confidentiality.

Not only may the components of some illnesses vary significantly between cultures, but there are cultural differences in how they are presented. A tendency to present emotional disorders as physical ailments — somatisation — seems clearer among Asians than among Afro-Caribbeans, whose 'low feelings' may refer to physical lassitude rather than a state of mind. Rack (1982, p. 101) postulates several reasons for somatisation: patients might consider that physical disease is what Western medicine is for, and consult other healers for different problems; somatisation may result from the use of customary metaphors, along the lines of the English 'my heart is heavy'; or because of the stigma attaching to mental illness, physical symptoms may be the only ones acceptable to the patient.

Language 'structures and verifies experience' and languages differ in the extent to which they provide for descriptions of internal states of mind. The language and culture of many Asian patients may be less concerned with what is going on in their own heads, more with their roles and positions in society and their interactions with others. If you can fulfil your obligations and your role, you are well; if you cannot, you are ill. Psychiatric conditions may be presented in these terms and questions about states of mind not well understood (Rack 1982, pp. 99–115).

Hallucinations and delusions are quite commonly reproduced hysterically by Asian women and girls wishing to draw attention to some problem they are unable to express. 'Madness is a disgrace affecting the whole family, so they are likely to succeed. It parallels the white girl's parasuicide' (Rack 1982, pp. 142–3).

Lau (1984) discusses family therapy with such 'pseudo-hallucinations', stressing the importance of knowledge of the cultural background for the therapist, who needs to know when cultural materials are used as defences, and when an item of behaviour may point to a delusion despite conforming to group norms. The patient should not automatically be assigned a psychotic role or label. Lau points to the pitfalls of therapy using Western assumptions about family boundaries, and:

> It is important on joining the family that the therapist confirms the parent's authority role with respect to the children. The family's sense of power needs to be mobilised and used effectively, and their competences elicited.

With Hodes (1985) she stresses the importance of interpreting the symptoms in a positive light, as evidence of concern about the family, rather than in terms of the individual's difficulties.

Rack (1982, p. 99) also instances the use of magical explanations, commonplace in peasant societies, as a diagnostic pitfall. A patient complaining of a headache goes on to say that it is caused by an enemy employing black magic against him. The headache may have a simple physical cause, in which case the other remarks are irrelevant. Or the headache, with a simple physical cause, may be worrying him so much that he has developed an anxiety state about it, and he is expressing his anxiety in a culturally normal way. Or he may have an anxiety state for some quite different reason, and the anxiety may be causing his headache. If the reason is a family quarrel, he would be right in saying that a relative is causing his headache. Or his fears about magic, and his headache, may both be due to a paranoid or depressive psychosis. There is an irreducible complexity: cultural beliefs can either be mistaken for illness, or conceal the existence of it. The confusion and marginality experienced in working across cultures parallels that often experienced by ethnic minority members themselves. Rack also suggests that the number of years that a patient has been educated in British schools should be taken into account when deciding the appropriateness of his behaviour.

Black professional staff may have widely different education, background and lifestyles to the patient, so both white and black staff may require training if they are not to respond to beliefs, which appear unscientific and delusional, in a self-centred way, in terms of 'are they true or false?' (for me) rather than 'are they normal for this patient, functional for his social group?'

Rack (1982, pp. 194—5) offers a way of translating magical concepts into psychological terms:

the magical explanation may be represented as
source (eg an enemy)   magic_____result (eg pain)
the psychological formulation is
source interpersonal relationship subject
(eg an enemy)

                                    psychosomatic
                                    relationship

                                    result (eg pain)

Patients do not go to practitioners of Western medicine for supernatural solutions, but to other healers; the psychological formulation provides more points at which it is possible to intervene therapeutically.

'What matters is not how odd a patient seems to you, a white middle class practitioner, but how odd he seems to his fellows' (Rack 1982, p. 119). Approved social workers from a different ethnic group to the patient may need the help of members of the same group to understand disturbed behaviour. In the following case they needed to remove the somewhat remote possibility of genuine religious possession:

The social worker with her student was called out at 9.00 pm by the police. Wife and children were gathered in the hallway of the house, the patient, in his late forties, was upstairs. The GP, from another Asian group, explained that the patient believed he was the next guru, and that morning had run to the temple to proclaim his message, throwing off his clothes along the way. Climbing over the closed temple gates he had cut himself badly. Sikhs had gone in and restrained and dressed him and returned him home, hoping he would improve. The GP was of the opinion that he ought to be admitted to hospital as an emergency. The social worker called to the patient from the foot of the stairs, whereupon he denounced her from a distant bedroom, shouting that it was totally forbidden for a woman to come in contact with the guru and threatening to attack her if she ascended. Two male relatives who had arrived strongly advised her not to ascend, as she was an unrelated woman, 'a woman from another family'. They escorted the (male) student upstairs and found the patient standing on a bed with a blanket wrapped round him, looking very distraught. His relatives contradicted his denial that he spoke English and the student spoke to him saying that it did not appear that he was very well, his doctor had decided that he ought to go to hospital, and asked him to come. The patient denounced him, shouting that he should not be prevented from giving his message. They returned downstairs. The relatives were certain that his role, his message and his mode of delivering it were inappropriate. The social workers explained to the family what a British psychiatric hospital was like and they agreed to committal, perhaps partly because the patient's current behaviour was a greater embarrassment than his hospitalisation. The forms were signed and an ambulance called. The patient was told that it had been decided that he was to go to hospital, he had no option. He was restrained and removed in handcuffs. Strangely, when these were removed on the ward, he became calm immediately. The social workers returned to the wife and relatives and described what had happened, the hospital ward and the staff in white coats, as a positive step. The children were brought in and everyone seemed quite pleased. The patient was actually back home in a few days apparently completely recovered.

Derbyshire (1984) points out the advantages of having translated versions of the forms available for information. Rack (1982) points out that manic or schizophreniform reactions in white British patients are correctly attributed to stress triggering a genetic predisposition. However in other cultures such reactions can be psychogenic, excitation states reactive to stress without an underlying biological predisposition. Sudden onset is followed by rapid recovery, and extended drug treatment is unnecessary. This indicates the importance of an adequate social history. Sometimes the general suspicion of outsiders and of outside authorities most of all, among these from peasant backgrounds, hinders the collection of material. At other times, when the worker's role has become clear or been clearly explained, clients are interested and co-operative, asking finally for an explanation of why the events have happened which they can consider alongside the explanations offered from within their own group.

Elderly people

The findings of the major studies of ethnic minority elderly people in Britain (Glendenning 1979, Berry *et al.* 1981, Bhalla and Blakemore 1981, Barker 1984, Norman 1985, Ahmed *et al.* forthcoming) are broadly consistent and compatible with each other. Because of the younger age profile of the ethnic minority population, only approximately 1 per cent of Britain's elderly population are black in contrast to the 3 per cent of the general population. There are as yet an even lower proportion of 'very old', the over-seventy-five age group, which tends to make the major demands on services.

As well as the usual diversity between different ethnic groups there is considerable diversity within each group in the life experience and position of elderly people. There are three major groups of originally 'immigrant' elderly: those who came here in the 1950s and 1960s and have now passed retirement age; those who arrived, often from sophisticated middle class backgrounds, as refugees from East Africa when they were already elderly or in their fifties; and those more recently admitted as elderly dependents. As regards the latter group, the immigration rules permit the entry of elderly parents of people already resident here, but only if they are already wholly or mainly financially dependent on their children in Britain and have no close relatives in their own country to turn to. The sponsoring descendant 'must be able and willing to maintain and accommodate his dependants without recourse to public funds in accommodation of his own or which he occupies himself', and has to swear an affidavit to this effect. 'Public funds' remained undefined until the 1985 draft immigration rules, which held that they constituted supplementary benefit, housing benefit and family income supplement. How entitlement can be affected by changing circumstances does not seem very clear.

There is thus a very wide range of life experience among ethnic minority elderly people, a wide variation in their reasons for coming here, and in their length of stay in Britain. Pension entitlement will be affected. Of those who came in the 1950s and 1960s, the West Indians employed in public services made full National Insurance (NI) contributions irrespective of their original intentions to return to their islands after some years. Asians may not have worked for such responsible employers, and their long-held intention to return may have disinclined them to feel concern on this score. Elderly refugees and dependants will have had little, or no, opportunity to make NI contributions. It is clear that only a very small proportion of ethnic minority elderly people have any serious intention of returning to their countries of origin, mainly because their children are living here. However if they do so, their NI pensions are excluded from the annual uprating, and frozen at the level obtaining when they leave the UK. Supplementary benefit, on which a larger proportion of the black elderly rely compared to the indigenous elderly, is not paid to persons living abroad.

The elderly people originating from the West Indies have similar residential circumstances to those of the white elderly in that roughly one-third live alone, another third with one other person, and another third with more than one other person, usually with their descendants. In contrast 80—85 per cent of Asian elderly people live with more than one other person, 70 per cent with their extended family of six or more people (Barker 1984, p. 22).

Whites may resist providing services for the ethnic minority elderly groups by over-reliance on the cultural explanation that black families 'look after their own'; but the operation of this cultural preference is crucially affected by the factors described in Chapter 3:

> One final point . . . concerns the nature and degree of family involvement in the lives of Black and Asian older people as it is widely believed that 'they look after their own'. From this survey, it is apparent that this has some truth to it but it needs to be qualified: the population profile of the Caribbean population mirrors that of the white population to the extent that those who have families tend to have considerable contact and to derive enormous amounts of care and support from them particularly in times of crisis. However they tend to live in small houses and flats in which it is impossible to provide unlimited space or day-to-day care and there are also many who have no accessible or surviving children.
>
> In the Asian populations, most do live with members of their family; however, younger family members are often very busy and there is undoubtedly much loneliness even in this setting, particularly among people who have come to Britain for the first time in old age to live with children who have been in Britain for a generation or more. However . . . no generalisations can be made about the Asian elderly; the group (who came in the 1950s and 1960s) include both people who are the patriarchs of the family and community, and people who were always proud, independent loners who crossed the world on their own and who are now living in isolation in old age, often unwilling to accept help from anyone (Barker 1984, p. 23).

Not being cared for within the extended family may be more stigmatising for Asian elderly than other groups, and persons in this group may be particularly at risk. Asian parents may sometimes acquiesce to their children's reinterpretation of traditional values partly through anxiety that too much strictness may result in isolation in their old age.

The ethnic minority elderly people interviewed by researchers feel that white family relationships in Britain are inferior to their own. Nevertheless their family systems have under-gone considerable adaptation to the different economic base, and in many cases have had to accommodate the change from rural to urban living. As a result, in addition to the usual losses of old age, these elderly people may feel the loss of some of the role that they might have expected to occupy had they remained in the first homeland. Those surviving into old age there would have been relatively few, their experience and knowledge highly valued. Most would not have been expected to 'retire' at sixty-five or sixty, but would have remained fully involved in all spheres of life as long as this remained physically possible.

West Indian elderly people in the UK may live some distance from their children, who have long hours of work, so that they may feel they have less contact with their grandchildren than they would like. The looser family ties may contribute to feelings of loneliness. There may be generational differences in reactions to the attitudes of the host society, the younger generations being less inclined to accept their difficulties with the equanimity of the elders.

Elderly Asians may find themselves left alone for much of the day when both husbands and wives are at work and grandchildren are at school. Those men who have recently arrived as dependants have to rely on their children for advice and pocket money and are unable to occupy their culturally preferred patriarchal role. Elderly women who expected to rely on the services of a devoted daughter-in-law may find instead that she is at work, so they are expected to help out. There may be tensions with more anglicised grandchildren.

These role losses may contribute to nostalgia for the homeland where, it is felt, people really care for the old:

> Mr R came to Britain in the 1970s. He speaks no English and cannot read his native Urdu. He worked on the land in Pakistan and came to join his son, daughter-in-law and grandchildren in Manchester. His son came to England in the 1960s.

Mr R goes out occasionally to visit the mosque and a few other men visit him at home. Most of the day he sits in front of his gas-fire or wanders around the local park and shops. Sometimes he stops for a kebab if he goes on a long walk. Mr R's wife has died and he feels that the semi-detached house is his son's. His daughter-in-law manages the household money and he doesn't like to ask for any. He has no pension entitlement and he receives no other state benefits. His son is out all day, working 'as an accountant and a taxi-driver' but provides Mr R's main source of company and conversations; they talk about the city, cricket, food, but never discuss the grandchildren (who hardly speak any Urdu and who wear English clothes) or Pakistan — 'it's all too painful' (Barker 1984, p. 9).

This loss of role for the elderly is of fundamental importance in understanding the effect of migration on family processes. Describing work with Asian extended families whose three-generational co-residence has not been interrupted by migration, Lau (1984, p. 103) states:

In the context then of the patterns of authority, continuity and interdependence found in the extended family, it becomes highly incongruent to regard the primary governing unit as the parents. Decisions made by parents must be supported by the authority of the grandparents — or other important family figures.

The honoured and influential position of elderly people, especially the very old, in the West Indies is also well attested (Glazier 1983).

The stereotype of families doing all the caring has the effect of discouraging service providers from offering services and from changing the services to fit the different needs of minority groups. The ethnic minority elderly can be seen as having many of the same difficulties as the white elderly, though their poverty, health and housing are likely to be worse, and most will also be suffering from the general deprivations of an inner-city location. Cooper (1979) and numerous others have convincingly shown, however, that ethnic minority elderly people do not generally see themselves as having much in common with white elderly people, with whom they have little contact:

[There were, in fact, indications that the respondents felt that the elderly white persons were particularly hostile to them and were more prejudiced than younger people, a feeling that is supported by research findings on the subject . . . . This identification with the West Indian and black community, rather than of themselves as 'elderly' persons, is particularly important when discussing any provision for elderly West Indians. It is clear that the isolation of one black person amongst white elderly persons, for example in a housing development for the elderly or in residential accommodation, should be avoided whenever possible unless the situation had been discussed in detail with the black person concerned and he or she has chosen this (Cooper 1979, p. 36).]

It is usual to find a very low take-up by black people of officially 'integrated' services. Pursuing a 'colour-blind' policy may appear to be non-discriminatory but effectively excludes black people from its provisions: an outcome that suggests 'passive racism':

The argument for total integration seems ludicrous for this age group . . . . Integration can more often mean assimilation into a dominant cultural way of life . . . integration only becomes an issue when it is forced upon people . . . . There are many ethnic elders who would in old age wish to be housed with people from their own culture. The provision of housing and welfare facilities to bring about integration has the effect of limiting choice and imposing, for example, certain types of food, leisure and other facilities totally unsuited to the needs of ethnic elders, while also limiting their opportunities to relate to others of their own culture (Barker, Age Concern/Help the Aged 1984, p.26).

There are very strong feelings among the ethnic minority groups that this particular department (social services) is specifically meant for the white indigenous population (Khan 1985, p. 21).

[Central . . . is the perception of many members of ethnic minority groups that local authority services are not meant for them. In some areas very few of the service providers are themselves members of ethnic minority groups . . . . An elderly or handicapped Gujerati woman with a limited command of English, for example, is unlikely to want to spend much time in an all-white day-centre where no one speaks her language or shares her experience of India or East Africa, where none of the food or publications to which she may be used are available. How should this be improved? One way ahead may be for local authorities and the voluntary sector to provide specialised facilities for specific groups. This is not a plea for special treatment, merely for special measures to ensure equal treatment. Neither is it the advocacy of some form of apartheid, but simply a recognition that some members of minority ethnic groups may feel unwelcome at facilities designed for, and overwhelmingly used by, peope with whom they share few experiences and with whom they cannot communicate (Keeble 1985a, p. 16).

Take-up is low whether or not services are known about. Afro-Caribbean elderly persons generally have an awareness of what services exist. This is not always the case with Asians. Many elderly Asians are illiterate in their own language, and facility with an acquired language tends to decline with age. There seems to be an unmet need for information and advice in their own languages about both services and benefits.

Conelly (1983) shows how the numbers of ethnic minority elderly in each ward may be calculated from the 1981 census in order to monitor proportionate use of services. Many services may be more sensitively provided at this time through ethnic voluntary organisations, but the tendency to provide for black people in this way, and to resist diversifying local authority provided services, may result in services for ethnic minorities being provided at a less adequate level than for whites:

what happens in practice is that money for voluntary organisations comes from a mishmash of sources with no clear policy and no future security and is often not sufficient to provide a decent service in terms either of accommodation or of staffing . . . ratecapping is beginning to bite, the GLC and the metropolitan counties are likely to go out of business and the Urban Programme is being increasingly directed to short-term capital projects in the economic sector . . . (Norman 1985, p. 129).

The present multiple sources of funding give some freedom from central control, but result in insecurity and time-wasting because of different expiry dates and criteria for record and account keeping, and different objectives in the grant-givers' mind (Tuck 1979). Manpower Services Commission (MSC) funding is liable to be cut arbitrarily and is difficult to co-ordinate with the Urban Programme. MSC workers are only for twelve months, so that the organisation has constantly to be starting again. S.11 funding could originally only be used to provide services for people who had been in this country for less than ten years, but lifting of this restriction in 1983 made it available to meet the needs of elderly settlers:

> The use of government money . . . must not be allowed to blur the fact that it is the responsibility of local authorities to see that elderly people from ethnic minority groups have access to services of the same quality and provided at the same level as those provided for the indigenous population. It is evident from the rapid proliferation of voluntary service in this field that investment though community-based initiatives is a quick and effective route to service provision in a situation in which local authorities are not yet able to offer appropriate mainstream services. It is however important that, if the voluntary sector is used in this way, local authorities should realise that it implies a commitment on their part not only to see that adequate funding is made available but also that the voluntary sector is included in planning and policy formulation (Norman 1985, p. 142).

Use of the voluntary sector is expensive in local authority staff time at senior level, and specialist appointments have been made. It is justified for its own sake, but not as a means of providing a cheap service that enables local authorities to evade their basic responsibility to see that all elderly people in their area have their needs appropriately met. Norman recommends that local authorities work out a clear policy on the level of basic services that should be provided to all elderly people who need them, so that equivalent responsibility to elderly members of ethnic minorities can be determined. If government funding for basic specialist services cannot be obtained, then full consideration should be given to providing an equitable share of mainstream funding. Otherwise services for white elderly are receiving a direct subsidy from black ratepayers, who form the majority in some wards.

Middleton (1982) and others have emphasised that the provision of ethnically diverse services should not mean that elderly people are assigned to different facilities on the basis of their skin colour, but on the basis of their own choice. Some black people may still prefer to use mainstream 'white' facilities for various reasons, and vice versa (Blakemore 1983).

Isolation of black individuals within mainstream residential provision adds an extra dimension to institutionalisation. The black person may feel unwelcome, and suffer from a general risk of hostility and physical violence. The diet may be unsatisfactory. Many West Indians find English food preparation unhygienic by their standards and the food rather tasteless. For Asians, dietary rules are not just culinary preferences but a part of religious observance. Language difficulties may compound the lack of knowledge and understanding. The likelihood of mental and physical deterioration is enhanced.

In authorities with black residential staff, in-service training may need to emphasise that there is nothing 'wrong' with the residents, which makes their extended families unwilling to look after them.

Blakemore (1983) suggests that the most practicable arrangements at present would be to allow certain large homes to specialise with ethnic elderly concentrated in certain units or wings. This might possibly avoid the problems with admissions policies and waiting lists, and of maintaining comparable standards, which might result from separate homes. The comparative numbers and types of provision needed are basic practical considerations.

Afro-Caribbeans with nursing qualifications are setting up a few 'ethnic' residential homes in the private sector.

The need for ethnic minority sheltered housing within their own areas of settlement can be inferred from the same considerations as for residential provision and from the housing issues discussed on pp. 44–50. There is a particular need for easy access to places of worship and food shops, protection from harassment, and support from people who speak the same language. Norman (1985) references detailed descriptions and reports of developments in accommodation schemes by ethnic minority voluntary groups and by housing associations.

Day-centres meet a particular need for people growing old in cramped accommodation in a cold climate, who, had they remained in their homelands could have been expected to meet others in similar circumstances frequently and informally. Bhalla and Blakemore (1981) show that Asian males tend to maintain their pattern of going out daily in spite of climatic difficulties, and Norman (1985) suggests that it may not be culturally acceptable for men to stay at home with unchaperoned female relatives, or else there may be no room at home to which they can invite friends.

Norman (1985) catalogues a great deal of day-centre provision generated by ethnic voluntary groups, which demonstrate not only the achievement, but also the potential for these communities to care for their own elderly. Premises are often poor in comparison with white equivalents; arrangements for sharing facilities with whites have often broken down in the face of hostility from white caretakers and other users, and there is a general wish to control a building of their own. West Indian centres are often set up by a church, an individual or a community organisation, have a predominantly female membership and a notably warm and enjoyable atmosphere. Asian centres are mainly for men. Only in one Sikh centre did women have comparable provision. When women are catered for this is usually on separate days or in a separate part of the building. There appear to be more elderly Asian men than women in the UK and in addition some Asian men may be 'elderly' in advance of their 'passport age'. They may have no exact record of their birth date and may have under-estimated their age in order to facilitate entry to the labour market in the UK, with resultant later difficulties. Opinions differ as to whether some Asian women would be too unaccustomed to going out to make use of any facility, or whether, if staff were Asian and female, transport was made available, and efforts were made to get to know them in their own homes first, such a provision would meet a desperate need. The requirements of different groups within each Asian community would need to be identified.

Meals-on-wheels services for ethnic elderly persons have also been provided in a variety of ways (Henley and Clayton 1982), ranging from mainstream provision with specialist staff, making use of day-centres, local restaurants, freezer technology, or recruiting a member of the community who will provide appropriate meals as part of a community care scheme (Norman 1985). The most effective means of provision will depend on numbers, the need to cater for individual medical diets, expense, and the control of quality and acceptability. Existing research on 'mainstream' meals-on-wheels is highly relevant (Conelly 1983).

The home-help service contains substantial numbers of West Indian workers in some authorities but we have not been aware of research on 'matching' preferences in either major community. Domiciliary help needs to be designed to support the extended family, and also to support the ethnic elderly who are without extended families. There does not appear to have been an account of a needs-based 'community-care' scheme directed at an ethnic minority elderly group. Nor does there seem to be an account of how 'patch' systems operate in ethnic minority areas.

Norman (1985, p. 146) complains that failure to differentiate services, persisting with wholly integrated services for people at a time of life when it is quite unrealistic for them to assimilate, generates a contradiction between theory and practice. The theory is: 'You are equal members of society with a right to equal consideration and equal use of services.' The practice is: 'If you can't make use of what is available it is just too bad. You will have to go without.' The implications of the demographic statistics should be faced, and services provided for the rapidly growing numbers of ethnic minority elderly people.

Disabled people

Many of the observations made on services for ethnic minority elderly people are equally applicable to services for disabled people, with whom they form an overlapping group. There is as yet little firm information on the incidence of disability in ethnic minority groups, but it is likely that the use made of services is disproportionately low, for similar reasons as for elderly people. One local authority has begun ethnic monitoring of the use made of occupational therapy services, and others have helped with transport schemes and the translation of information material.

In 1985 a National Council for Voluntary Organisations

Report (Dungate 1984) suggested a more active role for national voluntary organisations in co-operating with ethnic minority organisations such as offering to share facilities, exercises in joint fund raising, and regular consultation to reduce mistrust and build up good working relationships. A fact sheet subsequently produced by the Royal Association for Disability and Rehabilitation (Keeble 1985b) lists the initiatives of local authorities and voluntary agencies in the field of disability: it points out that severe disability allowances cannot be claimed when residence has been in the UK for less than ten of the previous twenty years.

Two disabling conditions have been found to occur disproportionately within the black community. The diet of certain Asian groups is deficient in vitamin D for a climate without much sunlight, and a national campaign was mounted by the DHSS to eradicate the resulting rickets through health education (DHSS 1983). Sickle-cell anaemia and thalassaemia are the unwanted side-effects of genetic traits that give some protection against malaria, and affect West Indians and Asians respectively (CRE 1979). There is a demand from the West Indian community, among whom one in 400 have the disease, for screening for sickle-cell anaemia, but the issue has been left to two ethnic minority voluntary associations. Don Smith (1985) describes the condition and the distress that can be caused if doctors or care staff fail to recognise it. A sufferer has some degree of pain in the joints at all times (often in the hands and feet), anaemia and enhanced susceptibility to infection. The pain and the anaemia can cause crises for which urgent hospital treatment is necessary. Further advice is given by the Commission for Racial Equality (1979).

Offenders
Difficulties between the police and the criminal justice system, and young black people, can be seen both as an outcome of the general social disadvantage detailed in Chapters 1 to 3, and as making an independent contribution to it. This hostility provides an uncertain foundation for social work with black offenders. Pitts (1984) refers to the need for social workers to equip themselves:

> to begin to navigate the space between the white, powerful authority figure and the black, young person whose only

power lies in the ability to resist or confound our often incomprehensible overtures.

The development of diversionary, reformative or rehabilitative provisions in Britain has been bound up with social class attitudes and has generally proceeded without much attention to comprehensibility to any client, white or black (Ely 1985). However to the white working class they are at least a long-standing and expected part of the system, whereas the black client may justifiably bring a more questioning approach. On the service providers' side, the very need for overtures may be difficult to incorporate into some current practice.

The results of a probation monitoring exercise (Taylor 1981) were briefly outlined on pp. 120–1. Staplehurst (1983) and NITFED (1985) reference a number of small-scale research studies on the distribution of black offenders in the penal system compared to white offenders. The findings are nearly all compatible with what could be anticipated from general studies of decision-making in the criminal justice system (for example, Bottomley 1973). The normal workings of the system would tend to result in worse outcomes for black offenders, independently of specifically racial contributions to this result.

In cases of juvenile arrest when black parents are called to the police station it may be that the police are less likely to see them as reassuring in terms of status and attitude, and more likely to interpret reactions of support or condemnation of their child as indicating a need for further action: thus making a caution or prosection more likely. Because of similar 'welfare' considerations, the greater incidence of one-parent families among West Indians would have an influence in the same direction. Black parents and children are less likely to have access to good legal advice and more difficulty in exercising their rights and understanding the proceedings. In tense, embarrassing situations, Afro-Caribbeans may smile, laugh or look away, which could make a poor impression on the Bench. Black juveniles will be more likely to have school problems of achievement and, among Afro-Caribbean males, of behaviour. They are more likely to have been suspended or expelled and, if so, to remain out of school for longer periods. This, together with the greater incidence of one-parent families among Afro-Caribbeans, would tend to the making of supervision orders at an early point in their offending careers. The same factors would tend towards relatively early care orders or committal to custody.

Adult black offenders are less likely to have good employment records than white offenders, and, if Afro-Caribbeans, are more likely to be homeless. Unemployment and homelessness are associated with a greater likelihood of remands in custody and custodial sentences. Some Afro-Caribbeans refuse to take any part in the proceedings, and comments by their supporters in the public section may also convey that the impartiality of police and sentencers is not beyond question, with obvious perils. In custody, homelessness may disadvantage parole applicants as may language difficulties, particularly in interviews with white independent representatives on parole review boards (Horabin 1978).

There is ample scope for racism to enhance all the effects listed above at every point of discretionary decision-making in the criminal justice system.

Proportionately fewer social enquiry reports seem to be available on black offenders. They seem less likely to respond to written invitations to co-operate in the compilation of pre-trial reports. Other reasons why reports are less often available are an issue to be monitored. WMPS (1985) describes an independent project using black volunteers at court to ensure that black defendants were aware of their rights, understood the legal aid system, and were introduced to the probation service in a positive way. They offered personal support during the court hearing and visited families and institutions afterwards, 'assisting with problems at a personal or practical level . . . they helped to bridge the gulf between black youth and white authority'. Their difficulty in getting on to basic qualifying courses perpetuates this *ad hoc* racial hierarchy in the Service. Social enquiries on black offenders are likely to be more time-consuming than on whites, which has resource implications. Some studies show reports on black offenders are less likely to conclude with positive recommendations, either for supervision or probation orders, or against custody: inconclusive recommendations making custody more likely.

Sometimes panels have been set up to screen reports for racist content or inappropriate material. In an important article Whitehouse (1983) describes in embarrassing detail the hopefully unintended consequences of report writing on lower class offenders of West Indian descent. Sentencers whose cultural preference is for married monogamy and ensured employment can be expected to view the client's 'strengths', such as their affection for children conceived outside marriage, their continuing involvement with the mothers of these children, or their work in the 'black economy', as further incriminating them. The interplay of cultural and structural factors entails that many offenders would be better off without reports written on traditional lines, as the value consensus necessary for an understanding reception of the information is absent. Drawing on his experience of the Handsworth Alternatives Project, Whitehouse advocates report writing and subsequent work oriented to the compensation of every kind of deprivation suffered by the client.

In the juvenile field, some authorities employ black staff and volunteers to run 'black' Intermediate Treatment (IT) groups with black consciousness-raising and cultural activities in the programme. However Pitts (1984) asks:

> while IT continues to chalk up successes in terms of white kids saved from the jaws of prison or CH(E), these institutions are filling up with young black people. Are we teetering on the edge of a situation where the community alternative is used primarily as a resource for white young people in trouble, while detention centres and youth custody develop as dumping grounds for young blacks?

Thomas (1984) suggests that IT should fight to get black referrals and his proposals have been largely incorporated in a policy paper (NITFED 1985), demanding ethnic monitoring, race training, and involving black people through authentic equal opportunities policies instead of confining them to unqualified or sessional work. Black people on management committees and in consultative roles can help develop meaningful programmes.

IT workers interviewing families to follow up poor attendance or other failures to conform might bear in mind that, among Asians particularly, to reprimand a child directly in the father's presence, instead of through the father, would be considered appallingly ill-mannered and insulting.

With regard to Afro-Caribbean adolescent/parent conflicts Staplehurst (1983, p. 31) comments:

> white probation officers need to be particularly aware of

the interplay between both cultural differences and social and economic constraints, and to avoid making assumptions based on their own cultural patterns. The probation officer who suggests to parents that it might be a good idea to relax discipline is likely to be seen as unhelpful and irresponsible.

Fletchman-Smith (1984, p. 124) suggests that 'the black child is likely to gain an understanding of the relationship between power and colour and needs to be helped to use this understanding without exploiting his parents'. BIC (1985) contains autobiographical accounts by children in care of how they used alliances with white social workers to undermine their parents and break up their families.

More often mentioned in relation to Asians are: language difficulties; the stigma that a supervision order casts on the parents and the resulting shaming effect on the family; the concept of professional social work assistance running contrary to traditional systems of extended family and community support; difficulty in understanding the dual role of social workers and probation officers in relation to both courts and social welfare; resistance to the infiltration of Western values into the family, and the threat this poses to the retention of their own beliefs and customs.

Their perception of the close relationship between probation and the legal and penal systems and the police is a central problem with black probation clients:

> One of the difficulties of predominantly white workers in probation is that of not being able to get under the skin of black clients. Additionally probation officers tend not to have formed relationships with black people other than their own clients . . . the use of one-to-one casework with black clients not only proved inadequate, but may also be a contributor to discriminatory practices in probation, since the probation officer is often applying social diagnostic techniques in a social and cultural situation in which his knowledge may be very limited. Probation officers tend to assess at the report stage for problems and will recommend probation when they consider their role will be one of problem-solving, often with an emotional component. We felt that there were many reasons why the black client could miss out on this and considered that the criteria for

recommending probation should also take into account the wider social considerations when there are not visible emotional or personal problems . . . .

A prerequisite of the Probation Order is often a good rapport. We then wondered about the case of the West Indian client who comes to the assessment interview with hostile feelings towards authority, sometimes quite legitimately held as a result of the arrest and the court proceedings, which are then acted out with the Probation Officer as a representative of a hostile white society . . . . We may well be under estimating the negative preconceived ideas that these clients bring. We may well be avoiding the issue of our role as court officers and perhaps deflecting the issue of white authority, in an unhelpful way. Perhaps we are not being sensitive to the way we are viewed and not recognising the powerful dynamics between the client and the worker and what the worker represents.

The social casework method discriminates against certain offenders since psycho-social diagnosis is usually concerned with the identification of internal emotional problems brought about by the failure of social systems and consequently the failure or inability of the individual's internal resources to deal with such breakdowns. Looking at this method, we make many assumptions about our supposed task, that the individual musters up internal resources in order to effect change in his life.

It is quite clear however with many clients, and in particular those from ethnic minorities, that the problems that face them of prejudice and discrimination in all aspects of their life are not internal . . . . Offenders who do not present with internal or emotional problems should not be denied probation because we are unable to work with them due to our shortcomings of training and organisation. Our responses should be systematically organised to accommodate these offenders and probation should adopt differential approaches to delinquency (ILPAS 1982, pp. 33—4).

Supervision can be made meaningful if it provides a service that the client values. Otherwise the irrelevance and worse of the diagnostic routines may contribute to lateness or failed appointments. Staplehurst (1983, p. 37) describes an officer who established a detached reporting centre in a youth club. His values were constantly tested but he gradually established his credibility by painstaking attention to clients' practical problems, in response to which clients seemed to 'grant rights of supervision'.

The Handsworth Alternative Scheme, supported by finance from the Home Office and the National Association for Care and Resettlement of Offenders, provides another example of a differentiated response to the needs of black offenders. At the social enquiry report stage the black staff negotiated access to a range of community resources in accommodation, employment, education, recreation and social support. They:

> developed an expertise in producing sharply focused reports to the courts offering immediate practical opportunities. The number of social enquiry reports on young black offenders increased, as did the number on probation and supervision orders.

As is usual with 'alternative' schemes, the extent to which it operates as an alternative to custody rather than to lesser sentences is unclear, but the general orientation of the work is appropriate for a wide range of offenders:

> The arguments for black staff dealing exclusively with black clients are controversial, but it was obvious that many young, black people found the relationships with the black workers more rewarding . . . (WMPS 1985, p. 46).

With Inner City Partnership money the West Midlands probation service has also established activity and cultural centres where clients can be referred, in accordance with requirements of their Orders, to take part in a very wide range of educational, trade, leisure, performing and visual arts activities, in districts where such resources are few. Though managed by the service, the centres are used by both offenders and non-offenders, and about 300 people are making use of the Handsworth Multi-Cultural Centre at any one time:

> We feel that there is a greater potential for equity in probation disposal with the development of a differential approach. This could serve to reduce selection in favour of clients who present with difficulties requiring our familiar psychodynamic response. It has been demonstrated by the West Midlands probation service that an offender's involve-

ment in an activities project could be his 'probation' and that the activities centre could be a viable form of supervision without any further probation input (ILPAS 1982, p. 36).

Some organisational arrangements would have to be constructed so that those clients who do have needs of more than one type can have them met from different parts of the service or elsewhere. However, having formed firm links with suitable organisations in the community, perhaps the service could consider copying aspects of the Dutch probation service's 'de-individualised' approach: instead of the provision of casework to offenders, community-based organisations are supported to extend their programmes to probation clients. Considerable changes in personnel and staff functions may be necessary to avoid tokenism and achieve relevance:

The Dance and Self-Defence Club aims to help and educate young people through leisure activities which develop their physical, mental and spiritual capacities. It occupies a redundant school and was conceived and set up in 1982 by a local black council tenant using his own money and a grant of £1,000 from the education department. By providing recreational facilities the Club aims to improve the conditions of life of the neighbourhood, and there are theatrical productions, singing classes, sculpture, fashion designing, dress-making, pool, football, table-tennis, basket-ball and many other activities. By 1984 over 700 young people, mainly black, were using the facility, and it was largely self-financing. In 1984 the existence of the club was threatened by plans to use the building for other part-time classes; though a small wooden building was offered, most Club activities would effectively cease.

Some two miles away an innovative Probation team introduced 'open reporting' sessions attended by a senior, a probation officer and an auxiliary and offering pool, table-tennis and darts. The average turnout by young black clients was five, so that there were frequently more staff than clients, and open reporting was abandoned. With jugs of orange juice and table tennis bats in hand, staff were ignorant of the existence of the Club and of the struggle in which it was engaged. They could have used their time more economically in an attempt to influence policy to save the Club, which provided opportunities for initiative, industriousness and the constructive use of leisure time, and was an expression of both the needs and the abilities of the black community.

In the field of community service orders, Taylor (1981, p. 44) describes an example of positive discrimination in favour of unemployed Rastafarians who were poor attenders on Saturdays because of late-night parties on Fridays. Sessions were concentrated on Thursdays and, using an old van, a mobile task force was set up which called for clients at home. 'This, on occasions, meant knocking on doors for five or ten minutes to get a reply and waiting another twenty minutes in the van. This situation improved as the group developed and now it seldom occurs'. Discussions in the van 'suggested abilities well beyond those that the clients are often thought to possess', and work performance was good. ILPAS (1982, p. 37) also mentions that, though they tend to get sentenced to community service lower on the tariff, once initial difficulties are overcome, black clients work through their hours 'as well if not better than their white counterparts'.

The 1985 rioting again concentrated minds on the Service's role in the inner cities. Central Council of Probation Committees (1986) referred to 'a long term undercurrent of hopelessness and helplessness among young people of all races, which has much to do with the expectation of unemployment'. Detailing the difficulties of the inner city population, though without mentioning racism, it recognises that the Service is not resourced to provide more than tokenistic palliatives to the situation. But it re-emphasises the Service's continued responsibility to try to help, and the futility of resentment that the population is not reciprocating with gratitude. It reiterates recommendations in its 1983 report that the Service should put more resources in the direction of Probation Rule 37 (v) 'it shall be part of the duties of a Probation Officer to participate . . . . in the community at large'. On the other hand it repeats assertions by the Home Secretary that the riots were caused by a few hundred 'alienated mostly black', youths. There is a problematic interpretation of one temporary 'shop front' project employing black ancilliaries set up at police request to advise on more sensitive police tactics. The Central Council seems to believe that the Service can detect and warn the Police of impending riots and undertake a certain degree of 'riot prevention' through the provision of alternative activities.

Probation Service Division, Home Office (1986) discusses the practical difficulty of encouraging inter-agency co-operation. What information and advice can be provided to the police if the Service is to sustain its ethical integrity, and not become a target itself? 'Strategic' policy discussions between inner-city agencies might be more fruitful than 'opportunistic' message-sending.

Investigating the degree of alienation among deprived black youth for the Home Office, Gaskell and Smith (1982) found that the aspirations of those unemployed were for skilled manual work, and were not unrealistic when compared to their abilities. They laid stress on accumulating material possessions, having a decent home and a car and a happy family life, aspirations for life-style that were almost identical to those of the white unemployed control group. Nor was their self-esteem lower than that of the white group. With the exception of politics, and of the police, they were 'not consciously alienated from the common values and provisions in Britain'. Nevertheless they saw these goals as more distant. They felt their deprivation keenly, and experienced considerable hopelessness and despair. They view society positively and desire to succeed in it but find they have little chance of realising their aspirations:

> Describing their condition in terms of alienation and other personal syndromes rather than the disparities and injustices of prevailing conditions flies in the face of reality and does nothing to suggest the type of policy which is required.

Notes

1 Bradford (1984b) gives guidance for white foster-parents of Muslim children on clothes, diet and religious observance.
2 Major tranquillisers used in the treatment of mania and schizophrenia.

Bibliography

Abbott, S. 1971, *The Prevention of Racial Discrimination in Britain*, London, Political and Economic Planning.

ABSWAP 1983, *Black Children in Care*, Evidence to the House of Commons Social Services Committee, London, Association of Black Social Workers and Allied Professionals.

ACOP 1985, *Recruitment, Training, Racial Discrimination and the Probation Service 1985*, London, Association of Chief Officers of Probation.

Adorno, T.W., Frenkel-Brunswick, E., Levinson, D.J. and Sanford, R.N. 1950, *The Authoritarian Personality*, New York, Harper and Row.

ADSS/CRE 1978, Association of Directors of Social Services and Commission for Racial Equality, *Multi-Racial Britain: The Social Services Response*, London, Commission for Racial Equality.

ADSS 1983, Association of Directors of Social Services, Training and Staff Development Sub-committee, *Social Services and Ethnic Minorities. Report of a Questionnaire Survey*, Newcastle upon Tyne, ADSS.

Ahmad, I. 1980, 'The Problem of Muslim Educational Backwardness in Comtemporary India: an Inferential Analysis', *Journal of the Institute of Muslim Minority Affairs*, vol. II, No. 2, winter, pp. 55–72.

Ahmed, S. 1982, 'Some Approaches to Recruitment and In-Service Training for Multi-Racial Social Work', in J. Cheetham, (ed.), *Social Work and Ethnicity*, London, George Allen and Unwin.

Ahmed, S. 1983, 'Blinkered by Background', *Community Care*, 13 October, pp. 20–2.

Ahmed, S., Blau, C. and Tilt, A. (forthcoming) *Perspectives of Asian Social Needs*, London, Department of Health and Social Security.

Allen, S. 1980, 'Perhaps a Seventh Person?', *Womens Studies International Quarterly*, vol. 3, pp. 325–38. Reprinted in C. Husband (ed.) 1982, *'Race' in Britain*, London, Hutchinson.

Anwar, M. 1979, *The Myth of Return: Pakistanis in*

Britain, London, Heinemann.

Antrobus, P. 1964, 'Coloured Children in Care — A Special Problem Group?', *Case Conference*, vol. 11, no. 2, pp. 39–45.

Arnold, E. 1982, 'The American Experience in Child Care', in J. Cheetham, *Social Work and Ethnicity*, London, George Allen and Unwin.

Bagley, C. and Young, L. 1982, 'Policy Dilemmas and the Adoption of Black Children', in J. Cheetham, *Social Work and Ethnicity*, London, George Allen and Unwin.

Baker, A. 1981–82, 'Ethnic Enterprise and Modern Capitalism', *New Community*, vol. 9, no. 3, pp. 478–86.

Ballard, C. 1979, 'Conflict, Continuity and Change. Second Generation South Asians', in V.S. Khan, (ed.), *Minority Families in Britain*, London, Macmillan.

Ballard, R. 1979, 'Ethnic Minorities and the Social Services. What Type of Service', in V.S. Khan (ed.), *Minority Families in Britain*, London, Macmillan.

Ballard, R. 1983, book review in *Ethnic and Racial Studies*, vol. 6, no. 3, pp. 372–4.

Banton, M. 1977, *The Idea of Race*, London, Tavistock.

Banton, M. and Harwood, J. 1975, *The Race Concept*, Newton Abbott, David and Charles.

Barker, J. 1984, *Black and Asian Old People in Britain*, Mitcham, Age Concern England.

Barrett, L.E. 1977, *The Rastafarians: the Dreadlocks of Jamaica*, London, Heinemann.

BASW 1982, *Social Work in Multi-Cultural Britain: Guidelines for Preparation and Practice*, Birmingham, British Association of Social Workers.

Bean, P. 1976, *Rehabilitation and Deviance*, London, Routledge and Kegan Paul.

Beetham, D. 1970, *Transport and Turbans. A Comparative Study in Local Politics*, London, Institute of Race Relations/Oxford University Press.

Benson, S. 1981, *Ambiguous Identity: Inter-racial Families in London*, Cambridge, Cambridge University Press.

Ben-Tovim, G. and Gabriel, J. 1979, 'The Politics of Race in Britain 1962–79', *Sage Race Relations Abstracts*, vol. 4, no. 4, pp. 1–56. Reprinted in C. Husband (ed.) 1982, *'Race' in Britain*, London, Hutchinson.

Berger, P.L. and Luckman, T. 1972, *The Social Construction of Reality: A Treatise on the Sociology of Knowledge,* Harmondsworth, Penguin Books.

Berry, S., Lee, M. and Griffiths S. 1981, *Report on a Survey of West Indian Pensioners in Nottingham,* Nottingham, Nottinghamshire County Council Social Services Department Research Section.

Bhachu, P. 1985, *Twice Migrants,* London, Tavistock.

Bhalla, A. and Blakemore, K. 1981, *Elders of Ethnic Minority Groups,* Birmingham, All Faiths For One Race (AFFOR).

BIC 1985, *Black and in Care,* Report of a Conference, London, Children's Legal Centre.

Blakemore, K. 1983, 'Their Needs are Different', *Community Care,* 10 February, no. 449, pp. 12–13.

Bottomley, A. Keith 1973, *Decisions in the Penal System,* London, Robertson.

Bourne, J. and Sivanandan, A. 1980, 'Cheerleaders and Ombudsmen: The Sociology of Race Relations in Britain', *Race and Class,* vol. 21, pp. 331–52.

Bradford 1982, Directorate of Social Services, 'A Survey of the Use of s.11 of the 1966 Local Government Act', *Clearing House for Local Authority Social Services Research,* Birmingham, 19 February, no. 1, pp. 61–75.

Bradford 1984a, City of Bradford Metropolitan Council, Social Services Committee, 28 June, *Social Services and Race Relations Policy,* Bradford, Social Services Department.

Bradford 1984b, Bradford Metropolitan Council, 'Fostering a Muslim Child', *Adoption and Fostering,* vol. 8, no. 1, pp. 46–7.

Brown, B. 1985, Lecture at the University of Kent at Canterbury.

Brown, C. 1984, *Black and White Britain. The Third PSI Survey,* London, Heinemann.

Burney, E. 1967, *Housing on Trial,* London, Institute of Race Relations/Oxford University Press.

Campbell, H. 1980, 'Rastafari: Culture of Resistance', *Race and Class,* vol. 22, no. 1, pp. 1–23.

Carrington, B. and Denney, D. 1981, 'Young Rastafarians and the Probation Service', *Probation Journal,* vol. 28, no. 4, pp. 111–17.

Cashmore, E.E. 1979, *Rastaman: the Rastafarian Movement*

in England, London, Allen and Unwin.

Cashmore, E.E. and Troyna, B. 1983, *Introduction to Race Relations*, London, Routledge and Kegan Paul.

CCCS 1983, *The Empire Strikes Back*, London, Centre for Contemporary Cultural Studies/Hutchinson.

CCPC 1983, *Probation: A Multi-Racial Approach*, London, Central Council of Probation Committees.

CCPC 1984, 'Probation: A Multi-Racial Approach', *Follow-up Letter* to Report, London Central Council of Probation Committees.

CCPC 1986, *Role of the Probation Service in the Inner Cities*, London, Central Council of Probation Committees.

Cheetham, J. 1972, *Social Work with Immigrants*, London, Routledge and Kegan Paul.

Cheetham, J. 1981, *Social Work Services for Ethnic Minorities in Britain and the USA* Report to the DHSS, Oxford, Barnett House.

Cheetham, J. 1982, *Social Work and Ethnicity*, London, National Institute for Social Work Training/George Allen and Unwin.

Cheetham, J., James, M., Loney, M., Mayor, B. and Prescott, W. (eds) *Social and Community Work in a Multi-Racial Society*, London, Harper and Row.

Cmd 2605 1965, *Report of the Committee on Housing in Greater London*, (Milner-Holland Report), London, HMSO.

Cmnd 2266 1964, *Second Report of the Commonwealth Immigrants Advisory Committee*, London, HMSO.

Cmnd 2739 1965, White Paper, *Immigration from the Commonwealth*, London, HMSO.

Cmnd 6845 1977, White Paper, *Policy for the Inner Cities*, London, HMSO.

Cmnd 8476 1981, *The Government Reply to the Home Affairs Committee Report on Racial Disadvantage*, London, HMSO.

Coard, B. 1971, *How the West Indian Child is made ESN in the British School System*, London, New Beacon Books.

Conelly, N. 1983, *The Asian and West Indian Old: Asking the Questions and Understanding the Answers*, London, Policy Studies Institute.

Conelly, N. 1984, 'Inequality and Race: Issues for Local Authority Social Services Departments', Seminar Paper,

Annual Conference, Social Administration Association.

Constantinides, P. 1977, 'The Greek Cypriots: Factors in the Maintenance of Ethnic Identity', in J.L. Watson (ed.), *Between Two Cultures,* Oxford, Basil Blackwell.

Cooper, J. 1979, 'West Indian Elderly in Leicester: A Case Study', in F. Glendenning (ed.), *The Elders in Ethnic Minorities,* Stoke on Trent, Beth Johnson Foundation/ University of Keele/CRE.

Cox, O.C. 1948, *Caste, Class and Race,* New York, Monthly Review Press.

CRC 1974, *Unemployment and Homelessness: A Report,* London, Community Relations Commission.

CRC 1975a, *Who Minds? A Study of Working Mothers and Childminding in Ethnic Minority Communities,* London, Community Relations Commission.

CRC 1975b, *Fostering Black Children: A Policy Document on the Needs of Ethnic Minority Group Children,* London, Community Relations Commission.

CRC 1976a, *Between Two Cultures: A Study of Relationships between Generations in the Asian Community in Britain,* London, Community Relations Commission.

CRC 1976b, *Aspects of Mental Health in a Multi-Cultural Society: Notes for the Guidance of Doctors and Social Workers,* also *Summary,* London, Community Relations Commission.

CRC 1976c, *A Guide to Asian Diets,* London, Community Relations Commission.

CRC 1976d, *Training Nursery Nurses for a Multi-Racial Community,* London, Community Relations Commission.

CRC 1976e, *Afro Hair, Skin Care and Recipes,* London, Community Relations Commission.

CRE 1977a, *Caring for Under-Fives in a Multi-Racial Society,* London, Commission for Racial Equality.

CRE 1977b, *A Home from Home? Some Policy Considerations on Black Children in Residential Care,* London, Commission for Racial Equality.

CRE 1979, *Sickle Cell Anaemia,* London, Commission for Racial Equality.

CRE 1981, *Code of Practice for the Elimination of Racial Discrimination and the Promotion of Equal Opportunities in Employment,* London, Commission for Racial Equality. See also *Implementing Equal Opportunity Policies,* CRE 1983.

Crewe, I. 1983, 'Representation and the Ethnic Minorities in Britain', in N. Glazer and K. Young, (eds), *Ethnic Pluralism and Public Policy*, London, Heinemann.

Cronin, K. 1985, *Children, Nationality and Immigration*, London, Children's Legal Centre.

Dahya, B. 1973, 'Pakistanis in Britain: Transients or Settlers?', *Race*, vol. 14, no. 3, pp. 241–77.

Dahya, B. 1974, 'The Nature of Pakistani Ethnicity in Industrial Cities in Britain', in A. Cohen (ed.), *Urban Ethnicity*, London, Tavistock.

Davey, A.G. 1975, 'Racial Awareness in Children and Teacher Education', *Education for Teaching*, no. 97, pp. 25–33.

Davey, A.G. 1983, *Learning to be Prejudiced*, London, Edward Arnold.

Davey, A.G. and Mullin, P.N. 1982, 'Inter-Ethnic Friendship in British Primary Schools', *Educational Research*, vol. 24, no. 2. pp. 83–92.

Davey, A.G. and Norburn, M.V. 1980, 'Ethnic Awareness and Ethnic Differentiation amongst Primary School Children', *New Community*, vol. 8, no. 1–2, pp. 51–60.

Deakin, N. (ed.) 1965, *Colour and the British Electorate 1964*, London, Institute of Race Relations/Pall Mall Press.

Dench, G. 1975, *Maltese in London*, London, Routledge and Kegan Paul.

Denney, D. 1983, 'Some Dominant Perspectives in the Literature Relating to Multi-Racial Social Work', *British Journal of Social Work*, vol. 13, pp. 149–74.

Derbyshire 1984, *A Study of Social Services Provision to Ethnic Minority Groups*, Derby, Derbyshire County Council Social Services Department.

DES 1977, Department of Education and Science, *Education in Schools – A Consultative Document*, London, HMSO.

DHSS 1982, *Survey of Children's Homes in London*, Report of Development Group, London, Department of Health and Social Security.

DHSS 1983, DHSS Asian Working Group, *Report of the Stop Rickets Campaign*, London, Save the Children Fund.

DHSS 1984, *Services for Under-Fives from Ethnic Minority Communities*, Inter-Departmental Consultative Group on Provision for Under-Fives, Report of Sub-Group on Provision of Services for Under-Fives from Ethnic Minority

Communities, London, Department of Health and Social Security.

DOE 1983, *Local Authorities and Racial Disadvantage*, Report of a Joint Government/Local Authority Association Working Group, London, Department of the Environment.

Dominelli, L. 1979, 'The Challenge to Social Work Education', *Social Work Today*, vol. 10, no. 25, pp. 27—9.

Dummett, M. and Dummett, A. 1969, 'The Role of Government in Britain's Racial Crisis', in L. Donelly (ed.) *Justice First*, London, Sheed and Ward, Reprinted in C. Husband (ed.) 1982. *'Race' in Britian*, London, Hutchinson.

Dumont, L. 1970, *Homo Hierarchicus. The Caste System and its Implications*, London, Weidenfeld and Nicholson. Reissued 1972, Paladin.

Dungate, M. 1984, *A Multi-Racial Society: The Role of the National Voluntary Organisations*, London, Bedford Square Press/National Council for Voluntary Organisations.

Edwards, J. 1986, *Positive Discrimination*, London, Tavistock.

Edwards, J. and Batley, R. 1978, *The Politics of Positive Discrimination: An Evaluation of the Urban Programme 1967—77*, London, Tavistock.

Edwards, V.K. 1979, *The West Indian Language Issue in British Schools*, London, Routledge and Kegan Paul.

Ellis, J. (ed.) 1978, *West African Families in Britain. A Meeting of Two Cultures*, London, Routledge and Kegan Paul.

Ely, P. 1985, 'Delinquency and Disillusion', in N. Manning (ed.), *Social Problems and Welfare Ideology*, Aldershot, Gower.

Eysenck, H.J. 1971, *Race, Intelligence and Education*, London, Temple Smith.

Farringdon, D.P. and Morris, A. 1983, 'Sex Sentencing and Reconviction', *British Journal of Criminology*, vol. 23, no. 3, pp. 229—48.

Fisher, M., Marsh, P., Phillips, D. and Sainsbury, E.E., 1986, *In and Out of Care — the experience of children, parents, and social workers*, London, Batsford.

Fitzherbert, K. 1967, *West Indian Children in London*, London, Bell.

Fletchman-Smith, B. 1984, 'Effects of Race on Adoption and Fostering', *International Journal of Social Psychiatry*, vol. 30, nos 1/2, spring, pp. 121—28.

Foner, N. 1977, 'The Jamaicans. Cultural and Social Change among Migrants in Britain', in J.L. Watson, (ed.), *Between two Cultures*, Oxford, Basil Blackwell.

Foner, N. 1979, *Jamaica Farewell. Jamaican Migrants in London*, London, Routledge and Kegan Paul.

Fox, R. 1967, *Kinship and Marriage — an Anthropological Perspective*, Harmondsworth, Penguin Books.

Francis, W. 1982, 'Out of the Textbooks and into the Consulting Room', *Community Care*, vol. 535, 25 October, pp. 19—20.

Fry, P. 1982, *Children Torn between Cultures*, Report submitted to the Central Council for Education and Training in Social Work, London, Unpublished.

Fryer, P. 1984, *Staying Power. The History of Black People in Britain*, London, Pluto Press.

Garvey, M. 1967, *The Philosophy and Opinions of Marcus Garvey*, London, Frank Cass.

Gaskell, G. and Smith, P. 1982, 'The Attitudes and Aspirations of Deprived Black Youth', Home Office, *Research Bulletin*, no. 13, pp. 7—9.

Gill, O. and Jackson, B. 1983, *Adoption and Race*, London, Batsford.

Gilroy, P. 1980, 'Managing the "Underclass": A Further Note on the Sociology of Race Relations in Britain', *Race and Class*, vol. 22, no. 1, pp. 47—62.

Glasgow, D. 1980 *The Black Underclass*, New York, Jossey Bass.

Glazier, S.D. 1983, 'Cultural Pluralism and Respectability in Trinidad', *Ethnic and Racial Studies*, vol. 6, no. 3, July, pp. 351—5.

Glendenning, F. (ed). 1979, *The Elders in Ethnic Minorities*, Stoke on Trent, Beth Johnson Foundation/Department of Adult Education, University of Keele/Commission for Racial Equality.

Gumperz, J.J., Jupp, T.C. and Roberts, C. 1979, *Crosstalk*, London, National Centre for Industrial Language Training.

Hall, S., Critcher, S., Jefferson, T., Clark, J. and Roberts, B. 1978, *Policing the Crisis: Mugging, the State, and Law and Order*, London, Macmillan.

Haralambos, M. 1980, with R. Heald, *Sociology, Themes and Perspectives,* Slough, University Tutorial Press.

Harrison, G.A. and Owen, J.J.T. 1964, 'Studies on the Inheritance of Human Skin Colour', *Annals of Human Genetics,* vol. 28, pp. 27–37.

Hawkins, P.M. undated, *Explanation of Asian Names,* Bradford, Community Relations Council.

HCP 424–I, 1981, *Racial Disadvantage,* Fifth Report from the Home Affairs Committee, House of Commons, session 1980/81, London, HMSO.

HCP 90–I 1982, *Immigration from the Indian Sub-Continent,* Report from the Home Affairs Committee, House of Commons, session 1981/82, London, HMSO.

HCP 360–I 1984, *Children in Care,* Second Report from the Social Services Committee, House of Commons, session 1983/4, London, HMSO.

HCP 102–I 1985, *Chinese Community in Britain,* Second Report from the Home Affairs Committee, House of Commons, session 1984/85, London, HMSO.

Helweg, A.W. 1979, *Sikhs in England. The Development of a Migrant Community,* Delhi, Oxford University Press.

Henley, A. and Clayton, J. 1982, 'Catering for All Tastes', *Health and Social Services Journal,* 22 July, pp. 888–9.

Higgins, J., Deakin N., Edwards, J. and Wicks, M. 1983, *Government and Urban Poverty: Inside the Policy-Making Process,* Oxford, Blackwell.

Hill, M.J. and Issacharoff, R.M. 1971, *Community Action and Race Relations: A Study of Community Relations Committees in Britain,* London, Institute of Race Relations/Oxford University Press.

HOC 1977, 'Probation and After-Care Service – Ethnic minorities', *Home Office Circular* no. 113, London, Home Office.

HOC 1982 'Section II of the Local Government Act 1966' *Home Office Circular,* no. 97, London, Home Office.

Hodes, M. 1985, 'Family Therapy and the Problem of Cultural Relativism: A Reply to Dr. Lau', *Journal of Family Therapy,* vol. 7, pp. 261–72.

Hollis, F. 1964, *Casework: A Psychosocial Therapy,* New York, Random House.

Holman, R. 1968, 'Immigrants and Child Care Policy', *Case Conference,* vol. 15, no. 7, pp. 225–8.

Holman, R. 1973, *Trading in Children — A Study of Private Fostering,* London, Routledge and Kegan Paul.

Holman, R. 1975, 'Unmarried Mothers, Social Deprivation and Child Separation', *Policy and Politics,* vol. 3 no. 4, pp. 25—41.

Holman, R. 1980 'Exclusive and Inclusive Concepts of Fostering', in J. Triseliotis, *New Developments in Fostering and Adoption,* London, Routledge and Kegan Paul.

Home Office 1981, *Racial Attacks,* Report of a Home Office Study, London, HMSO.

Home Office 1986, *The Implications for the Probation Service of the 1985 Inner Cities Disturbances,* London, Probation Service Division, Home Office.

Horabin, R. 1978, *Problems of Asians in Penal Institutions,* London, Runnymede Trust.

Husband, C. 1975, *White Media and Black Britain,* London, Arrow Books.

Husband, C. 1980, 'Culture, Context and Practice: Racism in Social Work', in R. Bailey, and M. Brake, (eds), *Radical Social Work and Practice,* London, Edward Arnold.

Husband, C. (ed.) 1982, *'Race' in Britain,* London, Hutchinson.

ILPAS 1982, *ILPAS in a Multi-Racial Society*, London, Inner London Probation and After Care Service.

Jackson, A. 1981, 'Just How Relevant and Accessible are Social Services Departments?' in J. Cheetham, W. James, M. Loney, B. Mayor and W. Prescott (eds), *Social and Community Work in a Multi-Racial Society,* London, Harper and Row.

Jackson, B. and Jackson, S. 1979, *Childminder: A Study in Action Research,* London, Routledge and Kegan Paul.

James, A.G. 1974, *Sikh Children in Britain,* London, Oxford University Press.

Janis, I.L. 1968, *Victims of Group Think: A Psychological Study of Foreign Policy Decisions and Fiascos,* Boston, Massachusetts, Houghton Mifflin.

Jenkins, R. 1963, 'The Fostering of Coloured Children', *Case Conference,* vol. 10, no. 5, pp. 129—34.

Jenkins, Rt Hon. R., MP 1966, *Address Given by the Home Secretary on 23 May 1966 . . . to a Meeting of Voluntary Liaison Committees,* London, National Committee for Commonwealth Immigrants.

John, G. 1972, 'The Social Worker and the Young Blacks', in J.P. Triseliotis, (ed.), *Social Work with Coloured Immigrants and their Families,* London Institute of Race Relations/Oxford University Press.

Joint Committee 1982, *Report of the Joint Committee for Refugees from Vietnam,* London, HMSO.

Jones, P.R. 1982, *Vietnamese Refugees,* Home Office Research and Planning Unit, Paper 13, London, Home Office.

Jordan, W.D. 1974, *The White Man's Burden,* Charleston, University of North Carolina Press. Adapted to 'First Impressions: Initial English Confrontations with Africans', in C. Husband (ed.), *'Race' in Britain,* London, Hutchinson.

Kapadia, K.M. 1966, *Marriage and the Family in India,* 3rd edn. London, Oxford University Press.

Karn, V. 1984, 'Race and Housing in Britain: The Role of the Major Institutions', in N. Glazer and K. Young (eds), *Ethnic Pluralism and Public Policy,* London, Heinemann.

Katznelson, I. 1973 'The Politics of Racial Buffering in Nottingham 1954–68', *Race,* vol. XI, no. 4, April.

Keeble, P. 1985a, 'Minority Ethnic Groups and the Royal Association for Disablement and Rehabilitation', *Contact,* no. 44, summer, pp. 15–17.

Keeble, P. 1985b, *Disability and Minority Ethnic Groups: A Factsheet of Issues and Initiatives,* London, Royal Association for Disability and Rehabilitation.

Khan, V. Saifullah (ed.) 1979, *Minority Families in Britain,* London, Macmillan.

Khan, V. Saifullah 1982, 'The Role of the Culture of Dominance in Structuring the Experience of Ethnic Minorities', in C. Husband (ed.), *'Race' in Britain,* London, Hutchinson.

Khan, Y. 1985, 'Disability Among Asian Communities', *Contact,* no. 44, summer, pp. 21–2.

Khare, R.S. 1985, *The Untouchable as Himself. Ideology, Identity and Pragmatism among the Lucknow Chamars,* Cambridge University Press.

Kirby, A. 1975, 'Race Today, Gone Tomorrow', in C. Husband (ed.), *White Media and Black Britain.* London, Arrow Books.

Kirp, D.L. 1979, *Doing Good by Doing Little — Race and Schooling in Britain,* Berkley, University of California Press.

Labov, W. 1972, *Languages in the Inner City*, Philadelphia, University of Pennsylvania Press.

Ladbury, S. 1977, 'The Turkish Cypriots: Ethnic Relations in London and Cyprus', in J.L. Watson (ed.), *Between Two Cultures*, London, Basil Blackwell.

Lal, B.B. 1983, 'Perspectives on Ethnicity: Old Wine in New Bottles', *Ethnic and Racial Studies*, vol. 6, no. 2, pp. 154–73.

LARRIE 1984, Local Authority Race Relations Information Exchange, *Information Sheet*, May, London, Policy Studies Institute.

Lau, A. 1984, 'Transcultural Issues in Family Therapy, *Journal of Family Therapy*, vol. 6, pp. 91–112.

Little, A. and Robbins, D. 1982, *Loading the Law*, London, Commission for Racial Equality.

Littlewood, R. and Lipsedge, M. 1982, *Aliens and Alienists. Ethnic Minorities and Psychiatry*, Harmondsworth, Penguin Books.

Liverpool, V. 1982, 'The Dilemmas and Contribution of Black Social Workers' in J. Cheetham (ed.), *Social Work and Ethnicity*, London, National Institute for Social Work Training/Heinemann.

Lorenz, K. 1966, *On Aggression*, translated by M. Latzke, London, Methuen.

Lowenthal, D. 1972, *West Indian Societies*, London, Oxford University Press.

Lustgarten, L. 1981, *Legal Control of Racial Discrimination*, London, Macmillan.

Middleton, L. 1982, 'Pride and Prejudice', *Social Work Today*, vol. 13, no. 38, 15 June p. 15.

Midgley, J. 1982, *Professional Imperialism*, London, Heinemann.

Miles, R. 1982, 'Racism and Nationalism in Britain', in C. Husband (ed.) *'Race' in Britain*, London, Hutchinson.

Moore, R. and Wallace, T. 1975, *Slamming the Door*, London, Martin Robertson.

Morris, S. 1968, *Indians in Uganda. Caste and Sect in a Plural Society*, London, Weidenfeld and Nicholson.

Mukherji, T. 1982, 'Sri Guru Singh Sabha: Southall', in A. Ohri, B. Manning, P. Curno (eds), *Community Work and Racism*, London, Routledge and Kegan Paul/Association of Community Workers.

Murray, N. 1984, 'A Cure for Colour Blindness?', *Community Care*, no. 525, 16 August pp. 16—17.

Myrdal, G. 1944, with R. Sterner and A Rose, *An American Dilemma: the Negro and Modern Democracy*, New York, Harper.

Nash, M. 1972, 'Race and the Ideology of Race', *Current Anthropology*, vol. 3 pp. 286—8, quoted in G.E. Simpson and J.M. Yinger 1965.

NBF 1983, Video, New Black Families Project, London.

Nettleford, R. 1970, *Mirror, Mirror: Identity, Race and Protest in Jamaica*, Kingston, Sangster and Collins.

NITFED 1985, *Anti-Racist Practice for Intermediate Treatment*, Report of a Working Party, London, National Intermediate Treatment Federation.

Norman, A. 1985, *Triple Jeopardy: Growing Old in a Second Homeland*, London, Centre for Policy on Ageing.

Norris, K. 1962, *Jamaica: the Search for an Identity*, London, Oxford University Press.

Ohri, A., Manning, B., Curno, P. 1982 *Community Work and Racism*, London, Routledge and Kegan Paul.

Ollereanshaw, S. 1984, 'The Promotion of Employment Equality in Britain', in N. Glazer and K. Young (eds), *Ethnic Pluralism and Public Policy*, London, Heinemann.

OPCS 1982, Office of Population Censuses and Surveys, 'Sources of Statistics on Ethnic Minorities', *OPCS Monitor*, PP 1, 81/2, 22 June.

Ouseley, H., Silverstone, D. and Prashar, U. 1981, *The System*, London, Runnymede Trust.

Parekh, B. 1984, 'Educational Opportunity in Multi-Ethnic Britain', in N. Glazer and K. Young (eds), *Ethnic Pluralism and Public Policy*, London, Heinemann.

Patterson, G. 1984, 'Millionaires Include 100 named Patel, Inland Revenue Report', *Daily Telegraph*, 2 November, p. 14.

Patterson, S. 1971, *Immigration and Race Relations in Britain 1960—1967*, London, Institute of Race Relations/ Oxford University Press.

Payne, S. 1983, *Long-Term Placement for the Black Child in Care*, Norwich, Social Work Monographs, University of East Anglia.

Peach, C. 1968, *West Indian Migration to Britain. A Social Geography*, London, Institute of Race Relations/Oxford

University Press.

PEP 1967, Political and Economic Planning Report, *Racial Discrimination in Britain.* Reissued as W.W. Daniel 1968, *Racial Discrimination in England,* Harmondsworth, Penguin Books.

PEP 1974, Political and Economic Planning Reports no. 544, *Racial Disadvantage in Employment,* and no. 547, *The Extent of Racial Discrimination.* Reissued as D. Smith 1977.

Pettigrew, J. 1975, *Robber Nobleman. A Study of the Political System of the Sikh Jats,* London, Routledge and Kegan Paul.

Phillips, M. 1982, 'Separatism or Black Control?', in A. Ohri, B. Manning and P. Curno (eds), *Community Work and Rascism,* London, Routledge and Kegan Paul/Association of Community Workers.

Philpott, S.B. 1977, 'The Montserratians: Migration Dependency and the Maintenance of Island Ties in England', in J.L. Watson (ed.), *Between Two Cultures,* Oxford, Basil Blackwell.

Pincus, A. and Minahan, A. 1973, *Social Work Practice. Model and Method,* Itasca, Illinois, Peacock.

Pinder, R. 1981, 'Ending Deprivation', *Community Care,* 27 August, pp. 12—13.

Pitts, J. 1984, 'Racism, Juvenile Justice and IT', *IT Mailing,* no. 17, July, pp. 4—5, Leicester, National Youth Bureau.

Pocock, D.F. 1973, *Kambi and Patidar,* London, Oxford University Press.

Poliakov, L. 1974, *The Aryan Myth. A History of Racist and Nationalist Ideas in Europe,* London, Chatto/Heinemann for Sussex University Press.

Poulter, S. 1986 *English Law and Ethnic Minority Customs,* London, Butterworth.

Powell, Rt Hon. J.E., MP 1968, 'Text of a Speech Delivered on 20 April in Birmingham', *Race,* vol. XI, no. 4, April.

Rack, P, 1982, *Race, Culture and Mental Disorder,* London, Tavistock.

Rashid, S.P. 1982, 'Home Is Where One Starts From', Reflections of an Ethnic Minority Social Worker, in J. Cheetham (ed.), *Social Work and Ethnicity,* London, George Allen and Unwin.

Reeves, F. 1983, *British Racial Discourse,* Cambridge, Cambridge University Press.

Rex, J. 1970, *Race Relations in Sociological Theory*, London, Weidenfeld and Nicholson.

Rex, J. 1973, *Race, Colonialism and the City*, London, Routledge and Kegan Paul.

Rex, J. 1979, 'Race Relations Research in an Academic Setting: A Personal Note', *Research Bulletin*, no. 8, pp. 29–30, London, Home Office Research Unit.

Rex, J. and Moore, R. 1967, *Race, Community and Conflict*, London, Institute for Race Relations/Oxford University Press.

Rex, J. and Tomlinson, S. 1979, *Colonial Immigrants in a British City*, London, Routledge and Kegan Paul.

Rogg, E.M. 1974, *The Assimilation of Cuban Exiles: the Role of Community and Class*, New York, Aberdeen Press.

Rooney, B. 1981, 'Active Mistakes – A Grass Roots Report', in J. Cheetham, et al (eds).

Rooney, B. 1982, 'Black Social Workers in White Departments', in J. Cheetham, (ed), *Social Work and Ethnicity*, London, National Institute for Social Work Training/Heinemann.

Rose, E.J.B. 1969, *Colour and Citizenship*, A Report on British Race Relations, London, Institute for Race Relations/Oxford University Press.

Roys, P. 1984, 'Ethnic Minorities and the Child Welfare System', *International Journal of Social Psychiatry*, vol. 30, nos 1/2, spring, pp. 102–121.

RSG 1980, Radical Statistics Group, *Britain's Black Population*, London, Runnymede Trust.

Rutter, M. 1972, *Maternal Deprivation Reassessed*, Harmondsworth, Penguin Books.

Scarman, Lord 1981, *The Brixton Disorders 10–12 April 1981*, London, HMSO. Reissued as *The Scarman Report*, Harmondsworth, Penguin Books.

Segal, R. 1976, *The Race War*, Harmondsworth, Penguin Books.

Shackman, J., 1985, *The Right to be Understood*, Cambridge, National Extension College.

Sharron, H. 1985, 'Rob the Poor – Give to the Rich', *Social Work Today*, vol. 16, no. 27, pp. 6–7.

Shyllon, F.O. 1977, *Black People in Britain 1555–1833*, London, Institute of Race Relations/Oxford University Press.

Simpson, G.E. and Yinger, J.M. (eds) 1965, *Racial and Cultural Minorities,* 3rd edn, New York, Harper and Row.

Sivanandan, A. 1976, 'Race, Class and the State: The Black Experience in Britain', *Race and Class,* vol. 17, no. 4 pp. 347−68.

Sivanandan, A. 1981, 'From Resistance to Rebellion: Asian and Afro-Caribbean Struggles in Britain', *Race and Class,* vol. 23, no. 2/3, pp. 111−52.

Small, J.W. 1984, 'The Crisis in Adoption', *International Journal of Social Psychiatry,* vol. 30, nos 1/2, spring, pp. 129−42.

Smith, D. 1977, *Racial Disadvantage in Britian,* Harmondsworth, Penguin Books.

Smith, Don 1985, 'Sickle Cell Anaemia', *Contact,* no. 44, summer, pp. 18−19.

Smith, D.J. and Whalley, A. 1975, *Racial Minorities and Council Housing,* London, Political and Economic Planning.

Smith, M.G., Augier, R. and Nettleford, R. 1967, 'The Rastafari Movement in Kingston, Jamaica', *Caribbean Quarterly,* vol. 13, no. 3, pp. 3−29 and vol. 13, no. 4, pp. 3−14.

Sondhi, R. 1982, 'The Asian Resource Centre, Birmingham', in A. Ohri, B. Manning and P. Curno (eds), *Community Work and Racism,* London, Routledge and Kegan Paul.

Staplehurst, A. 1983, *Working with Young Afro-Caribbean Offenders,* Norwich, Social Work Mongraphs, University of East Anglia.

Stern, C. 1973, *Principles of Human Genetics,* 3rd ed., San Francisco, W.H. Freeman.

Stewart, M. and Whitting, G. 1983, *Ethnic Minorities and the Urban Programme,* Bristol, School for Advanced Urban Studies, University of Bristol.

Street, H., Howe, G. and Bindman, G. 1967, *Report on Anti-Discrimination Legislation,* London, Political and Economic Planning.

Tajfel, H. 1978, 'The Social Psychology of Minorities', *Minority Rights Group Report no. 38,* London, Minority Rights Group, Reprinted in C. Husband (ed.), *'Race' in Britain,* London, Hutchinson.

Tambs-Lyche, H. 1980, *The London Patidars: A Case Study in Urban Ethnicity,* London, Routledge and Kegan Paul.

Taylor, W. 1981, *Probation and After-Care in a Multi-Racial*

Society, London, Commission for Racial Equality.

Thoburn, J. 1980, *Captive Clients. Social Work with Families of Children Home on Trial,* London, Routledge and Kegan Paul.

Thomas, J. 1984, 'Tiptoeing Round Racism and IT', *IT Mailing,* no. 17, July, pp. 6–7.

Thomas, L. 1984, 'Black and Proud of It', *Social Work Today,* vol. 16, no. 15, 10 December, pp. 16–17.

Thorpe, R. 1980, 'The Experiences of Children and Parents Living Apart', in J. Triseliotis, *New Developments in Fostering and Adoption,* London, Routledge and Kegan Paul.

Tierney, J. (ed.) 1982, *Race, Migration and Schooling,* New York, Holt Rinehart and Winston.

Tomlinson, S. 1981, *Educational Subnormality. A Study in Decision Making,* London, Routledge and Kegan Paul.

Tomlinson, S. 1984, *Ethnic Minorities in British Schools. A Review of the Literature 1960–82,* London, Heinemann.

Tuck, M. 1979, 'On Researching Self-help Groups: A Problem in Evaluation Research', *Research Bulletin,* no. 8, p. 22, London, Home Office.

Walvin, J. 1973, *Black and White: the Negro and English Society 1555–1945,* Harmondsworth, Penguin Books. Adapted to 'Black Caricature: The Roots of Racialism', in C. Husband (ed), 1982 *'Race' in Britain,* London, Hutchinson.

Watson, J.L. 1975, *Emigration and the Chinese Lineage. The Mans in Hong Kong and London,* London, California University Press.

Watson, J.L. (ed.) 1977, *Between Two Cultures. Migrants and Minorities in Britain,* Oxford, Basil Blackwell.

Weber, M. 1954, *Max Weber on Law in Economy and Society,* translated by E. Shils and M. Rheinstein, Cambridge, Massachusetts, Harvard University Press.

Werner, P. 1981, book review in *Ethnic and Racial Studies,* vol. 4, no. 4, pp. 503–4.

Whitehouse, P. 1983, 'Race, Bias, Social Enquiry Reports', *Probation Journal,* June, pp. 43–9.

Wilson, H. 1974, 'Delinquents and Non-Delinquents in the Inner City', *Social Work Today,* vol. 5, no. 15, pp. 446–9.

Wilson, H. 1980, 'Parental Supervision: A Neglected Aspect

of Juvenile Delinquency', *British Journal of Criminology*. vol. 20, no. 3, pp. 55–69.

WMPS 1985, *Challenge and Change. The West Midlands Probation Service, 1974–1984*, Birmingham, West Midlands Probation Service.

Young, K. and Conelly, N. 1981, *Policy and Practice in the Multi-Racial City*, London, Policy Studies Institute.

Index

8, 159—60;
and see social casework
separatism, 18, 115, 122—3
Shackman, J., 126
Sharron, H., 107
Shore, Peter, Rt. Hon., 35
sickle-cell, 190
Sikhs, 8, 13, 34, 42, 45, 57,
178, 188;
case example, 138—41;
family structures, 134—6;
inheritance rules, 135;
naming system, 136
Sivanandan, A., 7, 65—7
skin colour,
attitudes to, 11, 12—13;
biology of, 1—2;
of councillors, 43, 102,
172;
discrimination on grounds
of, 37, 43, 53, 60, 117;
and English language, 12
slavery, 11, 71
Small, J.W., 171
Smith D., 57
Smith Don, 190
Smith, M.G., Augier, R. &
Nettleford, R., 149
social casework, and discrimination, racism, 82—3,
84, 86, 89—90, 97—8
psycho-social model, 93,
95, 194—5;
racial, cultural and socio-
economic underpinnings
69, 82—3, 85—6, 89—90
193—6, 141—2, 144—5,
149, 194—5;
in social enquiry reports,
149—52, 194—5;
and see power; self-determination; social services

social work; probation
service
social class, *see* ethnicity,
and social class
social control, 10, 89, 137—
8
social enquiry reports, 127,
146—52, 192, 194—5
social services departments,
access to, 110, 117;
changing services,100—101,
102—19, 171—2;
'colour blind' policy, 43,
47—8, 49—50, 65, 88,
164, 169, 184, 189;
policy development, 100—
19, 168, 172;
policy review, 100—101,
102—3, 105—6, 117;
policy, and skin colour of
councillors, 43—4, 101,
172;
and see colour blind
policy; ethnic monitor-
ing
social work, and allocation
of scarce resources, 141—
2;
appropriate interventions,
125, 137—8, 146—7;
assimilationism in, 76, 84,
87, 88, 93, 94, 117—19,
151, 184, 194—6;
colour-blindness in, 108,
109, 194—5, 199;
and cultural differences
not taken seriously,
111;
and discrimination, racism,
82—3, 84, 86—7, 99—
100, 108, 170, 171,
184;